NEW YORK RANGERS

BROADWAY BLUES

Frank Brown

SAGAMORE PUBLISHING
Champaign, IL

Production supervision and interior design: Michelle R. Dressen
Dustjacket and photo insert design: Michelle R. Dressen
Editors: Susan M. McKinney, Russ Lake
Proofreader: Phyllis L. Bannon
All photos by Bruce Bennett Studios

Library of Congress Catalog Card Number: 93-85458
ISBN: 0-915611-85-6

Printed in the United States.

For Simon Fischler.
If the Rangers had his courage, they'd have won it all.

- CONTENTS -

-ACKNOWLEDGMENTS -

IN YOUR HANDS is a work that would not have come into being without the graciousness of someone who did not hesitate to help a virtual stranger when a catastrophe was in progress. The day I met Michael Geylin was the day he put a laptop computer in my hands and said, "Keep it as long as you need it."

Without his generosity, this book probably would have been finished in crayon on a roll of paper towels. This, no doubt, would have made angry people of the enduringly patient folks at Sagamore Publishing, specifically Joe Bannon, Jr., who remained incurably cordial as I missed deadline after deadline.

This was a learning experience. Writing a book is an agony I would wish only on people I dislike. I gained enough weight, during long nights and early mornings of stolen meals and sneaked snacks, to model a line of maternity clothing. And while this *was* a birth of sorts, the labor pains were joyless, hopeless, and endless hours long. This, to be sure, is a child of troubled ancestry, delivered nine months after the start of a rotten Rangers season better forgotten than immortalized.

Still, those who were asked for help gave it in abundance and to them I am grateful. From Barry Watkins of the Rangers communications department to his boss, Neil Smith, to his boss, Bob Gutkowski, every question was answered with as much candor as could be mustered.

Even Gutkowski's boss, Stanley Jaffe, who routinely dismisses my routine requests for an interview, contributed two entire sentences' worth of his take on last season. This was in Quebec City, before the NHL draft. As he sped from an escalator to a doorway, Jaffe said: "I'll let the results speak. Last year, they weren't wonderful."

Okay, so it wasn't the Gettysburg Address. It's not like this is Moby Dick. It's just a year in the life of a good team that went bad without stopping long enough to be mediocre.

Re-creation of the tale took a very long time, and a lot of good, kind, loving people were inconvenienced, shoved aside. To my friends, to my family, to everyone who had to say, "You're STILL not finished?!" my humble, heartfelt apologies. To those who supported me, provided insights or reassurance, or editing suggestions or creative ideas, there is no way to express the depth of my thanks.

One brief note:

In 1964, or thereabout, a young man named Richard Hochenberg shared the gift of hockey with an unknowing friend. His wrist shot was the first to strike my unpadded shins. His bedroom carpet was the site of pitched floor-hockey battles, refereed by his ferocious poodle, Pepe. His television was my first connection with those marvelous Saturday nights of Ranger hockey. His tickets, I am certain, provided my first exposure to the utterly captivating action and color of a hockey night at the old Madison Square Garden. His interest in the game sparked my unquenchable passion for it, started me on a career path that, to this day, I cannot believe has come into being.

The game has taken me around the world. It puts a roof over my head, puts clothes on my back, puts dollars in my wallet, puts food in my mouth. When the food puts holes in my teeth, I pay Dr. Richard Hochenberg, now my dentist, to fill them. He should know I am paying him with his own money. It can never be enough.

    —Frank Brown
    New York
    1993

THE COMPELLING THING about the Rangers is that they can be interesting even when they stink. And when you finish last, as the Rangers did in 1992-93, you stink. You sneak into fourth, maybe you're allowed an excuse. Maybe several. But when you finish last, you get "bum" tatooed on your butt.

When you do it the year after looking like a world-beater, it's interesting. When you bungee jump from first place to worst in 12 shocking months, with a payroll of more than $15 million, you raise eyebrows.

The coach and the captain were at odds, but only until the coach got fired — with the team two victories above .500, four points out of second place, with 44 games to play.

The same day he got fired, the coach got suspended for two days by the NHL. Barely two days after that, his dog died.

That's a bad week.

The best defenseman, Brian Leetch, signed a seven-year contract worth about 17 million bucks, then missed 34 games after attempting approximately the first bodycheck of his career. For $17 million, he can hire somebody to hit for him.

One of the goalies got sent to the minors, so did one of the assistant coaches.

They scored 11 goals in Pittsburgh, but only 10 against Montreal. They gave up 11 goals in Buffalo but held Quebec to 10 at Le Colisee.

They got snowed out of a game in Washington, which should not be confused with getting blown out of the Garden, 10-4, by Pittsburgh.

Then they won the Norman Vincent Peale award for positive thinking: On March 23, team president Neil Smith met with the team — which he virtually never does. Roused to a frothing frenzy by whatever he said, the Rangers lost 11 of the season's 12 remaining games. The victory was a 4-0 shutout, of course. On the road.

There always seemed to be a piece out of the puzzle. If the goaltending was good enough to keep the team in a close game, there were too many nights when the Rangers went without a game-breaking goal. Other nights, the goalies would give up the game-breaking goal. Or there wasn't enough emotion. Or there wasn't enough defense. There was always a gap, always a lapse someplace where it could be least afforded.

The fans, of course, are used to this kind of treatment. They came to last season expecting steak and the Rangers put cat food on their plates. But the fans come back. They always do and probably always will.

And when the Rangers finally win the Stanley Cup — hey, miracles happen — every one of the players should get a copy of this book, to remind them what can happen if you get a big head.

BLUEBLOODS

IN THE MORNING, there had been a buffet of eggs and bacon and sausage and potatoes and french toast and pastry and all the things you really shouldn't eat at the age most of these diners had reached.

In the afternoon, there had been golf — a hackers' frenzy, truth be told — and all kinds of laughs. The men would howl at the stories of days gone by, would scream with laughter at how low a person can sink when begging a golf ball to do his bidding. Some wiseguy brought a hockey net, regulation size, and placed it in the middle of a fairway a few hundred yards away; score a "goal" with your drive, you win a prize.

There was a great gab session in the clubhouse afterward. There was a cocktail hour, a dinner, chance after chance for the members of the Rangers Alumni Association to reminisce.

A platform was placed near the center of the dining room and a microphone was connected so everyone could hear the speakers' remarks. An old-style referee's sweater was given to Bill Chadwick, the Hall of Famer credited with introducing hand signals to describe penalties. The presenter was Jim Gordon, Chadwick's long-time partner in the TV booth. Dave Maloney gave a Rangers jersey to his teammate, Steve Vickers, who had played so large a role in the formation of the association.

Some of the men looked like they could still play. There was an expression in their eyes, as though if they walked past a clean new sheet of ice, they would pause for a minute and wonder if there were skates nearby — wonder if they should get out there and show the kids how the REAL game gets played. To many of them, that ice was a canvas, awaiting their brushes, their colors. And what pictures they painted!

Some of the men wobbled when they walked, enduring evidence of the bones and tendons and ligaments and cartilage they had sacrificed.

Some of their faces had lumpy scars; they would get bandaged or stitched up and get right back out there to earn their hundred bucks a night or whatever they got paid. Some of them earned a few thousand a month and thought they had it made.

There were 50-goal scorers, there were checking-line slugs. There were guys you couldn't recognize or remember until they introduced themselves.

No matter. Star or scrub, you could feel the spirit there, from the first sip of coffee to the brandy after dinner. There was a pride in every one of them to have worn the Ranger jersey, which merely was the deepest blue you ever saw. The most incredible blue. You could hold it in your hands and stare at it for hours, and someone could ask you to describe the color and there is only one way to answer:

It's Ranger blue.

No, not Maple Leafs blue. Not navy, not royal, not indigo. Ranger blue.

You pulled that sweater over your head, tied the little shoelace at the neck if you wanted, and you were ruler of your world. You'd have done it for nothing, in all likelihood. Playing the game may not have made your wallet fat, but it lifted your heart and freed your spirit because when you skate, you fly. You have a freedom no one else can have, no outsider could understand. There probably wasn't a guy in the room who could explain the physical action which causes a blade of cold steel to melt a strip of colder ice and push a player forward. All they knew was, you put on your skates, tied 'em good and tight, and the ice was your runway: You were clear for takeoff.

The men were bonded by The Freedom. They were bonded by The Sweater.

And there was something else that united these men of all shapes and sizes, all ages and hometowns.

Virtually all of them had come to New York, played, moved on . . . without once winning a Stanley Cup.

If there were Cup rings at The Fenway Country Club on September 9, 1992, they bore the crests of other teams. You might see them and look away, as you'd look away from a sixth finger or a sixth toe, not wanting to make the owners feel like freaks just because they had The Ring you never got to wear.

The whole day was so pleasant, really, but sitting at dinner that night and seeing all the Rangers made you think the logical next thought:

Stanley should be here.

On a big table with a white cloth.

Stanley should be here.

With a light shining, just right, in the way that makes it sparkle — the way that blinds you for an instant, takes your sight away and takes your speech away and just melts you, like the bad guy who looked into the sacred Ark in the Indiana Jones movie.

Stanley is why they played, why they strived — just so they could touch it once, so they could pick it up and skate with that sterling icon. You could swear a bolt of lightning comes down straight from heaven and jolts the hearts of those so honored and so privileged to lift it. Win that thing, you live forever, because your name goes on it in those little block letters and no one can ever rub them off.

To see the names of the last Rangers to win Stanley, to hoist him high, you must travel to Toronto. The Hockey Hall of Fame, on Yonge Street, used to be a bank; the original Cup — the punch bowl part, which is all Lord Stanley of Preston donated 100 years ago — sits, spotlit, on the right side of what used to be the vault.

Along the far wall, the left wall, is a display case where the 1940 Ranger panel is nailed to what looks like black velvet. The Cup has been won so many times since then, they had to take off some panels to clear space for the names of the new winners. So the tomb of that 1940 team, that last Ranger champion, is in Toronto, in that brick vault with the heavy steel doors.

It isn't that big a vault. Back when the place was a bank, people must not have had much money. If you took the 19 men whose names are etched on that panel and brought them all in to look at it, they'd pretty well fill the place.

There are three Patricks: Lester, Lynn and Muzz. There are two Colvilles, Mac and Neil; two Smiths, Clint and Sanford. Davey Kerr was the goalie, Frank Boucher was the coach. There are Ott Heller, Alf Pike and Babe Pratt. The engraver must have appreciated the short names — fewer letters to pound into the silver. Art Coulter . . . Bryan Hextall . . . Dutch Hiller . . . Kilby

McDonald . . . Alex Shibicky . . . Phil Watson . . . Harry Westerby, the trainer.

A lot of them are dead, of course; 1940 was a long, long time ago. There have been 23 different Ranger coaches in the years since Boucher, eight different general managers since Lester Patrick. And every blessed one of them has gone home at the end of the season and wondered what it would take to win that last game, just once.

Do they need more speed or more scoring or better defense or a younger goalie? Do they need a new coach? Do they need minor changes, or do they need to tear it all down and start over? Would they have won if their star hadn't been hurt, if they'd been able to play their home games in the Garden, if there hadn't been a player strike?

The players would go home for the summer and ask themselves, What if I hadn't missed the net? What if I'd scored on that breakaway? What if I'd blocked that shot? What if I hadn't taken that penalty?

The funny thing is, guys who have won it ask the same questions — even guys who never played for the Rangers or worked for them, guys who were not at The Fenway this day but whose testimony qualified as expert.

Terry Crisp played on the Philadelphia Flyers teams that won in 1974 and 1975, and coached the Calgary Flames team that won it in 1989.

"When you sit back after you've won it," Crisp once said, "you look at different things that could have gone wrong, where you dodged a bullet — where you had injuries and guys played hurt, or the other team had a key injury that put them out. There are so many variables along that road that have to drop into place for you to win.

"There's so many teams that could have and should have and didn't win it, and there's just some fine little thing that caused them not to. And it may never come around again," he added.

"The first year we won it, I remember (coach) Fred Shero telling us, 'You know what? You guys won't realize what you've done until 10 years down the road. You won't appreciate it as much — what you all have done together to win the Stanley Cup — until 10 years later.'

"At that given time, it's the hoopla and the party time and the parade time and the ring time, and when it's going on, you think it's not going to end," Crisp added. "You think, 'This is great.' But it's when you've all gone your other ways and you're watching the playoffs another year on TV and some other team's winning that you say, 'Hey. WE were there. We know that feeling. I know what those guys are experiencing.' Freddie was right about that."

Shero spent so much of his life in the Rangers' organization, coaching them, ultimately, after those two Cups in Philadelphia. He was a Ranger near-miss who had to go to another city to taste ultimate triumph.

Wayne Cashman did it the other way, coming to the Rangers as an assistant coach more than a decade after his Stanley Cup days in Boston.

"As soon as it sinks in, it's like the completion of the dreams you had as a kid growing up," said Cashman, who with the 1972 Bruins won his second ring at the Rangers' expense. "It's the greatest feeling you can have, because it makes everything you've ever done worthwhile — all the hours you put into hockey, the times you got up early in the morning, the bruises and the bangs.

"Every team starts out in the fall, everybody's pulling in the same direction, and that direction is toward the Stanley Cup," he said. "And if you're one degree off as you're going, the ultimate result is like shooting at the stars. If you start from here, to go to the stars, and you're a mile off, by the time you get to the stars, do you know how far away you are? It doesn't take much for you NOT to win it."

Every man at The Fenway knew that, only too well.

"Once you've done it, though, you have that feeling forever, the confidence forever, that you can win it again," Cashman said. "The Stanley Cup is the ultimate of confidence. Once people learn how to win, they never forget it, because the feeling is so great. The Cup is yours. You've got it. You're part of a team that got it.

"The Stanley Cup is nothing but a hunk of silver, but it's the fact of what it takes to win it, and you've done that. It's the fact that so many great players and teams, that's what they LIVED for. That's what you've lived your whole life for, to lift that trophy over your head," Cashman said. "When you lift that Cup, you're lifting the weight of 20 years of hard work, and it feels lighter than you do.

"Let's face it: Sports is emotion, and this is the greatest emotional feeling you can have," Cashman added. "Each thing you receive afterward adds to it, makes it more great. You say, 'Oh boy. It was greater than I thought!' That's why you never forget it, why it becomes, to you, the ultimate. That's why guys who have won it are willing to go that extra to win it again — because they realize there is a difference, there is a GREAT difference, between winning it and losing it. If you haven't experienced the winning part, you don't know.

"No matter where you go or what you're doing or how things are going, you sit back and you've got that ring on your finger," Cashman said. "Sometimes I just sit and twirl it, and it gives me a relaxed feeling, a confident feeling. I can think back to that time, and it helps me. It's not the ring, it's the thoughts and memories it brings back."

You get them while you can. Cashman's Bruins beat the Rangers in the '72 finals for the ultimate joy. Cashman's Bruins lost to the Flyers of Shero and Crisp in the finals of 1974, the ultimate sadness. It can change that quickly, on a bad call or a bad break or a bad game. Sometimes you get another chance at it; more often, you don't. So you go home miserable, your boss goes home miserable, and the fans go home utterly devastated.

You would think after all this losing, all this disappointment, that you could fit all the remaining Ranger fans in that vault with the original Cup. You would think by now the group is so demoralized that you could not find enough of them for a softball team or a jury pool.

To think that would be very foolish.

Because, by now, these people have a point to prove. You do not question their heart, you do not question their devotion.

"Fans may come and fans may go, but I will never leave," Claire Prevot says. "You see, I bleed Ranger Blue."

Peter Taubkin works in Albany, N.Y. as an associate counsel in the State Assembly. His curly hair is kept in conservative trim, his eyeglasses embellish a scholarly appearance. He appears normal, and for a Ranger fan, he is entirely normal — right down to the seven pairs of Ranger boxer shorts his fiancee bought so Taubkin will have one pair for every day of the week.

When he went to prep school in Pottstown, Pennsylvania, Taubkin would take a bus to Philadelphia, then ride Amtrak to Penn Station, which sits underneath Madison Square Garden. Three hours, each way, every home game he could get to. And you know he made way more than he missed.

Taubkin went to college in Waterville, Maine — an eight-hour drive from campus to center ice.

"Never minded it," Taubkin says, "even after a loss."

He went to law school in Boston, a four-hour trip each way. The commute from Albany, barely three hours by car, is a joyride by comparison.

Taubkin has season tickets, of course. When he has extra, he gives them to people.

"I look at it," he says, "as a method of recruiting."

Recruiting new Ranger fans?

You mean there could be others out there as devoted?

You wouldn't believe it.

There was a Rangers Fan Club bus trip in February, 1983. The gang was headed for Montreal, which is pretty much an annual stop for them.

"I had four buses all lined up when the weatherman decided to drop 20 inches of snow on New York City," recalls Frank Schmitt, who was Trips Chairman that year.

Two of the buses departed, with general orders to use the George Washington Bridge and specific orders to stay away from the snarled traffic in the Bronx. Schmitt's bus and one other stayed behind to wait for stragglers, keeping in touch with the other buses by CB radio.

"Those two buses did, indeed, end up in the Bronx — stuck on the Major Deegan (expressway) near Yankee Stadium, until 9:30 the next morning," Schmitt says. "Needless to say, they never made it to Montreal.

"Meanwhile, we ended up getting stuck in uptown Manhattan, about 10 blocks from the Bridge. We were stuck there for three hours, and after I quelled a near-rebellion on my bus, I took a good look at the jam-up in front of us and realized about 10 non-moving cars were all that stood between us and the Bridge.

"I then got about 15 guys off the two buses, and we pushed those cars out of our way — despite protests from the drivers," Schmitt continues. "We were out of there and over the Bridge at 4:30 a.m.

"I stayed awake all night and talked to my driver so he wouldn't fall asleep, and we got to our hotel at 1:30 p.m. I was left with a lot of unused tickets, but there was a happy ending. The Rangers won, 3-2."

Surprised by this devotion? You shouldn't be.

"In December of 1986, my mother had heart bypass surgery. I missed a game because of it, stopping a streak of 248 straight," said Bill King, a 40-year-old maintenance man from Elizabeth, N.J. "To this day, I sometimes wonder if I should either have gone late to the game, or gone to the game and then left at the first stoppage of play — just to keep the streak going.

"You've got to put certain things ahead of hockey, but not many," King continues. "I must admit, I did miss a few weddings and family gatherings along the way, but — hey! — what are you doing scheduling something on a night the Rangers are home?"

For seven years, Debbie Rockower made banners that hung from the facade at the Seventh Avenue end of the Garden. They would take two or three hours to prepare at home, another hour before the game to get the pieces in place.

"When the players would skate out for pre-game warmups," she said, "their eyes would all be focused up to the banner, to see what it said."

Then, for an Islander game in 1979, someone else decided to make a banner. One with profanity in it.

That was the last time a banner was seen at a Garden sporting event.

"I was devastated," Rockower said.

But she kept coming back.

"I've made too many friends because of the Rangers," she says, "and the thought of suffering home alone, in front of a television, just won't do it for this die-hard Ranger fan.

"Maybe I've become numb to the losses, the disappointments. It's expected," she says. "Maybe this is how it's supposed to be. Maybe this is why there is such a strong bond among the Rangers and their fans. Everyone loves a loser."

Rob Friedman, a season ticketholder since 1970, will tell you how deep that love can be. In 1981, during what he called "a bitter and acrimonious divorce," Friedman and his lawyer met with his soon-to-be-ex and her attorney in an attempt to divide any jointly-held property.

"In a soliloquy worthy of an Emmy, she went on about how she looked forward to every game (not true) and had contributed financially to the cost of the tickets (true) and was, in fact, more of a Ranger fan than I!" Friedman recalled. "I calmly asked her to name three current Rangers.

"After a moment of hesitation, she asked, 'Rod Gilbert?'

"Rod Gilbert, all-time great, hero of my youth, had retired the previous season.

"I kept the tickets."

There is a P.S. to the story:

"My first date with my wife of three-plus years was a Rangers-Islanders game," Friedman says. "And we got engaged after a game in the Spectrum."

That also is not uncommon. There are those who literally have had a life-long love affair with the team — or because of it.

Claire Prevot joined the Rangers Fan Club in 1952 and met her husband, John, through its activities. Together, they brought four new Rangers fans to the planet.

"Being pregnant with me wasn't about to stop my mother from going to the games, even on her due date," says Joyce Prevot, Claire's daughter. "I almost entered this world at the old Garden, during the playoffs in 1962. Fortunately for everyone, I was born 10 days late . . . on an off-day."

Joyce would meet her husband through the fan club; two of her brothers would meet their wives in the same fashion. Mary Ann Principato and Janet Esposito experienced similar events.

"During the 1986-87 season, the Rangers Fan Club made a road trip to Detroit," Principato remembered. "I was on the welcoming committee for the 'For 'Em (Red Wings booster) Club."

One of the visitors she greeted would become her husband. Now, they make frequent road trips to Ranger games.

"It doesn't matter where the game is. We just love the game so much and want to give our support to the team," she says. "It's a part of me that I will never give up."

Esposito met her husband on a trip to Montreal, delivered her first son during the 1981 all-star game.

"So you see," Esposito says, "the Rangers already have their next generation of Ranger fans covered."

That's the way these people are. They find a reason for hope.

"I was born a Ranger, I was raised and lived as a Ranger, and I am proud that I will die as a Ranger," says Bob Comas, of Brooklyn. "They could go 83 years without a Cup and I will still be a Ranger."

Bob Comas puts on a white Ranger jersey at the home games. On his head, he wears a feathered headdress, which is a signal for everyone in the mezzanine to abuse the heck out of him.

"Next to God, country and family," he says, "the Rangers are the love of my life and the reason to live."

Where else can you get this kind of entertainment?

"Being a Ranger fan means so many things," Schmitt says. "It means endless wondering if the team will EVER win the Cup in our lifetime. It means watching a team that always teases you; they play well and get your hopes up, then self-destruct.

"It means watching players that get booed out of the Garden go on to win Stanley Cups with other teams, while players who won Cups elsewhere are brought here, only to fizzle.

"It means watching teams that don't forecheck enough or backcheck enough and who treat their goalies like they were meant to be targets. It means watching as proven goal scorers become unable to score a goal if their lives depended on it in a crucial game.

"Would I change any of this if I could? Sure: The RANGERS would have won those four straight Stanley Cups — not the Islanders," Schmitt says. "There's a Cup out there for us somewhere in the future, though, and when it does arrive, it will have been worth every minute of this."

In September, players gathered at the Fenway to remember old times and to think of what could have been. In October, young folks and old would join hands again at the Garden to cheer what they hope will be.

"My girlfriend has been my seat-partner for 12 years," says Steven Dorio, of Weehauken, N.J. "We're waiting for the Rangers to win the Stanley Cup to get married."

Fill in your own punchline.

CHAPTER 1

SWEPT AWAY

MADISON SQUARE GARDEN does not know night or day; it knows only light or dim. And it knows that when there is light, it is showtime.

When the lights are shining in the big, round building, there is the brightness and sparkle of a perfect smile. There is the electric sense that something, anything, can happen — that you've come to see something and the Garden will show you something because it always does. The Garden always comes up big, the people who fill it do the same. And the challenge, to those who perform there, is to come through the way the building does and the people do.

In New York, you have to come through every day just to have a fighting chance at tomorrow. On your way to the Garden, you say no to at least some of the homeless people who want your change, no to the scalpers who want your tickets, no to the thieves who want your wallet. You say, "New York, I won't let you beat me. I've got a Ranger game tonight and nothing else matters."

Without its lights, the Garden slumbers. Though huge when bustling with ushers and vendors and 18,200 hockey fans, it seems larger still — a bowl big enough for football — in the shadows after the show. Giant bulbs give way to smaller lamps that drain the building of its color. Everything goes gray. You lose the lavender and the teal of the seats, the cream and orange of the spoked ceiling.

Sometimes, when the Rangers score, you wonder what keeps that wheel of a roof from flying right into the sky on the power of the cheers and the howls New Yorkers let loose.

Sometimes you think the noise is what lights the building. You don't flip a switch, you just open the doors and let in the people and they take care of the rest. The people are the light. Their joy slaps you on the back; their anger squeezes your stomach.

When they are gone, the Garden is the biggest garbage can in New York. There are half-eaten hot dogs and melting ice creams and spilled sodas and crumpled napkins. There are left-behind programs and empty cups and ticket stubs and price tags from the T-shirt dad just bought junior at the youngster's first Ranger game. And of course there are people whose careers in show business consist of sweeping that stuff toward the aisles, then shovelling it down the steps, then scooping it into great gray wagons to be taken wherever all the memories go that nobody wanted to take home. Empty cups drop down stairs, making little popping, plopping noises on the concrete until they settle in growing mounds at the nearest promenade.

It is a place rather like the Colosseum in Rome, albeit some 1900 years younger. Gladiators fought to the death at the Colosseum, a round, roofless wonder the emperor Vespasian ordered built in 72 A.D.. There were archery competitions and boxing and swordsmen. There were chariot races and wild beast shows. No hockey, of course, no ice — even if there are Ranger nights that seem to combine all those ancient attractions into one jolting surge of modern energy and excitement. The nights they win are the nights the Garden lights burn brightest, the nights the Rangers are one step nearer the exit from purgatory, one triumph closer to ending their curse of five-plus decades.

On April 13, 1940, at Maple Leaf Gardens in Toronto, Bryan Hextall Sr. scored at 2:07 of overtime, and the Rangers were Stanley Cup champions for the third time in their history. On the wall of his office, facing his desk, Rangers president/GM Neil Smith has a photograph of the celebration at the Royal York Hotel that night, the last night a Ranger team felt that ultimate joy. On the same wall, a bit below and to the left, is a photo of the team standing shoulder-to-shoulder, the autograph of each player in white on black-and-white of the picture.

Every time he lifts his eyes from the papers on his desk, Neil Smith can't help but see those photographs. He might be on the phone with another general manager, with his coach, with an agent. He might be pondering a trade, might be considering a draft choice. If his gaze shifts around the room, away from the huge bulletin board to his left or the shelved black case crammed with books and mementos to his right, Smith is bound to focus on the task that rests across the room, literally in front of him. The challenge is to put a color photo on that wall, a photo with his face in it, a photo of the party he puts on when the Rangers are the champions and the whole rest of the hockey world can shut the heck up because at last the cruel joke has another team's name for a punchline.

Smith's office is on the fourth floor of Four Penn Plaza, on the 31st Street side of the sprawling complex that stretches from Seventh Avenue to Eighth, from 31st Street to 33rd in Manhattan. Though they have long been referred to as "the Broadway Blues," the nickname never has been more than half-correct. True, the team has worn blue uniform jerseys, either at home or on the road, since it was founded in 1926. But neither the current Garden nor its venerable predecessor — which occupied the square block from 49th to 50th Streets, Eighth Avenue to Ninth — actually was located on Broadway.

The "Broadway" aspect had more to do with the show-business following the team attracted. Babe Ruth and Lou Gehrig, the Yankee immortals, were frequent visitors to the dressing room in the team's early years. Such show business megastars as Humphrey Bogart, Edward G. Robinson, Lucille Ball and Desi Arnaz were seen at the Garden, as were various society matrons and masters. In fact, before they were the Broadway Blues, the team was referred to as "The Park Avenue Rangers," in deference to the evening-gown crowd that occupied the best seats.

If he strides quickly from his den, Smith can be backstage at the arena in minutes. He walks through a couple of corridors, up an unmarked flight of stairs, and emerges on the fifth floor. To his left are the laundry machines where sweaty uniforms and soaked towels are washed. The network of cinderblock bunkers to his right forms the makeshift TV studios where players are interviewed.

Ahead on his left is the carpenters' workshop and a generator room. Straight ahead is the massive service elevator that glides between floors, slow and stinky as an elephant. One more right turn, a stride through heavy double doors, and he's there, between the dressing rooms, facing the rubber-matted walkway to the ice.

Two hours before the game, there is no better place to taste the flinty flavor of the event ahead. Down a hallway to the left is the door to the Rangers' dressing room, in front of which rests a waist-high wooden cabinet, painted dark blue. At one corner of the station is a vise in which players will anchor their sticks and tailor them.

Every player has sticks made to his exact specifications, yet when they arrive from the factory, the sticks never seem to be "just right." They are always too long or too curved or not curved enough. Or the heel is too square. Or the blade is too long. A player or a trainer will slide the edge of a scissors down the heavy plastic cocoon in which a dozen sticks arrive, will cut through the heavy plastic binding tape that bundles the six sticks on top to the six on the bottom. Then the player will grab a stick, test its strength and its flex. Rarely will he smile, nod, wink or evince any pleasure whatever. It almost seems part of the show that the player will make a face or shake his head, then reach into the cupboard for the saw.

He will trim away a millimeter from the tip of the blade or an inch from the top of the knob. He will reach for sandpaper to smooth away the rough edges. He will reach for the torch which will heat the blade, will make the treated wood malleable. He will adjust the blade's curvature by placing its tip in the hinge of a doorway and bending the hot wood until satisfied it is the wand that will make magic this night. Heartier souls don't bother with the doorway; they pin the blade under their shower sandals and pull upward. Stouter souls with tougher soles don't even wear sandals; they perform this mystical ritual barefoot.

For all the good the factory customizing has done them, the players might just as well have stopped at Gerry Cosby's sporting goods store in the Garden lobby and picked up a stick or two on the way upstairs. It seems that even if the stick WAS perfect, a player would find something wrong with it in order to have something to do with his time and his hands as the game approaches and the bubbles begin boiling in his belly. He is going out to skate and shoot and hit, perhaps to fight. He is going before dozens who will report his performance in the media, thousands who have forked over big dollars to watch in person, hundreds of thousands who will watch on TV in the New York area, countless more who will scout him on a satellite dish. On game night, you go in front of the hockey world with millions on the line and harsh judgments in store.

The carpenters ply their craft in a corridor lined with photographs of Garden events. Over here, John Davidson makes an artful save. Over there, Rangers soar over the boards from the bench to celebrate their 1979 playoff conquest of the Islanders. Over here, Pete Stemkowski is mobbed after a triple-overtime goal that beat the Blackhawks in Game 6 during the '71 semifinals. Further down, by the Knicks' dressing room, the theme shifts to basketball.

From the sound system in the dressing room, music fills the hallway and mixes with the noise from the construction work. The music is loud and aggressive, hard rock for the hard business ahead. Players sit at their dressing spots or lie on the gray-black carpet, a huge Ranger crest in its center, and stretch.

Outside, as the hacking and rasping proceeds, little snowdrifts of sawdust form at the players' feet. Stick-knobs fall lightly to the floor, followed by the heavy thunk of a saw being plunked on top of the hollow box. No one ever finishes the work and gently places the saw where it had been; another player will want it next, so there's no point making him look for it.

The next player will walk out of the dressing room with a few sticks in one hand, a partly-filled cup in the other. The challenge will be to determine whether the dark liquid in the bottom of his white foam container is the remainder of the player's coffee or the salivary residue of his chaw. The Rangers aren't smokers, but the odd can of tobacco has been seen in the clubhouse. It would classify as a serious rookie blunder to accept a cup of black "coffee" from any veteran you did not trust to the limit.

Right wing Tony Amonte, his baseball cap on backward, comes out to do his sticks. Then maybe Darren Turcotte or Joe Kocur or James Patrick. Always, at some point, Mark Messier appears — wearing a Ranger jacket or a Ranger sweatshirt or a Ranger hat. He is interviewed on camera regularly before games and the team name or the logo always are present at those moments. Messier may not have his pants on, but your TV screen at home always will flash the Rangers' colors someplace. It may have to do with the fact he is a paid spokesman for the sportwear line that makes most of these items. Still, you see him in enough interviews that the unspoken message is clear: the Rangers are Messier, Messier is the Rangers.

Of course that can be good and bad. By the end of his first two seasons with the team, Messier will have known the outer limits of both.

Messier has the posture and carriage of a captain, of the

main man, of the go-to guy. There is a swagger to him, the shoulders and head back, the chin tucked like a boxer in the ring. There seems an immense strength to him — a stallion's strength that, properly harnessed, helped pull the Rangers toward greatness in 1991-92.

But this April night in 1993, the stallion's just a plowhorse in a Ranger pullover. It all has gone bad, so horribly bad for him and his team, which has contracted a terminal case of Broadway blues. In the Rangers' Colosseum this night, you wonder how different it will be for them from those days when Vespasian's gladiators faced thumbs up or thumbs down. The biggest difference, of course, is they can lose and live to lose again.

These 1992-93 Rangers would live to lose a lot. They would lose 39 times and the night of this 38th defeat, the last night of the season at the Garden, Neil Smith is not in attendance. Neil Smith is outside Toronto, convincing Mike Keenan to become his coach. Because 39 losses is 14 more than Smith's Rangers had suffered the year before, eight more losses than the worst of his Ranger teams had compiled in Smith's first two seasons, 1989-90 and 1990-91.

The performance would leave a taste so foul that monstrous lakes of mouthwash could not have gargled it away. The night of April 14, 1993, or 53 years plus one day since the high point of modern Ranger history, the Garden fans would sneer and jeer a pathetic 2-0 loss to the Washington Capitals. For the second consecutive contest, the Rangers would not even score a goal.

Despite an announced attendance of 17,897, the joint is barely half-full. Those who come bring their anger. They are in strong voice, too, booing Messier every time he touches the puck. When Messier's face appears on the scoreboard video screen, they boo. He gets one shot and goes minus-2, which, of course, is the maximum possible in a two-goal loss.

They yell "Last place," a taunt usually reserved for hated opponents. They even yell "Nine-teen for-ty," the most despicable epithet you can utter around a Ranger; the Islander fans do it at Nassau Coliseum and they will do it until Neil Smith gets a more modern photo for his wall. And the fact at least some Ranger fans howl it this last lousy, losing night tells all you need to know about the contempt that had built inside them. They are die-hard fans, these people who have endured decades of misery, but this year's death has been harder than ever.

There is another intriguing display. The night of this last Ranger home game, there are lots of empty seats in Section 54, where the top brass sits. Garden president Bob Gutkowski, silver-haired, bearded, always elegantly dressed, is a fixture there. So is his boss, Stanley Jaffe, chief operating officer of Paramount Communications. Paramount owns the Garden, the Garden owns the Rangers.

Jaffe is the other end of the spectrum from Gutkowski. He is clean-shaven, his crown completely bald; what hair he has is close-cropped. He is more conservative than Gutkowski from a fashion standpoint, far more energetic in his rooting. Gutkowski may stand and applaud, but Jaffe on joyous occasions will jump from his seat and pump his arms skyward.

"Stanley sits right in front of me, so I never have to look at the scoreboard," Gutkowski jibed playfully. "I can tell how the game's going by the color of his head."

This last night at the Garden, Gutkowski is in Ontario with Smith and Jaffe's head is unavailable for inspection. You lose 38, you lose 39, it's still way too many in an 84-game season that was supposed to be a big one. The team went from first to worst in just a few months, a tale too absurd to be true. This night, the brass has better things to do.

The fans come. They boo. They leave. Light becomes dim at the Garden. The temporary seats are removed, and the metal lids are lifted off two pits in the floor at the Eighth Avenue end of the building. Clouds of steam waft from the holes; they seem to form two spectral hands that wave from the gateway of hockey hell, beckoning this awful season to its rightful resting place there.

As the brine pipes in the floor are heated, the ice becomes a milky mush and onto it roll two motorized carts, each conducted by a two-man crew. The first sled bears at its front a sharp, V-shaped device which digs into the melting mass, plowing it into shiny crumbs. The trail sled funnels the ice and water and paint toward either of those two yawning chasms. The debris disappears with the noise of waves at the beach.

It is leisurely work. The men have all kinds of time. It is barely 10 past one when the Eighth Avenue blue line begins to vanish. Not long after, the Garden crests at diagonal ends of the neutral zone are gone. So are the two giant Ranger insignias, one pointing east from the center circle, one pointing west. Large patches of slate floor come into view after the trailing sled has made a few passes. The scene starts to look more like a place where, when the Ringling Brothers Circus performance begins in a few hours, acrobats will tumble and horses will prance and wild beasts will snarl as they did in far-away arenas nearly 2,000 years ago.

Mike Junick sits in one of the loge seats, pulls on a cigarette and watches his men work. General foreman of all 31 shifts, Junick virtually lives with this ice, his ice, during hockey season.

"It's gotten more attention the last three years than my wife has," Junick says, bidding his frozen friend farewell — too early, again.

"One year we'll win the Stanley Cup," Junick assures, "and we won't have to take the ice off. The fans will take it with them."

This was supposed to be the year. The Rangers were going to ride Messier and Brian Leetch to hockey's mountaintop. You can't finish higher than first place overall, which is where they finished the year before; the next step up is the division playoff title, then the conference, then The Big One.

They had the horses, they knew they did. Even if arbitrator Larry Bertuzzi had denied them the rights to Eric Lindros, all that meant was the Rangers would keep a top goalie in John Vanbiesbrouck, two fine right wings in Alexei Kovalev and Tony Amonte, and a good young center in Doug Weight. They would keep twelve of Paramount's millions in their treasury, two first-round picks in their future. It was a win-win proposition.

This was the year.

In the 80-game joyride that was 1991-92, the Rangers had won a team-record 50 games — 22 of them on the road. They had scored a team-record 321 goals, a club-record five players providing 30 or more. They had given up 246 goals, fewest in 20 years. They had OWNED the Garden, losing just eight times there.

Messier had been voted MVP, not only of the team, but of the league. Leetch had been elected the NHL's top defenseman. Almost everything that happened in 1991-92 was superlative, a "best" or a "most" or a "fewest." The only similarity with past seasons was the shortfall at the end, when it mattered most, in the playoffs — and that would change this year, for sure. Steeled by the painful lesson Pittsburgh taught them in the second round, the players had to know every night in 1992-93 would call for sacrifice and selflessness; would demand that they give above and beyond the call of duty.

And they would give it.

For oh, at least the first 10 games.

CHAPTER 2

WARNING SIGNS

EVEN WHEN A TEAM WINS the Stanley Cup, management will make changes because it serves no purpose to stand pat. The rest of the league will try to get better and beat you next season; you can't sit and let them catch up.

When you DON'T win, when you flop like fish in the playoffs as the Rangers did in 1991-92 — when you don't even come near coming close — change is a more obvious mandate. Even if the Penguins were the defending champions, and the eventual repeat winners, they were there to be had by the Rangers in the second round and the job simply did not get done.

The thing is, how do you change a team that won 50 games, finished first overall and unmistakably was the class of its league before the first leaguewide player strike in NHL history?

Firing the coach would be a tough sell, even if there is an unwritten clause in every contract a coach signs. "When a team wins, it's the players' fault," the saying goes. "When a team loses, it's the coach's fault."

The Rangers had won and won and won for Roger Neilson in 1991-92. Their first-place finish marked the second time in three seasons the team had won the regular-season title in the Patrick Division, so based on regular-season play, Neil Smith hardly could cry about results.

The big payoff comes in the playoffs, however, and the track record under Neilson had been consistent in its futility. After that first-place campaign in their first season under Neilson, the Rangers had steamrolled the Islanders in five games, but then had been stunned in five second-round contests by a Washington team they should have beaten.

The following season, 1990-91, the team went 2-8-1 down the stretch and finished second at 36-31-13 — the same record that snatched the top spot in 1989-90. Not only did the Rangers blow first place with that nosedive in '91, but they were outperformed, by Washington again, in six first-round games. With all due respect to someone who has forgotten more hockey in an hour than many of us ever will know, Neilson was beginning to look like a golfer who could drive the ball 325 yards but who had no stroke whatever when he got to the green. When the going got tough, his Rangers got beat.

You go out early once, well, those things happen; in his first season, Neilson took a mediocre team on pretty short notice when Smith was hired barely two months before training camp.

You go out early twice? Well, it better not happen again.

Three times — the third with a team that won 50 games? That's a problem. Rick Bowness got a far less-talented Boston Bruins team to the playoff semifinals in 1991-92, and HE got fired; how do you keep Neilson after the Rangers bowed out (bow-wowed out) one round earlier?

Once the Penguins undid them in the division final of the 1991-92 tournament, the Rangers had been in the playoffs three times under Neilson and had won exactly two rounds. In the case of each victory, the Rangers had been prohibitive favorites; an argument could be made they also were favorites, or should have been, the three rounds they lost.

To make one unarguable point, the Rangers never under Neilson won a series in which they were prohibitive underdogs. With Dave "Tiger" Williams leading the bashing and crashing, Neilson guided the Toronto Maple Leafs past a Cup-minded Islanders team in the 1978 quarter-finals. And in 1982, with Williams' bark again the loudest in his kennel, Neilson reached his playoff pinnacle: he steered a 77-point Vancouver Canucks team into the final against an Islander squad that then paid him and Williams back for that Toronto indignity with a four-game sweep.

It hardly mattered, of course, that the Canucks got trampled as they did. They had become classic "overachievers" and had captured the imagination of the hockey world. They had "King" Richard Brodeur in goal, Harold Snepsts and Colin Campbell on defense. And they had Neilson, who one night in Chicago was so disgusted with the referee's work that he grabbed a towel and waved it in mock surrender from the bench — to the rage of the officials and the enduring admiration of the Canucks' fans. By the time the finals ended, a giant white flag, eternally defiant, flew taut in the wind from the mast atop Pacific Coliseum in Vancouver.

And if he just could have pulled off one of those upsets with the Rangers, it seems likely Neilson still would be coaching them.

That did not happen, though, and there is only so much patience that can be expected in a city that is impatient by its nature, but is appropriately restless when it comes to the failure of its oldest hockey team to win the playoff championship of its league. The Islanders, created in 1972, have won the Stanley Cup four times, have been to one other final and have reached the semifinals four other occasions. When they won the 1991 Cup, the Penguins became the fifth team to enter the NHL since 1967 and win it all without significant interference from the Rangers.

Look at it another way: From 1940 to 1967, when the league doubled in size to 12 teams, only five other clubs could win the Stanley Cup and they all did — even the Chicago Blackhawks, who have avoided the status of league laughingstock strictly by virtue of the Cup they won in 1960-61. That title, to which Al Arbour contributed as a player, is the only one the Blackhawks have managed since 1937-38. Imagine the abuse the Ranger fans would be only too happy to rain on Chicago rooters! Imagine the pent-up abuse they would love to heap on ANYBODY.

And they just can't.

Until their team wins again.

Just once.

"I want to be there when the Rangers win the Stanley Cup, so I can tell future generations, 'Yes, I was there '" says Scott Rosenbaum, a long-time resident of section 305 at the Garden and a long-time member of the Rangers Fan Club. "It would be frustrating to have gone to all the games in the past, stop going, then have the Rangers finally do it without me."

To his credit, Neilson's 1982 trip to the finals came three years after the Rangers' past visit there. The expectation, a reasonable one, given their regular season, was that 1992 would mark their final-series return — and his.

Except this playoff loss wasn't that cut-and-dried.

First of all, in 1991-92, the NHL celebrated its 75th anniversary and endured the agonies of that player strike. The dispute disrupted the entire league, the Rangers probably more so than most, because they were playing so well before it occurred. Neilson is accountable for a lot of things, but there is no way to hold against him the strike and its hideous after-effects any more than you'd point a finger his way if Halley's Comet landed on the Rangers' dressing room.

The team's last game before the strike was against the Islanders at Nassau Coliseum (a loss, naturally) on Saturday, March 28. After that, the Rangers had a four-day break in the schedule and virtually had been ordered to stay away from the rink for a couple of days.

During that time, the strike began. Initially, most players foraged in their garages for equipment and came up with enough to stage informal group workouts. The players dropped a few dollars each into a hat to cover the cost of some ice time at Rye. Piles of clean towels, rolls of tape and a bucket of pucks — they must have been left there by accident — materialized in the tiny, weathered dressing rooms the players scavenged upstairs at the Rye Playland practice facility.

The workouts lasted until the Hilton Head contingent returned home on Tuesday.

The morning after the Islander game, Messier had headed for his summer home in Hilton Head, South Carolina, just to get away for a couple of days and recharge the batteries for his first playoff drive with the Rangers. Messier had been brought to New York for a specific reason, to bring the sparkly silver bowl to Broadway, and The Big Test was not far away. The hope was that the labor dispute would be resolved quickly — at least in time for the playoffs, if not for the conclusion of the regular season the first week in April.

For company on his trip, Messier brought his protege, Leetch, plus Tony Amonte and Mike Richter. Once the strike began, however, the group returned to New York.

Messier walked into Playland during a workout, got a load of his union brothers in their rag-tag getups, and snarled disdainfully about how unprofessional it all looked. If you want to make a point to management, he said, why should we allow them the comfort of thinking we're staying in shape? The dispute will be over faster if the owners know we're losing our conditioning base.

The informal workouts stopped almost instantly, and Messier proved quite correct. In the 10 days of the strike, the team's game conditioning vanished.

And it was a very, very long time coming back. It was all the Rangers could do to survive the New Jersey Devils in a first round that included what certainly seemed some odd Neilson decisions when it came to starting goalies.

John Vanbiesbrouck finished the season with an 8-0-1 run, during which he permitted only 11 goals. He mounted a 12-0-3 streak his final 15 Garden starts and concluded the campaign tied for second in the league with a .910 save percentage. He was a natural to start the playoffs against the Devils, and reaffirmed as much with a splendid showing in a 2-1 Game 1 triumph at the Garden.

When the Rangers were throttled 7-3 the next game, however, Neilson ran for the hook and threw Richter into Game 3. Richter lost, 3-1, at the Meadowlands, but it seemed a no-brainer that Vanbiesbrouck would be the goalie to seek the split in Game 4.

Neilson, instead, gave Richter the nod, reasoning Richter deserved to battle back after a loss. The decision was nothing if not inconsistent; Vanbiesbrouck lost for the first time in 16 home starts and received no such consideration.

Nonetheless, Neilson's decision proved entirely prudent when Richter responded with a 3-0 shutout — a victory which served as a springboard to an 8-5 Ranger romp in Game 5 at the Garden. Richter started Game 6, naturally. But when he was ordinary at best in a 5-3 loss that forced a Game 7 showdown, Neilson was in a bit of a corner.

Vanbiesbrouck's last start before the strike had come on March 24; his first start after it was April 16, or 23 days later. He then played Games 1 and 2 against the Devils, which meant three starts in 28 days, before taking a seat. You had to think that for Game 7, Neilson would go with Richter, who at least had played four straight. To play Vanbiesbrouck would be to pin your hopes, in an ultimate game — the high-pressure point of the season — on a guy who would be starting for only the fourth time in more than five weeks.

By extension, Neilson also was in an extremely awkward position. Though not in so many words, necessarily, he had said to Vanbiesbrouck, "We didn't think you could win Game 3, but would you be so kind as to win us Game 7?"

But Neilson did it and the Rangers won. They survived an 8-4 decision and advanced to the division final against Pittsburgh. Sometimes gambles work, this one did, and it took moxie. If it results in a victory, any coaching move is a brilliant coaching move. Vanbiesbrouck, nothing if not well-rested, came through — earning a vote of confidence that lasted all the way to the end of Game 1 of the next round.

Then the Penguins won 4-2 and Vanbiesbrouck was bye-bye again.

Now here's Vanbiesbrouck, the guy who ignored some very weird treatment and came through in Game 7 against New Jersey. Maybe he had pulled a rock in the opener against Pittsburgh, but Richter had pulled a rock in Game 3 of the first round and Richter had gotten a chance at redemption.

Vanbiesbrouck got no such consideration in Game 2 against Pittsburgh. All Vanbiesbrouck got was a seat on the Garden bench, no more than a few dozen feet from where Adam Graves slashed Mario Lemieux.

Even if Pittsburgh was the defending Stanley Cup champion, the common philosophy is, when you play the first two games of a series on the road, you come to the other guy's rink just looking for a split. Well, by winning Game 1 at the Garden, the Penguins already had their split.

And they got on an early roll in Game 2. In fact, they got on a roll BEFORE it, when Messier — the Rangers' Lemieux — was sidelined by back spasms for the first of two contests.

It got better for Pittsburgh when Kevin Stevens tallied just 1:29 into the match. So when referee Dan Marouelli penalized Rangers defenseman Joe Cirella for elbowing at 4:59, the Penguins' power play was given a chance to provide an early stranglehold. A power-play goal by Pittsburgh there and the Penguins, up 2-0 in the game, can start thinking about checking their way to a 2-0 lead in the series. Lemieux jumped over the boards as soon as the penalty was called and assumed his position at the left point, directly in front of the Rangers' bench.

Off the draw, in the circle to Richter's right, the puck came to Lemieux and Graves raced to him. Lemieux turned slightly and crouched somewhat, using his body to try to protect the puck. Graves, wielding his stick like a bat, chopped Lemieux across the hands. The puck was several feet south of Lemieux's hands when Graves chose this course of action, one for which there seemed no reasonable explanation.

Lemieux, in addition to being a player of stunning skill, is one of exceptional smarts. Unless he is very busy scoring, Lemieux rarely misses an opportunity to embellish an opponent's foul by falling to the ice in agony or cradling the part of his body which has just been bludgeoned. This pretty much guarantees the referee will be aware that some untoward event has occurred.

A few seasons earlier, not far from the very spot where Graves whacked him, Lemieux was chopped across the chest by Rangers defenseman David Shaw and dropped like a ton of bricks — although the exact spot where Shaw's stick had made contact could not be determined immediately. Shaw was suspended 12 games for that incident, but it had involved a high stick, dangerously near the face; the Graves hit clearly was lower.

Thus when Lemieux went down this time, it was easy to imagine he had done the smart thing. The Penguins, up a man, up a goal, up a win, now were going to be up two.

Except Lemieux's left hand was swollen by the time he got to the bench. Later, X-rays of the area showed intelligence had played no role in Lemieux dropping to the ice. Those X-rays disclosed a fracture that would leave the defending Stanley Cup champions without the most dangerous force in the game.

Graves, the son of a policeman, was showered with media garbage for days. Graves was a criminal, nothing more. Scum, basically. A murderer. An assassin. And Neilson, who obviously ordered the 'hit' on Lemieux, was no better. It was bad enough the Rangers had hurt Lemieux, even more galling they didn't even have the decency to lose Game 2 out of collective guilt for Graves' brutality.

In fact, the Rangers won 4-2, so the series was tied when it shifted to Pittsburgh for Games 3 and 4.

Whether they felt good about it or not, the Rangers were in pretty good shape. As it was, Lemieux had missed time during the first round against Washington because of back spasms. As it was, the Penguins had to rally from a 3-1 deficit in games to reach this round. With the Penguins coming off an 87-point season and not playing particularly well, with Lemieux out, with the Rangers appearing to be regaining game condition, it certainly seemed the defending champs were teetering.

Newspaper columnists, who see three games a year and proclaim themselves hockey experts, declared the Rangers' first Stanley Cup in 53 years would be a tainted one. If they had to sink to the level of Graves' despicable act, maybe the Cup wasn't worth winning. Certainly, no Ranger could take pride in winning it by such methods.

There are a lot of really stupid columnists out there.

These are the Rangers, after all.

They have been known to mess up in the playoffs.

It's a good idea to play the games, see what happens, then make the high-and-mighty pronouncements.

So they played the games.

They played Game 3, in fact, before the NHL got around to suspending Graves, which was absurd. If that wasn't bad enough, Graves scored just 3:45 into the game. If THAT wasn't bad enough, the Rangers ended up winning in overtime on a shot that didn't even come from in front of the net. It came on a centering pass Kris King banked into the net off the legpad of Penguins goalie Tom Barrasso.

So now, the city of Pittsburgh is really cranky. Mario's in a cast because of the Ranger thugs, and now the Rangers are ahead in the series because Graves — the criminal — was allowed to butcher Lemieux in one game and score a goal in the next. And now the Rangers are two victories from the semifinals, 10 victories from their tainted Cup. Game 4 could be the last time you see the Penguins on the ice in Pittsburgh this season.

Except by Game 4, it had become clear if Graves was going to hurt anybody, he should have hurt Ron Francis.

It's the third period. The Rangers lead two victories to one and have taken a 4-2 lead on two goals by Messier, who is back in the lineup.

So here are the Rangers, with their captain back, going for the Penguins' necks. They are fewer than 15 minutes from being up 3-1 in games and going back to the Garden, where they dominated all year, for the clincher.

And at 5:19, Penguins defenseman Gordie Roberts gets a major penalty for cross-checking Paul Broten. The Rangers get a five-minute power play, during which they can score all they want; the Penguins don't get the man back.

The Rangers can blow the doors off. It is right there for them.

Brian Leetch, the quarterback on the power play, stays on the ice the whole five minutes.

Nevertheless, the power play stinks. The Rangers barely get a shot on Barrasso. It stays 4-2.

Eight seconds after the penalty expires, Francis, killing time in the neutral zone, flips the puck at the goal from 65 feet away.

As a memorial to their late and beloved coach, Bob Johnson, who steered them to their first Stanley Cup, the Penguins have stencilled onto the ice surface the slogan that was his trademark. The slogan is, "It's a great day for hockey," and it is from the middle of the slogan that Francis shoots.

Because you never know what may happen if you get the puck to the net. You never know when the Rangers might remember they're the Rangers.

The puck goes in. It dips under Richter and the Rangers are done.

They're still ahead, 4-3, still ahead two victories to one in a best-of-seven series, but you know they're done. You know they are not going to win another game because of who they are and who they are playing. You know that if Bob Johnson's ghost is going to reach down through the Civic Arena's arched roof and place his hands over Mike Richter's eyes while Ron Francis' shot flutters toward him, destiny is going to carry Pittsburgh onward.

You know two other things:

You know there isn't a Penguin on the planet who looks at his Stanley Cup ring today and thinks it is tainted because the Rangers choked.

And you know a goalie blowing a shot from 65 feet doesn't make Roger Neilson a bad coach.

He may not have been responsible for that debacle, but Neilson unmistakably was accountable for it. With fairly blistering candor, Neilson admitted as such the morning after the series had been lost. Neilson sat at Rye, looked back at the playoff with an unblinking eye, then looked ahead.

"A coach's job is to get each player to play to the best of his abilities, and maybe their team did a better job there," he said with astonishing frankness. "I feel, on paper, we had a better team."

On ice, they did, too — until the third period of Game 4.

"You can't afford to let two games slip away in a seven-game series like we did. We have no one to blame but ourselves," he said. "In Game 3, they had 50 shots (at Richter) and lost. We had them in Game 4. It was 4-2 and they were done. We could easily have been out of the series in five games and waiting for Boston."

Not quite. Boston completed a four-game sweep of Montreal in the Adams Division Final on May 9; the Rangers didn't play their fifth game against Pittsburgh until May 11. That does not dismiss Neilson's point.

Boston and Montreal, two of the "Original Six" NHL teams, are life-long, knock-down, drag-out rivals. A sweep of the Canadiens is like a pseudo-Cup; the team that wins two playoff games in the Forum, then finishes the job in the minimum time, is bound for a letdown the next series against a team from another division — a team it can't possibly hate as much.

From a purist's standpoint, Rangers-Bruins would have been neat; it would have been another "Original Six" matchup. And with Chicago on a tear in the other conference, you're looking at a guaranteed "Original Six" final next round to cap a season in which the NHL is celebrating its 75th anniversary.

Boston seemed beatable. Chicago, too.

"We feel if we win this game," Neilson said of Game 6 in Pittsburgh, "we're going to win the Stanley Cup."

Neilson might just as well have gotten out the hammer and chisel right then, because you KNEW that one was going on his Ranger tombstone.

There are several absolutely immutable facts in pro sports and one of them, bad grammar notwithstanding, is: you better not assume you will pick up where you left off. Players and executives are completely mistaken when they say, "We had a great season. We'll have to build on that next year."

It doesn't work that way, and you'd be foolish to believe it does. You never know which of your players had their best seasons the year everyone wants "to build on." A season isn't like a house, where you add a room or a garage. When the season ends, the house gets levelled and the only thing that stays in place is the foundation.

A guy who got 40 goals one season doesn't start at 40 goals the next season. He starts at zero goals. He has to score 40 again just to be as good as he was the year before, and he has to score at least 41 to keep from sliding backward. It's the same with a team: A team that gets to the second round one year isn't even guaranteed a playoff spot the next year. You don't start with the 105 points the Rangers got in 1991-92, you start with zero and just hope you can find a way or make a way to even come close to that in 1992-93.

So, more than anything else, when the tournament is wide open and the Cup is right there to be had, you've got to win it. Because things could be completely different at playoff time next year. One of your key players might be hurt. One of your key players might be suspended.

And remember, Montreal, which had won the Adams Division, had been beaten by Boston. Detroit, the Norris Division champion, had been beaten by Chicago. Vancouver won the Smythe with a record of 42-26-12, and had lost in the second round to an Edmonton club that had gone 36-34-10.

If three other first-place teams are out, if you're the only first-place team left and winning Game 6 stands between you and eliminating the defending champ to clear the playoff field, you find a way to win it or you die trying.

"We didn't come through in the key parts of the series," Neilson said. "Overall, we had an edge in the play, but they (the Penguins) had an edge in goal in the series, their defensemen played better than our defensemen, and their top four or five players probably played better than our top four or five players.

"When we needed to kill a penalty early in a game, we couldn't do it," Neilson summed up. "When we needed a power-play goal, we couldn't get it. Whether it was the breaks or not, we just couldn't come through like we needed to. The other team seemed to come up with the big plays.

"We never got on a roll in the playoffs. Some people look back and blame the strike, but once we got past the first series, you'd have to write that off," he said.

Now, the objective was to keep it from happening again. You need 16 victories to win a Stanley Cup; in the three playoff seasons — remember, following two first-place finishes and a second — the Rangers had managed 13.

Which just won't do. Three trips to the playoffs had produced just 16 home games for the Garden, 16 sellouts for Paramount, which really means more revenue losses than gains.

When a team enters the playoffs, arena dates have to be blocked out; when a team is eliminated from the playoffs, it is virtually impossible to book an event into the building. When a team is eliminated and the building goes dark, the ticket sellers and ticket takers don't work and neither do the ushers, neither do the vendors. The ice crew doesn't work because there is no ice.

Nobody has to clean up the garbage after the game, nobody has to change the toilet paper in the restrooms.

When the building goes dark, the pizza place across the street doesn't sell as much product, nor does the deli or the hamburger joint or the Chinese takeout. No visiting team — with its entourage of announcers, news crews and reporters — comes to stay in the city's hotels, eat in the city's restaurants, shop in its stores. The financial disaster is a giant tree with roots that extend deep into the city's soil.

"Maybe something we should do next year is mix-and-match the lines a bit, because that happens in the playoffs," Neilson said.

In the 105-point season, Neilson had been uncomfortable with the predictable nature of his lines. You knew Messier with Graves and Amonte was the scoring line. You knew Turcotte with Kris King and Paul Broten was the checking line. You figured Sergei Nemchinov, with Jan Erixon on the left and Mike Gartner on the right was the swing line and Kocur or Domi would find their way onto the fourth line with Randy Gilhen or Doug Weight. Brian Leetch and Jeff Beukeboom were the top defense pair, Mark Hardy and James Patrick manned the second set, Joe Cirella and Jay Wells filled the 5-6 slots.

Sure it was predictable, but it was a very simple proposition: You knew who was coming, but you still had to stop them. In 1991-92, a lot of teams tried and a lot of teams failed. They didn't have the depth and they didn't have the skill. When it came to their best hockey against the Rangers' best hockey, the Rangers' best hockey was better three nights out of four.

Do you think you need more speed?

"No," Neilson replied. "Two things you're looking at are toughness and speed. I think we have enough of that to survive the Patrick Division."

More scoring?

"I always wondered if we had enough."

Defense?

"I must admit, our defensive play always concerned me. In the playoffs, everybody tightens up (defensively), and we didn't seem to," Neilson said. "Where New Jersey and Pittsburgh tried to beat us was on the counter-attack. I would think, next year, we'll be stressing more of the defensive part of the game. A player like Mark Messier or Wayne Gretzky or Eric Lindros, you've got to let them freelance a bit. You've got to let them do their own thing a bit. But it would apply to all our players to tighten up defensively."

Though the goals-against total had been remarkably low, fourth-best in the league with 246 in 80 games, the work of Richter and Vanbiesbrouck had stolen points on a regular basis. Richter had three shutouts, Vanbiesbrouck two. Of the 40 games in the second half, the opposition was limited to two goals or fewer 15 times. Often that was because the Rangers seemed to have the puck all night; other times, it was as though the goalies were the only members of their team to report for work.

When you have the league MVP on your team, and the top defenseman and one of the top rookies, you might figure to do well. You get goaltending like that, you might figure to do well. You get 95 goals from your first three centers (Nemchinov and Turcotte added 30 each to Messier's 35) and 75 from your top two right wings, you might figure to do well. And 88 goals from the top three right wings (Gartner 40, Amonte 35, Broten 13) aren't going to set you back. You get the saves virtually every night and you can get league-leading penalty killing, so you can play as rough as you want and not give a darn.

You put it all together, you can get 105 points.

But that doesn't mean you can do it again.

A simple fact of the 1990s is, teams that jump 20-odd points in one season have found it difficult to sustain such dramatic improvement. Often, they return nearer the level of the season prior to the big jump. In 1989-90, the Chicago Blackhawks had 88 points, then jumped to 106 the next season before settling back to 87 in 1991-92. In that same three-season span, the Los Angeles Kings went 75-102-84, and the St. Louis Blues went 83-105-83.

Put it another way: Since the Detroit Red Wings had the first set of 100-or-more point consecutive seasons (1950-51 and 1951-52), only 11 teams have recorded consecutive 100-point seasons. And since the 1989-90 season, only the Bruins had managed consecutive 100-point showings in the '90s, starting with 101 that season and following with 100. Calgary deserves honorary mention, though, since its 100-point season in 1990-91 came on the heels of a 99-point showing.

Anyway, a hundred points is a LOT of points; and the NHL in 1992-93 would be a season in which it was extremely difficult to win.

"I want to knee-jerk it today," Colin Campbell said that May day. "I really want to knee-jerk it. I really want to punch a wall. But you can't; you just can't. You've got to assess it properly, because there are three other first-place teams that want to do the same thing.

"It's a situation that calls for a temper tantrum," Campbell continued. "You want to get mad at somebody, some thing — your team, the other team. I mean, the top five teams are GONE.

"You come a long way, you strive to go on, and all of a sudden, there's nothing there when you get there, and it's another whole year before you get the chance to get there again," Campbell added. "You wonder, what do you do? Do you prepare for a marathon when you've got to sprint at the end?"

Nope, you lay one foot in front of the other at a steady rate and pace until you pass the finish line, whenever and wherever that is.

There was another thing to consider. Because of the Stanley Cup drought and its attendant pressure to win, because of the "off with his head" manner in which the Rangers and the Garden had interacted with the Paramount people for years, Rangers coaches were fired with relative regularity. Neil Smith didn't want to be just like the others who had preceded him. He had run on a platform of political stability in the volatile Garden environment; to guillotine Neilson would be to give the fans a message. "Here we go again."

So Neil Smith brought Neilson back, gave him a three-year deal worth about a million bucks.

And once Smith brought Neilson back, you had to figure Neilson would be around all season — that he might well be fired before the end of the new contract, but that he'd be judged, for sure, on what his team did in the playoffs in 1992-93.

CHAPTER 3

BATTLE STATIONS

WHILE NEILSON SAT IN ONE part of the Rye training base and owned up to the unacceptably poor playoff performance by himself and his team, captain Messier stood on the other side of the wall, in the dressing room, and — by implication — agreed enthusiastically with Neilson's assessment.

Although this breakup-day gathering was an opportunity to salute the role Neilson had played in a season of extensive achievement, Messier passed on the chance — providing the first signal all was not well, suggesting for the first time these two very different men differed more profoundly than anyone imagined.

When their association began, Messier was an experienced 30, Neilson a fatherly 57 — notwithstanding the fact that watching music videos on MTV was among Neilson's favorite activities. It should be noted, as well, that despite the huge age difference, Neilson sported an owl's nest of hair the color of seasoned salt; Messier had earned honorary captaincy of the All-Scalp team.

Though Edmonton-born, Messier gained big-city savvy in his years with Oilers GM Glen Sather, whose hockey IQ was sharp as his wardrobe. Neilson retained the conservatism of his Toronto birthplace, preferring dry wit and understatement.

Messier, tall, muscular, leaned toward cutting-edge fashion; Neilson had dozens of neckties, if not hundreds, and bragged he had not spent more than three bucks on a single one of them.

Unmistakably, jewelry presented the most graphic contrast between Messier and his boss. Although never seen wearing any of them — "That's history. I'm a Ranger now," he often declared, shoving Oiler cards aside when asked to sign them — Messier had those five Stanley Cup rings. Neilson had as many Cup rings as his beloved dog, Mike.

Neilson had come close only that one time, that 1982 Stanley Cup final. But it was over in four games, before the Canucks knew what hit them. Just getting there had been their Stanley Cup.

Does losing a final make you a bad coach? Does it make your desire to win any less than that of someone who has won? Does it push you off the high wire that stretches between being a loser and simply being a non-winner?

No.

On the other hand, was a coach ever hired NOT to win it all?

Those issues started coming to the forefront May 14.

The Knicks, the Rangers' basketball brethren in the Garden sports group, still were involved in their playoffs. The Knicks are not coached so much as they are choreographed by Pat Riley, a tall, elegant man who radiates charisma and success. There is a stunning energy to him, a total commitment to and immersion in the event, such that the players would have to work very hard to outwork him on a gamenight. He calls plays, shouts instructions, directs action. And when referees need educating, Riley always makes sure to stand very close to them, so that the pronounced difference in their relative heights is unmistakable.

There seem barely a handful of moments when Riley simply stands on the sideline and lets the action unfold of its own free will. Those times, he will fan the fabric of his jacket like a cape, rest his fists on the hips of his slacks, and watch expectantly. Or, absorbed, he will stretch one arm across his chest and rest the elbow of the other arm on it, leaving one hand free to knead the skin of his chin. As he prowls the sidelines, Riley's appearance is of someone who already has seen the game — someone who has jumped ahead in time, has watched the contest, and has returned to the present filled with foreboding that the night will be lost if the players fail to do his bidding.

Contrast that with Neilson's philosophy:

"If I don't feel I could coach the other team, put the right players from the other team out in the right spots, I don't feel I'm as prepared as I should be," Neilson said. "I should know the other team well enough that I could go behind their bench and coach them, and they wouldn't notice any difference between me and their coach. That would be the perfect situation."

Sounds similar, doesn't it?

You cannot watch Riley work without wondering how much his clothes cost. You wonder whether he actually wears the Armani suit or the shirt or the tie a second time, or whether the appearance of a single wrinkle signals impending expulsion from his wardrobe. Riley knows drape, texture, tone; would not blow his nose in a $3 tie, much less wear one.

In his appearance, Riley is all the things Neilson characteristically has not been: Strong. Powerful. Commanding. Dominant. Determined. Demanding.

And, oh yes . . . a champion.

Riley makes things larger than life, Neilson makes them smaller; there are fewer flourishes from him when the game is on. If Riley is The Cashmere Coach, Neilson is more like canvas or burlap.

Nonetheless, the mindsets seem matched, and coaching is a job of substance over style — even if it helps to have both. Even in overalls, Riley would be an exceptional coach. Even in a tuxedo, Neilson's credentials cannot be questioned.

Yet despite almost identical seasons and identical nicknames — each has been tagged "Captain Video" for passionate study of game tapes — cracks started showing in the ice under Neilson, while Riley, in his first season with the Knicks, was walking on water.

Riley's team went 51-31, a .622 winning percentage.

Neilson's team went 50-25-5, a .625 winning percentage.

Riley's team survived a winner-take-all fifth game from the Detroit Pistons in the first round, then lost to Chicago's defending league champions.

Neilson's team survived a winner-take-all seventh game against the Devils in the first round, then lost to Pittsburgh's defending league champions.

Riley finished second in Coach of the Year voting, behind Don Nelson of Golden State.

Neilson finished second, behind Pat Quinn of Vancouver.

Riley's team jumped 12 victories from the prior season's total and finished tied for first.

Neilson's team jumped 14 and won the division by seven points.

It comes down to this: In 1982, the year of Neilson's losing trip to the finals, Riley was winning the first of four championships with the Lakers. Neilson's favorite player that season was

Dave "Tiger" Williams, who was no-field, all hit — who said he couldn't score because by the time the message went from his head to his hands, the game was over. Riley's favorite was Earvin "Magic" Johnson; who could make a perfect fast-break pass while wearing snowshoes and carrying a set of dishes.

And, on his first day with the team, Pat Riley was more "New York" than Neilson ever was or ever will be. It's not a big thing, but it matters.

"What do the Rangers need to win it all? They need to be a real New York team," says a fan, Lisa Yancey of Brooklyn. "Look back at the Yankees of the Seventies, the Mets and Giants of the Eighties, and the Knicks now.

"What have they got in common? ATTITUDE! Nothing, I mean nothing, comes close to New York attitude.

"It's Reggie Jackson watching his home run go over the wall and taking a slow run around the bases. It's Lawrence Taylor sacking the quarterback for the third time, standing over his fallen body, pointing a finger in his face and saying, 'I own your ass!' It's John Starks in Michael Jordan's face, never backing down.

"Some hockey teams think the Rangers do have that New York attitude, but they don't yet," Yancey continued. "They need to take on the identity of the city, that feeling of being bigger, better, smarter, faster — that 'Get out of my face and get out of my way' feeling . . . the attitude that, 'I will always win, no matter what, because I have to.'

"Hate it or love it, it's what makes New York what it is, and all the championship teams that have come and gone over the years have had it," Yancey said. "A little can take you all the way."

If Messier played for the Knicks, the captain-coach thing would have been bliss. This breakup day, Messier invoked Riley's name but never Neilson's.

"Obviously, he has proven he's an incredible coach at this time of year," Messier said, speaking of Riley, "and on top of that, he's got the commitment of the players."

Did Neilson enjoy that same commitment?

"Definitely we were committed to a cause, for sure, this year," came Messier's reply. "One of the reasons we really kind of came together and grew together was, there was a good chemistry on the team and I think that was a really important part."

Asked about the Rangers' commitment to Neilson, Messier replied about being committed to a cause. Moreover, by declaring Riley "an incredible coach at this time of year" and not mentioning Neilson, there was an implication Neilson did not meet that standard.

Of course, history would support that contention.

Still, Messier had ample opportunity to throw out a typical, gratuitous, "We all had a great year, from the coaching staff to the trainers, but we fell short of our objective, which was to win the Stanley Cup."

Messier did not take that opportunity. He said things that came relatively close, but never the bare bones of, " . . . and I feel for Roger and the coaches, who worked so hard this year. . . "

If coach and captain do not read from the same page of the same book, every victory serves, nonetheless, as a solid steel girder in the bridge across any gap that might exist. Teams can win in spite of real or perceived friction; teams can win BE-CAUSE of it, as there is always pepper in the stew and the pot never cools. Captain and coach don't have to like each other for a club to do well, but mutual respect helps, and performance by the player is a minimum condition. If you can't play for the coach, at least play for yourself, your teammates, the fans; if the results are there, little else matters.

From an on-ice standpoint, Messier could not have done much more in 1991-92. He scored 35 goals, set a team record for assists in a season by a center with 72, and became the fifth scorer in Rangers history to collect 100 points or more. He ran off a 15-game point streak from February 5 to March 7, managed a point or more in 64 of the 79 games in which he played, helped the Rangers jump 20 standings points to 105, and increase from 36 victories to 50.

Off-ice, Messier organized the team Christmas party at a lavish Manhattan hotel. During a West Coast trip, he set up a team outing to his prestigious country club, Sherwood, in Thousand Oaks, California. When team meetings had to be called, when the right things had to be said and listened to, Messier called the meetings and made the speeches.

Pretty much, he became Mister Everything. Messier was the emblem player, the focus of virtually all attention not only in New York but every Ranger stop around the league. And the more the spotlight was on him, the more he seemed to accomplish in its glare.

One example was a game at Edmonton on January 23, when Messier walloped a rocket of a slap shot over Bill Ranford's left glove from the right-wing circle. Naturally, it was the winning goal, the fourth of six such scores Messier would collect during his first Rangers season. Naturally, it came in his return to his hometown, to the place where he built a legend for leadership — where he became all the things the Rangers characteristically have not been: Strong. Powerful. Commanding. Dominant. Determined. Demanding.

And, oh yes. . . a champion.

So when Messier spoke, he wasn't just a player, he was The Captain.

He was The Guy Who Knows What It Takes To Win.

He also was The Big Guy Who Has Won (even if the coach hasn't).

If this person stops short of ringing endorsement for the coach, mentions the coach of another team — not his own — the ground under that player's coach begins eroding instantly unless at least one of the following occurs:

— The coach stands up for himself. Firmly.

— Upper management stands up for the coach. Firmly.

Players always are testing coaches or management. It ends up being part of a team's dynamic. They want to know what the rules are, how firm the control is, where the boundaries are. No matter how large the field is, they will run all the way to the fence; when they reach it, the fence better be high enough to contain them.

Is it a player's right or privilege to hire or fire a coach? Moreover, is it any of his business? By definition, of course not. General managers manage generally. Coaches coach. Players play — unless, of course, they have been brought in with a mandate to Show The Winning Way, which unarguably was the case with Messier. If you ask that of a player, then he does what he thinks you've asked of him, don't try to make it his fault if the fur starts flying.

Is it a captain's obligation to make noise if he feels the coach and the team are not the right fit? Absolutely. Usually, the noise gets made behind the scenes first, then gets made in front of them only after other avenues have failed. Later, Messier would admit his lobbying began in November, a good six months before breakup day.

As everyone sat around the team's Rye training base that day, the coaching staff seemed to be crumbling anyway. Assistant coach Wayne Cashman's contract had expired; he would not be back. Assistant coach Colin Campbell had head coaching aspirations, and jobs would be coming open over the summer, so there was no guarantee he would return. Coming off the come-from-ahead loss the team had suffered to Pittsburgh, facing the loss of two assistants, anyway, Smith could have canned the whole staff and not raised many eyebrows.

Smith had made significant changes in player personnel the year before, after the outrage of the first-round loss to Washington. They always say, "You can't fire two dozen players, so you fire the coach." But Smith had fired players. He flat-out fired captain Kelly Kisio and Brian Mullen by leaving them available for claim in the 1991 expansion process. He signed Adam Graves, surrendering Troy Mallette as compensation. He traded Bernie Nicholls, Louie DeBrusk, Steven Rice and, ultimately, David Shaw in the Messier deal.

You have that kind of player turnover one summer, the place you go to work the next summer is behind your bench. Neil Smith's eyes seemed focused in that direction on breakup day, but he handled the pleasantries better.

"I can't imagine a guy could have done a better job than Roger did this season," Smith said. "But it's up to us to analyze every aspect of the organization."

A qualified endorsement was not exactly what Neilson needed at that stage, but Smith was in a corner. Neilson was a finalist for Coach of the Year. How do you fire him, then watch him walk on a stage to accept his award?

Smith could have waited, made his move after the award was handed to Vancouver's Pat Quinn. But still, Neilson WAS runner-up. There were 22 coaches in the business and 20 of them lined up behind Neilson in the election. How do you fire him and not second-guess yourself?

Further, Messier was named the league's Most Valuable Player in voting by the Pro Hockey Writers' Association. He was named league MVP by *The Sporting News*. He was voted the Lester B. Pearson Award as league MVP by the members of the NHL Players' Association.

Messier's right wing, Tony Amonte, was a finalist in the PHWA Rookie of the Year voting, made the Upper Deck All-

Rookie team and won the rookie prize from *The Sporting News* —
leading a field that included Vancouver's electrifying Pavel Bure
and Detroit defenseman Nicklas Lidstrom.

Clearly stimulated by Messier's influence, Brian Leetch,
meanwhile, ended up with career-high totals of 80 assists (a team
record for defensemen) and 102 points — which made him only
the fifth defenseman in NHL history to surpass the century mark
in points. Leetch won the Norris Trophy as the outstanding
player at his position.

Could Neilson have had nothing to do with these accomplishments?

Messier was a three-tiered MVP. His protege, Leetch, won
the Norris. Amonte won top rookie honors from *The Sporting
News*. The common joke claimed Messier was just bitter HE
didn't win Coach of the Year.

The night of the NHL awards show, an Oscars-style production in Toronto that is televised nationally in Canada, all media
ears tuned eagerly to every word Messier uttered. The world
would learn this night if his failure to mention Neilson on
breakup day merely had been an oversight the morning after a
crushing loss stamped a premature end to a glorious season.
Weeks removed from the disappointment, the expectation was
that Messier's head had cleared and that he would correct the
error — if, in fact, there had been one.

The chance was right there for Messier to clear up any
confusion, right across Canada. He could have stared into the
nation's living rooms and taken the fuse out of the bomb that had
begun to tick.

He didn't do it.

Later, in the interview area, Messier's tone was somewhat
different.

"I have to laugh a little bit at those accusations," Messier
said, as people started wondering about possible differences
with Neilson. "I certainly wouldn't have intended (people to
think that). The first thing that came to my mind (on breakup day)
was the fact that Pat Riley did a fantastic job.

"When you lose," he added, "you have to go back and assess
what are your strong points and what are your weak points."

Funny, isn't it? Neil Smith had said the same thing on
breakup day, but the remark had a decidedly less-pointed tone.
Smith said it as administrator of the large company the Rangers

are, and the comment seemed appropriate. Messier said it as an employee, and it was perceived as totally inappropriate.

Anyway, finding accusations laughable does not declare them untrue. Messier had 107 points in the regular season, 14 in the playoffs. Now, he seemed to be making one more point — one that was difficult to miss, one that banged hard on the soft wood of the door to the coaches' office.

Colin Campbell heard the unmistakable knock.

"In sports, there always seem to be turbulent offseasons because changes are always happening," Campbell said. "It's always nice to go into a summer knowing, 'We had a great year, we're going to be back, let's enjoy it,' and I was hoping to have a great summer after the year we had. But obviously, from the awards on, with Mess not acknowledging Roger, there seemed to be tension.

"And probably, other people focused in on it more than Mess or Roger," Campbell added. "They had their opinions, and they're very strongly opinionated people about their hockey thoughts. It seemed like when you were a kid; you're riding in the car and your parents had had a fight. There was that tension between them, and it made you feel uneasy. They wouldn't say anything, but you knew there was something wrong; you just wished they'd be back together again and not having that tension.

"They talked about it in training camp and they talked about a couple of things during the season. And it's interesting: They were both gentlemen enough not to put their own opinions and stubbornness of philosophy ahead of the team. And yet they weren't going to abandon it, either," Campbell said. "As much as was made out of it, there was no real yelling and screaming. That wasn't there. It just seemed from the day of the awards that there was supposed to be a rift.

"And after Mess's year (in 1991-92) — and Leetchie's, too — not too often does an MVP, particularly at his age, repeat a year like that," Campbell said. "So when he didn't come back at the start of the year, playing like he did, people are going to point to, 'Well, that (friction) is the reason. We're not winning, and that's the reason.'

"I don't think that's the reason," Campbell said. "I think, when it gets right down to it, that when you get a new face, a new voice, new drills and a different suit behind the bench, players just seem to revel in new blood and new life. That's the tough part about our coaching profession. Unfortunately in our business, change seems to be the hallmark that's screamed for every three years."

CHAPTER 4

MONEY TALKS

THOUGH NEILSON AGREED to the terms of his contract in August, announcement of the deal was delayed for months while various documents were exchanged between the Rangers' lawyers and Neilson's. It wasn't so much a contract as a treatise, a festival of clauses and conditions — all of which had to be worded acceptably for both sides.

Neil Smith spent a small mountain of other dollars over the summer because there were gaps in his lineup and he needed to patch them.

Attending to the defense, Smith added Peter Andersson and Sergei Zubov to the depth chart on the left side and, in rather a surprise, brought swingman Per Djoos from his self-imposed exile in Sweden.

Andersson had been a fourth-round draft choice by Craig Patrick in 1983, back when the Rangers' fabulous European scout, Lars-Erik Sjoberg, still was alive. But neither Patrick nor his successor, Phil Esposito, had extricated Andersson from contracts with club teams in Farjestad and Malmo in the Swedish Elite League; so it was only now, at age 27, that he would wear Ranger colors.

Zubov had been a fifth-round selection in Smith's first draft, 1990, but had remained with the CSKA (Red Army) team in Moscow. When political conditions cleared the way for Russian players to join NHL teams more easily, Smith did what had to be done to speed Zubov's emigration.

Then he brought back Djoos, though the defenseman had been nothing more than a spare part with some power-play skills in the preceding season. Djoos had appeared in 50 games with the Rangers but was disappointed with his playing time. On break-up day, after the Pittsburgh series, he virtually had promised he would not be back.

The lure of an NHL job overcame him, however. Djoos figured if he was not one of Neilson's favorite players, he might just play well enough that some other club would make a deal for him. So when training camp workouts began in upstate Glens Falls, New York, Djoos was on the ice.

If those three weren't enough, Smith also signed free-agent Dave Marcinyshyn. Except for Jeff Beukeboom, there wasn't much size on the Rangers' defense and there wasn't much anger, either. Though an imposing specimen at 6-3, 210 pounds, Marcinyshyn was more likely to add the former than the latter; he had washed out in New Jersey and Quebec for being a big man who wouldn't use his size and it was doubtful this toothless tiger would change stripes.

There was other business to conduct up front.

Tie Domi had played out the option season of his contract in 1991-92, and the Rangers were in 'danger' of losing the scrappy right wing to the Tampa Bay Lightning, which was making noise about signing him as a free agent. Unwilling to place the policeman's role entirely on Joe Kocur's shoulders (and fists), Smith signed Domi for the three years at around $1.4 million.

Domi had been a willing enforcer for Neilson, but still had all kinds of rough edges that needed smoothing. Domi unmistakably had some hand skills with his gloves on. He was an eager hitter who made people hurry plays. He had some speed — without the puck — and could make a better pass than you might expect. But he also had a target on his back. Neilson hardly could trust him for a regular shift, so the coach used Domi in fight/intimidation situations; Domi would jump over the boards, the Garden crowd would buzz and eyes would scan the opponents' skaters quickly to see who might be the target of some mayhem.

The referee's hand would be in the air before many seconds passed.

Domi usually did a pretty good job of making sure that if he went to the penalty box, an opponent went with him. He could prove an infuriating foe and at times was roughly as infuriating a teammate; Domi never minded crawling along the floor during a team meal and giving a teammate a "shoe shine" using French dressing or chocolate sauce from the buffet.

But Domi did not play much, and was increasingly cranky about it.

"I don't want to be a spare part any more. I want to be a regular," said Domi, the target of constant jibes because of a crew-cut head that is disproportionately large for his body. "I don't want to be sitting up in a press box, pulling out the hair I don't have."

Domi's 42 game appearances represented barely half the schedule; his two goals, four assists, and six points (2-4-6) looked eminently symmetrical next to his penalty-minute total, 246. When Domi re-signed with the Rangers, it appeared that the Rangers were tacitly making some guarantee of ice time.

They wouldn't give a guy $400,000 a year and not play him, would they?

With Domi's round face in the crowd on the right side, along with Mike Gartner, Tony Amonte, Alexei Kovalev, Paul Broten and Joe Kocur, Smith looked to his left flank. And he didn't see quite as much depth because of a different raid by Tampa Bay.

Because of injuries, Jan Erixon tended to miss lots more games than he played, which left the port side somewhat threadbare behind Graves and Kris King. So Smith brought back Dave Archibald, who had been obtained from Minnesota for defenseman Jayson More in 1989 and who afterward had meandered from Flint (IHL) to the Canadian National Team to the Canadian Olympic Team to Italy — making time, in the interim, for a brief retirement.

The other spot on the left had been intended for Rob Zamuner, who, like Domi, had played out the option year and had become a free agent.

Zamuner had been claimed by interim GM Joe Bucchino in the third round of the 1989 draft. Esposito was fired in May that year and Neil Smith was not hired until July 17, which left Bucchino, who had been Esposito's assistant, to conduct the selection at the Met Center in Bloomington, Minnesota, that June.

With the Rangers' No. 1 choice, 20th overall, Bucchino picked Steven Rice — a hard-hitting right wing who along with Louie DeBrusk (Bucchino's fourth pick) ended up going to Edmonton in the 1991 trade for Messier. With his second pick, Bucchino over-rated a right wing named Jason Prosofsky and with the third, he picked Zamuner, a lanky 6-2, 202 forward who at the time was coming off a 46-goal season with Guelph of the Ontario League.

Zamuner spent time with the Rangers' Flint affiliate in the International League, then its Binghamton team in the American League, and didn't see the same prospect for advancement that the Rangers were promising him. Tampa was offering more than $300,000, and at age 23, Zamuner was convinced that front-line playing time on an expansion team was better than occasional duty with New York, albeit at the same pay rate.

The Rangers were entitled to compensation from Tampa for the loss of Zamuner and received a third-round pick. But since you can't put skates and a sweater on a person you haven't claimed yet, Smith needed to bulk up on the left side.

So he signed Phil Bourque, off the roster of the Pittsburgh team that had beaten him and had gone on to its second Stanley Cup.

Smith likes Stanley Cup rings in his dressing room, and the addition of Bourque brought two more to the Ranger vault. Messier had won five, Beukeboom three, while Randy Gilhen and Adam Graves threw in one apiece.

The day he signed, Bourque was introduced to the New York media by a conference call, the method the team's media relations department uses to save new Rangers from having to return 20 or 30 individual interview requests. There was no mistaking the anticipation in Bourque's voice, which may have had to do with the terms of employment: four years, $2 million.

But in his eagerness to answer questions candidly, Bourque inadvertently put both feet in his mouth. He pretty much trashed Neilson's game plan for the Pittsburgh series and essentially confirmed media suspicions that the Rangers' increasingly physical play against the Penguins had been improper strategy. It may have worked for Neilson's Maple Leafs against the Islanders in 1978, but it wasn't going to work for Neilson's Rangers against the Penguins in 1992.

"As the series went on, we could see they (the Rangers) were getting more and more aggressive, trying to make a statement in each game by punishing us," Bourque explained. "As soon as a guy would come running at us, we would chip the puck by him. We'd have two-on-one and three-on-two rushes all night.

"There's a lot of discipline involved in playoff hockey," Bourque added. "If you take an unnecessary penalty in a playoff game, you could cost your team the game. You can't let things bother you. You've got to be focused on what the goal is.

"In Game 4, the Rangers had the Penguins where they wanted them and lost. I'm sure it was a hard lesson for them," said Bourque, absolutely correct yet again. "Everybody is waiting to see what the Rangers can do after losing a tough series. It's time to prove themselves. They're the best team in hockey. We should go in with the attitude nobody can beat us. There's every ingredient on this team to win the Stanley Cup."

Bourque just didn't get it. These are the Rangers. Regardless the attitude, ANYBODY can beat them. And to win the Stanley Cup, you have to make the playoffs. First things first.

■■■

When Neilson opened his fourth Rangers training camp, at Glens Falls on September 13, 1992, he was one of only seven coaches to have been in that position a mere 18 months earlier; more than two-thirds of the league's head coaching jobs had turned over in that span.

And of those "Magnificent Seven," Neilson was third in seniority. Chicago had hired Mike Keenan June 9, 1988, and the Islanders had brought Al Arbour back December 7 that year. The other four in the group were Washington's Terry Murray (January 15, 1990), Minnesota's Bob Gainey (June 19, 1990), Detroit's Bryan Murray (July 13, 1990) and Vancouver's Pat Quinn (January 31, 1991). Those last three had some built-in job security, as they also acted as general managers of their teams.

That track record makes it clear there is only one time when a coach isn't hanging by a thread. That is when he is GM as well; then he is hanging by two threads. Neilson, coming off a 50-victory season, is hanging by one thread and one hair as his club begins workouts at the Glens Falls Civic Center.

The coach has to take a group of players in training camp and decide which of them can make his team the best it can be. Then he must decide, each game night, which of them will provide the best chance of winning. He must determine which tactics are best suited to his personnel and which are most likely to disturb the plans of the opponent. He must plan practices that embellish the team's strengths and build up the weaknesses. He must believe in what he says and what he thinks, and he must convince the players constantly that his way is the right way.

And even if he convinces them today, there is every chance in the world he might lose them tomorrow. In pro team sports, a time almost always comes when the 1,100-pound horse figures out it's bigger than its 110-pound jockey; the challenge before the coach is to stay in the saddle, to have his horse run its race without ever needing the whip.

That, essentially, was the way things had gone for Neilson and the Rangers in 1991-92. The team had lost its season-opening game on a Thursday night in Boston, then had gone to Montreal — to find Messier, gift-wrapped and waiting, when they got to the dressing room at the Forum for practice Friday afternoon. From there, they had stormed to that remarkable regular season in a manner no one could have expected.

After all, a year earlier, Messier had been a mere fantasy; now he was a reality, the hub where all the spokes joined in the Ranger wheel. Now, he would be a factor in the planning and the program right from the get-go — he would show the way from the first minute of the first scrimmage in 1992-93 . . . assuming a way could be found to bring him closer to Neilson from a philosophical standpoint.

Toward that end, the men met the Friday night before training camp began and started working on damage control.

"I think we can work with each other and help each other out," Messier said. "I certainly respect my coach, as I've been taught my whole career, and I told Roger, 'I've come to play my butt off, as I did last year.'

"It was really good to sit down and talk, because of all the things that went on during the summer," Messier said, as though observers had created his apparent non-support of the coach. "I know there's a mutual respect between us, and that's important. More important is, he is coach of the team and I'm a player, and I don't think that has been or ever was in doubt — certainly not in my mind.

"We talked a little about the differences in philosophy, and I think that's OK. I don't think that's a problem," Messier said. "Basically, if I can help in certain areas and we can blend some ideas, it will be best for the team. Ultimately, he's the one who makes the decisions. He's the one who sets the tone for the team and the style of play and the personality of the club. That's the way it should be."

It still seemed, however, as though Messier was taking medicine instead of eagerly embracing and supporting the program.

Messier is a skater who plays a skating game. Almost everywhere he looked in the dressing room, he saw speed or skating skill, from Tony Amonte to Mike Gartner to Brian Leetch to Darren Turcotte to Alexei Kovalev, and Messier's contention was a simple one: "If you have a great wide receiver, you don't turn him into a defensive end. If you've got a fast-skating team, you can play that kind of style."

You play that kind of style because not many teams in the league can match it. Team speed is a relatively rare commodity, and the number of fast skaters the Rangers had was extremely high; Neilson could deploy at least one elite speedster on each line. By not exploiting the speed, you keep yourself back in the pack and let other people catch you, which doesn't make sense. Messier believed Neilson chose that plan too often.

"The one thing that got lost over the summer was that I really enjoyed last year and I really enjoyed Roger," he said, at last. "There were a lot more positives than negatives last year. I never blamed any of the coaches for us losing last spring."

Neilson, almost never one to wear his heart on his sleeve, seemed relatively satisfied.

"There is no issue. Things get blown up. All's well," he said. "He (Messier) said there is no problem whatsoever, and all he wants to do is play and have another great year. He made it very clear that he supports the coaching staff fully."

Thus the off-season turmoil was portrayed as water under a very high bridge. Nonetheless, it seemed a most prudent idea to have a raft stocked with provisions nearby, because you never knew if the river might rise.

And anyway, there were other things about which to worry.

FIRST, the team was more talented than ever and expectations were higher. The Rangers weren't going to be sneaking up on opponents, catching any teams by surprise. Everybody was going to want to knock the regular-season champions down a notch, were going to be more "psyched" to play them, because that is the nature of the sports beast. You spend all your time trying to make that climb to the top, and when you get there, the whole world spends every waking moment trying to think up ways to knock you off that pedestal.

SECOND, the team was at a crossroads from an intangible standpoint. It is one thing to handle disappointment and failure and underachievement, another thing entirely to confront the challenge posed by success. Unmistakably, it is safer to be on the sad end.

You never win anything of significance, "but at least you gave it that old college try, and isn't that, really, what sports is all about?" Of course, that is as big a load of crap as anyone ever could think up, but people buy it and players buy into it.

Which is how trouble starts.

When you've won something like a regular-season title, and have shown the promise of winning something — like the first Stanley Cup in more than five decades — you have to make constant demands on yourself to stay at or above the level of expectation that has been set. You have to create new challenges, new ways to win . . . ways which generally extract far more effort than finding new ways to lose. It isn't a matter of overachieving, because there is no such thing. Rather, there are people and teams who achieve — who reap the rewards of playing to maximum skill and effort, individually and within the team framework — and there are those who do not.

If you've won by one goal one night, maybe you want to try to win by two the next. If you've won one in a row, or three, or five, you want to try to win one or three or five more. Of course, it's artificial. But it keeps a long season interesting, gives the players an objective every game night, which varies the menu, so to speak. When you eat the same meal time after time, it loses some flavor.

THIRD, there was an enormous temptation to disregard totally the regular season. After all, 1991-92 had been a parade of victories and successes, of building hopes — only to have them dashed to splinters after the strike. The Rangers HAD to believe that while the division had improved, they still had enough talent to manage a finish better than at least two divisional rivals. After winning 50 games in the regular season and washing out in the playoffs, how could it not enter your head that April and May would be the only months to matter?

"You've got to go out and do the best you can every game," Neilson said. "We owe that to the fans and we owe it to ourselves.

"We want to do the very best we can," he added. "We want to repeat as first-place finishers if we can. The team that comes out of our division will likely repeat as Stanley Cup champion, and we'd certainly like it to be us."

Messier also felt some value could be found in the regular season.

"You can use the schedule for a lot of purposes," he said. "The competition in the league is so good, there are a lot of close games. And you have to learn under all kinds of circumstances."

Then you use those lessons, including the bitter one of last spring, in April and May.

"I don't think we should forget about it (the loss to Pittsburgh). We should learn from it and use it," Messier said. "We have to do everything in our power to make the team better going into the playoffs this year."

The fact was, while Messier was on his summer vacation, Neil Smith had done everything in his power to make the team better going into the season. Smith had taken his best shot at making The Blockbuster Deal of the '90s.

And he nearly pulled it off.

CHAPTER 5

LET'S MAKE A DEAL

THE MORNING OF AUGUST 31, cars began filling the parking lots at Winged Foot Golf Club in Mamaroneck, New York. Drivers eased up the pathway, paused for a nod of clearance from the security guard, skimmed slowly to a stop.

These cars were not, by any means, family clunkers. These cars made the cushioned sounds of luxury and workmanship when drivers pushed the button that opened the trunk from the glove compartment. These cars, many in all-business colors of flat gray or smoky charcoal, suggested their passengers were people of at least some wealth, success, or power. When the trunks opened, golf bags and clubs and shoes of spectacular expense were revealed.

Of course, when you are staging a fund-raiser, there is not much point to inviting people who are short on funds. This sizzling Monday of blazing sunshine was the day Ice Hockey in Harlem passed the hat for outreach programs that bring the sport to areas away from the frozen mainstream. With its own rink and its own classroom facilities the ultimate aim, there is little worry the project will ever be overfunded.

Ice Hockey In Harlem teaches underprivileged kids to skate toward their futures. Ice Hockey In Harlem wants young athletes to reach their potentials on an intellectual level as much as a physical one. A kid may not be able to relate to today's classroom methods, but if he can look at a map and point out where the Philadelphia Flyers play or where the Vancouver Canucks play, he still is studying geography. Isn't he? And if he can compute the number of miles between Philadelphia and Vancouver, he's doing mathematics. Isn't he? And if he can tell you who won the Stanley Cup in 1940, then he's doing history. Right? Some might say he's studying ancient history.

If a kid can do those things, he might want to look elsewhere on the globe. He might want to go beyond the limits of simple math. Maybe he'll be intrigued by history beyond the legends of the Stanley Cup. Kids need to know someone out there wants success for them — that someone cares about what they do in the hours they aren't at school, someone cares about who they are and who they can be, wants to help them reach the goals they set for themselves.

You've got to start somewhere, and Winged Foot was where the season's money drive began for Ice Hockey in Harlem. Where it finishes is determined by the dollars the program raises from its sponsors, by the drive of the youngsters to hurdle their obstacles and to make their lives matter.

A round of golf at a well-known club always draws people, and a round with a celebrity in your foursome usually will bring out those people's wallets. So several former and current Rangers turned out, as did a curly-haired youngster with shoulders broad as a fairway.

Eric Lindros handed his clubs to a caddy and surveyed the scene.

"Nice course," he remembers thinking to himself that day. "If I played in New York, I could play it a lot."

Lindros would play in New York in 1992-93, but only as a member of a visiting team, only as an invited guest. And that very fact was one of the biggest dominos to topple during what became the most bizarre season in modern Rangers history.

On June 20, barely two months earlier, the Rangers traded with Quebec for the rights to Lindros, the most sought-after junior player since Mario Lemieux went to Pittsburgh in 1984. They sent the Nordiques goalie John Vanbiesbrouck, right wings Tony Amonte and Alexei Kovalev, center Doug Weight and first-round picks in 1993 and 1995. To sweeten the pot, they agreed to contribute $12 million to the Quebec team's treasury. Neil Smith and Quebec GM Pierre Page agreed on the players, Jaffe and Nordiques boss Marcel Aubut agreed on the money. The announcement was going to be made at the Montreal Forum on June 20, before or during the NHL entry draft.

This is how set things were: Knowing he had traded Amonte and Kovalev, Smith also knew he had depleted his scoring and depth on right wing. From the draft floor, Smith spotted Steve Bartlett, the agent for right wing Jean-Yves Roy, a free agent who in three seasons with the University of Maine never had scored fewer than 32 goals despite unspectacular size at 5-10, 185 pounds. Smith waved the agent over and said, "How much for Roy?" The agent named his numbers and Smith agreed on the spot.

The signing of Roy would not be announced for a month; deservedly so. It was a minnow of a transaction compared to the whopping whale of a deal Smith had on his hook. The Forum had seen any number of exceptional hockey events in its years as the home of the sport's most honored champions, the Canadiens; the Rangers' acquisition of Lindros simply would lengthen the list.

The Forum had hosted another Ranger announcement of monstrous significance only a few months before. On October 4, 1991, at the Mise au Jeu (Faceoff) restaurant behind the glossy red loge seats of the fabled arena, Smith had introduced the newest Ranger, Mark Messier. Now, after the record-breaking season Messier had spearheaded, Smith was going to announce the addition of the next Messier — Lindros, the 6-5, 235-pound guest house on skates who would lead the team to the next century.

■■■

Though aging and smallish (it would seem to fit easily inside Detroit's vast Joe Louis Arena or Edmonton's cavernous Northlands Coliseum), the Forum is a glorious venue. Its roof is not especially high, which is a bonus in two ways. First, you barely have to tilt your head to see the two dozen white flags that commemorate Canadiens championships. Second, the lighting of the action below always seems impeccable; and there would be plenty of action on the Forum floor on June 20, though it would involve men in business suits and expensive loafers rather than the more customary skates and pads.

In winter, the Forum either is hosting a hockey game or looking forward, hungrily, to the next. If there isn't a game, at least there must be a Canadiens practice, for hockey is the blood in the Forum's veins and the air to its brain. Hockey makes the building live, renews it. If the NHL announced the entire league season would be played at the Forum, in 24-hour shifts starting at 3 a.m. tomorrow, Montrealers could be counted on to fill the place for every contest — after asking why it took someone so long to get the idea.

There must be people in Montreal who have no interest in hockey, who can't stand the Canadiens, who couldn't care less about the Forum and its well-earned reputation as a tabernacle of the game. Those folks tend to avoid, or at least ignore, the square block downtown that runs along rue Atwater and rue Closse from Ste. Catherine to de Maissoneuve.

Within that hallowed rectangle, Montrealers smoke millions of hockey cigarettes, drink tankers of hockey coffee, eat truckloads of hockey hot dogs. They shriek in amazement that anyone with the nerve to hit a Canadiens player is not ejected immediately from the ice, from the game, from the province. Deported. Executed. There is only one word and one note on the sheet music when so base an event occurs; the chorus sings a high-pitched, well-practiced "Hey," as in, "Hey ref! You missed ANOTHER one." They always start and finish together, as though prompted by the baton of some spirited conductor.

They are wounded, to their souls, when a Canadiens player is penalized. Canadiens players do not commit fouls. By waving a Canadiens player to the penalty box, a referee is committing an offense against all Montreal's aged, poor and infirm, all the city's orphans and pets, all the war veterans — unless an opposing player has been punished at least twice as severely.

And yet, the only thing worse than a Canadiens penalty in the Forum is a Canadiens loss there. Much as they hate to admit it, opponents will cheat enough or connive enough to score an occasional goal; the fans can live with one or two of those illicit events, for a period or two, but they do not handle it well when the enemy's total is greater than the Canadiens' at the end. Such an occurrence is met with resentment so frosted, so Arctic, only a polar bear would fail to notice.

"We knock ourselves out for you. We score the goals, we block the shots, we fight their tough guys and kill your penalties and you . . . you . . . you LOSE?!!!" they seem to say. If the Canadiens drop the first game of a Stanley Cup Final at the Forum, the faithful leave the rink wondering who they should name to coach Game 2.

So this warm June day at the draft, it is entirely appropriate that the dasher boards are in place, surrounding the Forum floor, and a mob of spectators has filled virtually every seat. The Forum is a hockey place 12 months a year, not just when the season is in progress. When Neil Diamond or Leonard Cohen does a concert at the Forum, he is a transient, a guest. Get in, set up, do your show, move on. All business. When hockey is involved, the pulse quickens and the passion is unmistakable: Stay as long as you want.

This day, instead of the reds and whites and blues of the ice — instead of the lines and dots and circles and arcs of the playing surface — there are four rows of tables, covered by cloths bearing the colors and crests of the teams that will sit at them. There are six teams to each row, the arrangement matching the order of draft selection, starting with the expansion clubs, continuing with the teams that had the worst records in 1991-92, and finishing with the best, the Rangers, who would claim 24th.

The newcomers from Tampa Bay and Ottawa, who would choose first and second, led the first row in front of the stage. When NHL president John Ziegler stepped to the podium, to open the final entry draft of his tenure, the Lightning and the Senators were to his immediate right. To his left, Ziegler would see San Jose's table, then Quebec's — the Nordiques having gone 20-48-12, a .325 winning percentage better only than the Sharks' .244.

Toronto and Calgary filled out the front row and Philadelphia was the first table in the second row, along the boards and directly behind the expansion teams. The Rangers were all the way on the other sideboards, the last table in the area, farthest from the podium and the stage.

So if a game were in progress, the Flyers would have been located near the end of the Canadiens' bench. The Nordiques would have been in front of the net the Canadiens defend twice. The Rangers' table (actually a few tables, pushed together) was in front of the penalty boxes, near the tiny, foot-wide door in the boards that the visiting goalie has to step through sideways to reach the ice.

Barry Watkins, the team's director of communications, brought to the draft a folder of Lindros-related information, including awards Lindros had won, the names of current NHL players who had skated with or against Lindros during his junior career with the Oshawa Generals, in World Junior Championships, in the Olympics, in the Canada Cup. Watkins wanted to have volumes of data available when the trade was announced. In the moments before the draft began, he had the folder open and its contents spread on the table.

Thinking the draft floor had been cleared of media visitors, thinking of a thousand things, preparing for the onslaught he would be facing shortly, Watkins looked up from the table and was horrified to see Walter MacPeek and Sherry Ross standing nearby. At that moment, no deal had been announced. The Lindros data, in plain sight, hardly was confidential information, but its presence certainly would suggest the Rangers were on the verge of The Big Deal. MacPeek, veteran of decades on the Rangers beat for the *Newark Star-Ledger*, is one of the top snoops in the field. Ross, meanwhile, is secretary-treasurer for the Pro Hockey Writers' Association.

Watkins feared his secret was a secret no longer, then learned he was mistaken. MacPeek and Ross had come only to present the awards the PHWA had voted his media guide and media services. Watkins accepted the first plaque and placed it directly on top of the Lindros data, covering it; then he took the second award and held his breath until his benefactors had left the area.

Of course, those moments proved a waste of perfectly good tension. The only Lindros-related press release Watkins ever would issue would be dated June 30, 1992. Entitled, "Statements by Rangers president and general manager Neil Smith," it occupied barely an inch on a page of stationery bearing the team logo.

"The New York Rangers are naturally disappointed by the arbitrator's decision," the statement began. "However, we have an exciting, young, winning team and will continue to pursue every opportunity to make it even better."

After 10 days of hearings, arbitrator Larry Bertuzzi had ruled the Rangers made a trade that wasn't a trade. Lindros would be slipping a black-and-orange Philadelphia Flyers jersey over his shoulders.

Watkins had ordered a white Rangers jersey bearing Lindros' name, preparing for the player's first Rangers news conference, but it would become a collector's item. It would become another symbol of the futility with which the organization is all too familiar — another case where you can't fault the effort, only the outcome.

Bertuzzi essentially said as much in the eight-page finding that explained his decision.

"I find that Messrs. Jaffe and Smith operated in a manner which is fair and proper and above criticism," Bertuzzi said.

To which Messrs. Jaffe and Smith said, Gee, thanks.

If it had meant bringing Lindros to New York, Messrs. Jaffe and Smith happily could have accepted being branded as villains in Bertuzzi's findings. The objective was to get the big guy and it didn't happen.

"It's simple economics: You get a kid like Lindros, it's going to help your business," said Garden president Bob Gutkowski. "If he becomes a superstar — and that's certainly the 'if' going into this — that's going to help your hockey team and the business of hockey. And that's why Philadelphia went out for it, and Chicago and the others. We didn't come up with better reasons than the other guys. It's just sheer good business."

Lindros sells T-shirts. Lindros sells hats and posters. Lindros makes commercials, enlarges the Rangers' already-large footprint around the league, the continent, the hockey world. Lindros means higher prices for ad time on TV and radio broadcasts. He is a money-making tree with all kinds of branches.

And he can play a little hockey. You get him, your team is better. Your team is younger. Your team is stronger. Barring injury, your team is set with a franchise player for a lot of years. Your team just might go a little farther in the playoffs than the patently unsatisfying one- and two-round visits they had been making since their fantastic voyage to the semifinals in 1986. The Rangers wanted Lindros, for all those things.

The Rangers went for him. To this day, they believe they got him.

And to this day, there are others who believe the Rangers did not get Lindros either because they waited too long to wade into the battle, or because some type of bogus corporate crap got in the way.

The latter position stems from the perception that being owned by a corporation, as the Rangers are by Paramount Communications, is entirely different from having the shots called by one man in charge—a Bruce McNall in Los Angeles, for example, or a William Wirtz in Chicago.

The Garden's position, expressed by Gutkowski, argues that point.

"If the guy who runs the team needs a quick decision, he'll get a decision, in the time frame that's necessary, because Paramount knows how important that is," Gutkowski said. "Nothing was going to pass us by because we weren't fast enough.

"On the Lindros deal, people said we didn't move quickly enough, and that is the only thing I get upset about. We moved VERY quickly," he said. "We were right there. We were very aggressive. We were there right from the beginning and right to the end. And if Marcel Aubut doesn't make the fatal flaw of saying to people, 'You can't talk to Lindros' family until I have a deal,' Lindros is a Ranger."

Lindros is a Flyer because at 10:30 Saturday morning, draft day, about 80 minutes before he completed his deal with the Rangers, Aubut gave Flyers president Jay Snider permission to call Lindros. Bertuzzi ruled that once such permission had been granted, an enforceable trade had been consummated between Quebec and Philadelphia.

"If Aubut intended the contact with the Lindros family to be something other than confirmation of the deal, he did not make that point clear to Philadelphia or Lindros' agent," said Bertuzzi's decision, a document that will hang forever in the Rangers' Hall of Agony. "Aubut did not have the capacity to conclude the New York Rangers' arrangement."

So, in fact, when he made the subsequent deal with the Rangers, Aubut was trying to move something he no longer owned. The store already had closed, even if Aubut, the shopkeeper, contended in the arbitration hearing that such was not the case.

"At approximately noon (draft day), Aubut came to Snider's suite and announced he was taking a New York offer, stating his Board said he had to take it," Bertuzzi's decision said. "Quebec suggests no deal was made with Philadelphia in that there was no meeting of the minds."

Aubut's mind was a difficult book to read on this subject. The Quebec president unmistakably was focused on getting every player and penny he could from the Lindros auction, but it remains difficult to conceive how Aubut could trade a player to one team at 10:30 a.m., then to another at 11:50.

Aubut's assertion was that Philadelphia and New York had become the finalists in the sweepstakes. In giving Lindros' telephone number to the Flyers, Aubut apparently believed he was creating an equal playing field for Philadelphia, because the Rangers already had secured a signed document granting them 48 hours to sign Lindros, or to be satisfied they could sign Lindros, before the exchange of players, drafts and cash would take effect.

While Snider was on the phone with the Lindros family, around 11:30 or 11:40, Aubut came to Philadelphia's hotel suite and asked how things were going. Snider flashed a thumbs up sign and Aubut left, convinced now that a choice was his to make in the minutes that remained before the draft. The Flyers' offer included the day's seventh overall pick; the final details would have to be ironed out in the little time that remained.

■■■

Over his personal objections, and despite his guarantee he never would play for them, the Nordiques had made Lindros the first player claimed at the entry draft in Buffalo's Memorial Auditorium June 9, 1991.

Then they issued a two-page news release that concluded with a hopeful expression by Page.

"Eric had constantly reminded people that he wants to be happy, he wants to win, and that he wants to be paid at his worth," Page's statement said. "The Quebec Nordiques have negotiated contracts which needed a lot of imagination in the past, such as the ones wth Peter Stastny, Michel Goulet, Guy Lafleur, Mats Sundin, Owen Nolan, and, more recently, Valeri Kamensky. We are all confident it (Lindros contract talk) will be a positive negotiation."

Of course, there was no chance of that. Lindros had made it clear, his father, Carl, had made it clear, and his mother, Bonnie, had made it clear.

But there was one passage elsewhere in Page's statement that proved prophetic, indeed:

"There is no doubt," he asserted, "that you can find more solutions through negotiations."

Ultimately, the Nordiques found more solutions than they were allowed.

■■■

If he wasn't going to sign with Quebec, at least he could be turned into several high-caliber players who WOULD play for the Nordiques. Lindros was a formidable foundation for a deal, a formidable foundation for a team. There may have been teams who neither could afford the money it would cost to sign him nor the players it would cost to get him, but there wasn't a manager worth his paycheck who couldn't at least make an offer and hope for the best.

With Paramount's backing, the Rangers certainly had the money. Given the season they just had concluded, they seemed to have the players, as well.

"It was a lot of money and a lot of players, and it was a deal that needed the support of Paramount to go forward," Gutkowski recalled, sitting in his 14th-floor office in the building in front of the Garden. "Certainly, as good owners, they (Paramount) would be part of that process. It was a very collaborative, cooperative effort.

"We all sat down and said, 'Does this make sense? Does this not make sense? Economically, does this make sense? From a personnel standpoint, does it make sense?'" Gutkowski continued. "The question we asked, over and over, both I asked and the Paramount executives asked, is 'Neil, is this going to split your team up? The second you say, This does not make sense, and this could tax the performance of the team, then you don't go forward with it.' We all were concerned. We had to keep asking ourselves those questions.

"We always knew a player like Lindros does not come along too often," Gutkowski said. "The kid was 18-19 years old. If he was 24-25, I don't think we would have had the aggressive conversations we had. We all wanted to do this, but it was enough of a concern that we kept asking each of ourselves, 'Does this make sense? Does this make sense?'

"Ultimately, the decision was to go forward," Gutkowski said. "It didn't wind up positively, but we were very aggressive."

Of course, team managements elsewhere in the league were coming to the same conclusion. Cliff Fletcher was in there, pitching for his Toronto Maple Leafs. Mike Keenan was involved on behalf of the Chicago Blackhawks. The New Jersey Devils inquired, as did the Detroit Red Wings and the Calgary Flames. If Lindros was going to go anyplace other than New York, of course the Rangers would prefer that it be outside the Patrick Division. Anyone with a sense of Ranger history would endorse anyplace but the Patrick Division — and Calgary.

Doug Risebrough is the Flames' GM, and Doug Risebrough is another of the many names that live in Ranger infamy. He had driven a spike into the Rangers' hearts once before in Montreal, and it would be too cruel for him to steal the Lindros deal and do it to the Rangers in Montreal again.

In 1979, the Rangers had ridden John Davdison's goaltending to triumph in the "Battle Of New York" playoff series with the Islanders. It seemed only a matter of time before the Islanders won a title, but this Ranger bunch, coached by the legendary Fred Shero, derailed the Islander express for a year. Given the blow Neilson's Maple Leafs dealt them the season before, the defeat by their Big City rivals was a numbing punch to the Islanders' heads.

The Rangers could not have cared less. They were on their way to the finals, against a Montreal team that had advanced past Boston in the semis only because the Bruins had been caught with too many men on the ice in the dying minutes of Game 7. Guy Lafleur converted the power play, tied the score, and the Canadiens won.

Still, Hall of Fame goaltender Ken Dryden had not played to his standards in the Boston series. And when the Rangers beat him in Game 1, pulling within three victories of ending their 39-year drought, Canadiens coach Scotty Bowman decided enough was enough. He named Michel "Bunny" Larocque to start Game 2.

Larocque was a fine goaltender, but he was no Dryden. He was mortal. If the Rangers could get past him, they would be going home, to the bedlam of the Garden, with a 2-0 lead in a best-of-seven title series.

Then, in the pre-game warmup, Risebrough cranked a shot that struck Larocque in the forehead and knocked him unconscious. When the game began, Larocque was being revived and Dryden was back in the net at about the same place in the Forum where the Nordiques' table would stand a mere 13 years later. Dryden allowed two early goals, then snuffed the Rangers the next four games.

All because of Doug Risebrough.

And here was that pest again, reportedly trying to get Lindros for left wing Paul Ranheim, defenseman Gary Suter, center Joe Nieuwendyk, goalie Mike Vernon, the Flames' first-round pick at the 1992 draft, and a 1991 draft choice, defenseman Francois Groleau.

■■■

The Nordiques had played the situation like a violin. They had to move Lindros, who had vowed never to play for them, because he already had been their property for a year — a contentious year, at that — and would go back into next season's draft pool if not signed soon. Montreal was the perfect site for a bidding war. The entire league was there; negotiations could be conducted virtually to the last second and consummated right on the trade floor, if necessary.

"The process was, 'Okay, clubs: If you're interested, give us your best shot,'" Gutkowski explained, "But everybody knew that no matter what you offered and what you said initially, it was not going to be good enough. So it was a cat-and-mouse game. You had to represent enough (of an offer) that it would intrigue them, as far as saying, 'I think I can get more,' or 'I think there might be an opportunity to deal here.'"

So Quebec had set up a command post in a hotel and the chariot race had begun, with various teams lining up their strongest horses to give the Nordiques what they wanted for this young star.

But while there would be no deal without sacrifice, there were teams who needed a commitment from the Nordiques, as well. On August 30, 1989, Lindros' Ontario Hockey League rights had been drafted by the Sault Ste. Marie Greyhounds, and Lindros had declared he would not play in the Sault. Of course, Lindros had done the same thing to the Nordiques. Now, just about any GM about to give up a half-dozen assets to get this kid wanted assurance he would be able to sign him; no way do you give up six players for the rights to a guy who isn't going to play for you, either.

Complicating the issue was the fact that Quebec would not allow teams to talk to Lindros to ascertain his willingness to play for a given team.

"Aubut was concerned," Bertuzzi's decision stated, "that to do otherwise would create a free-for-all and would detract from the heated competition he was intent on creating."

So Aubut held all the cards. He had Lindros and he had the league's general managers in a black hole. They couldn't call Lindros, because that would be tampering. They couldn't be sure Lindros would sign with them, because he had blown off two other teams and never looked the worse for wear. You know one GM wasn't going to tell another GM what was being offered. You know it is only reasonable business to get a written guarantee that any deal would be cancelled if Lindros, reached at long last, refused to sign with his new team.

Three weeks before the merde hit the fans, the Rangers actually obtained such a document. It is an interesting souvenir, but it is not evidence that they made a Lindros deal before the Flyers did. It is evidence a Rangers-Nordiques trade would become final only when Lindros signed a contract with New York.

New York is still waiting.

■■■

Smith picks up the narrative:

"The thing I remember most vividly was, Quebec had never really given a solid indication that they definitely would trade the guy. I was after Pierre Page every time I saw him, to make sure he got to us if he was going to trade him. They never really rang our phone. I knew there were people from other teams running in there and trying to solicit Pierre, and I never felt that was the way it was going to be (when the trade was made). I felt what was going to happen was, they were going to come to us and say, 'Here it is: If you want him, this is the price.'

"And I was basically right in the end. There was no sense flying up to Quebec and trying to take them out to dinner and try to get all over them about Lindros early. They were going to wait until the last hour, like everybody waits at a trading deadline.

"I was staying at the Ritz-Carlton, and I called Pierre (Page) a couple of times to see if I could talk to him about this. I got a call from (Quebec chief scout) Pierre Gauthier, who was a good friend of mine from our scouting days. He said, 'Neil, I'm calling you as a friend, to tell you you've got a chance to get this guy.' I said, 'I do?' He said, 'Pierre's going to call you later with a proposal that we've put together.'

"Pierre Gauthier said, 'You can do this trade. You can do it. You'll come out of it okay, and you'll have this guy. This guy's going to be incredible.' I hung up the phone and Pierre Page got me, and that started me into the two sleepless nights.

"I met him at something like 8 o'clock (Thursday night). I went to Le Grand Hotel. They had the whole floor. When you got off the elevator, they had a security guard there, and as you looked to the left, they had those temporary walls you can put up to make work stations in an office. Those things are blocking the hallways. I eventually did get down to that area a few times, because I was living there for a few days, and down there, they had everything set up. They had food rooms — cafeteria-style rooms — set up for everybody to have meetings in and sit and have dinner.

"Pierre (Page) takes me into this room, and I sit there with him and Marcel Aubut and Marcel does a little of his salesmanship, and then he left. Marcel's got his tie half-undone, his shirt undone, all coming out. He's in a sweat, and he's just running in a nervous frenzy.

"Pierre (Page) says to me, 'Here's who we would need from your team.' And he starts to write down the names. And I'm swallowing hard. Because through this whole process, I'm going against every grain of how I've been brought up in this business. And that is, the way you build a team is, you draft and develop. You don't draft, develop and trade five for one. Maybe modern-day sports is getting that way now, but it shook my whole upbringing that this was the way I was going to be doing it.

"Remember, I've already done it once with the Messier trade: I've already traded (Ranger-developed prospects) Louie DeBrusk and Steven Rice for Messier. And I'd already traded (Ranger-developed) Troy Mallette for Adam Graves. And I'd gotten Bernie Nicholls before that for a couple of players (Tomas Sandstrom and Tony Granato) produced by the Ranger system.

"Every trade I make, even for a John McIntyre or a Mike Hartman, I don't take it lightly. I don't play this job like a hockey pool. You get to a deal like this, you really are trembling about it. Your life is flashing in front of your eyes.

"So I'm not feeling good about it, in any case. But knowing that things change, you go forward and try to do it. Pierre gave me the names in the first proposal, and I said, 'Let's look at how that affects our team,' and I wrote down our roster on a piece of paper, and I said, 'Well, that means we'll have nobody at all on left wing. Nobody.'"

The problem there, according to someone else familiar with the discussions, was that the Nordiques wanted Adam Graves. Smith refused outright.

"Then we started to talk, and it went on, literally all night, about variations of this trade," Smith said. "I kept trying to pull people out of the trade, and he kept trying to push certain people back into the trade.

"And it was at about 4:30 in the morning (Friday) when he had left me alone in that room. He kept going out and not coming back for exorbitant lengths of time, and I found out later that was because they were working on other teams at the same time. I'm sitting there like a jerk, waiting, thinking I was the only person there interviewing and not knowing I was just being kept in a holding tank.

"He comes back and he says, 'You know, my people like this one.' And it was six Rangers for three Nordiques, one of them being Lindros. And I said, 'You know, Pierre, I came here to get Eric Lindros. I didn't come here to get these other two guys, and I didn't come here to give up half my team. We just came off the best season we've ever had. I don't want to destroy this team this way. So I'm just going to leave, because you're not going to get me to do this. You're not going to get me to say yes to this tonight. It's too much. It's too big. It's too everything.'"

Talks were recessed until Friday night. Smith went out for an Italian dinner and called the Nordiques twice from the pay phone in the restaurant, asking when discussions would resume.

Not much later, they would.

"I'm sitting with Pierre Page. We get the player component down, then, at the last minute, Pierre says, 'I want Tie Domi.' I said, 'You can't have Domi.' He says, 'I'll give you Jacques Cloutier. You need a backup goalie.' I said, 'Give me Cloutier. I'm not giving you Domi, though.' So he says, 'No, no. I can't do that.' I say, 'Fine. I don't give a shit.'"

■■■

"Friday night, I fall asleep in my room," Barry Watkins recalled. "Two o'clock in the morning, Neil knocks on the door. He's got this grin on his face. He says, 'We're going to get him.'

"I can't believe it. He says, 'I'm telling you. We're going to get him. It's in our court.'"

Smith and Watkins head to the hotel lobby, where they bump into Smith's assistant, Mark Piazza. They leave the hotel and head for the Four Seasons Hotel, where assistant GM/farm director Larry Pleau is stationed.

"Larry Pleau is waiting at the Four Seasons," Watkins said. "He's probably waiting the same way I was — by sleeping.

"Neil has me call Roger and Colin Campbell," Watkins continued. "I call Roger, wake him up. He says, 'If you want to get him, just get him already. What are you bothering me for?' Typical Roger.

"Five in the morning, Neil goes around the table. He says to me, 'Not that I give a shit what you think, but do you think this is a no-lose thing from a public relations standpoint?'

"Then he goes to Roger, 'As coach of the team, how can this affect the team next year? Is it going to bring us down a little bit before it brings us back up? Can we win right away?'

"He goes to Coley, same thing: 'Can you make him work hard? Can you keep him away from all the crap in New York?'

"Then he went to Larry Pleau: 'Larry — How does this affect our system? With the young players we're losing and the draft picks, can the scouting staff compensate?'

"Then he looks at Mark Piazza. He had gone around the room and asked everyone else in the room their opinion, so he HAS to ask Mark. He goes, 'All right, Mark, let's ask the toughest question of all: 'How does this affect your appetite?'

"It's 5:30 in the morning. The sun is coming up. At eight in the morning, we call Pierre and say it's done. I've got a list of stuff to do — press conference preparations, make sure the office in New York is staffed. We get to the draft and we're ready to announce it."

There would be an announcement that day, but it would be made by the league, not the Rangers.

"Two competing proposals for the services of Eric Lindros will be submitted to arbitration for resolution pursuant to the National Hockey League Constitution," the statement began.

"The parties to the arbitration are the New York Rangers, the Philadelphia Flyers, and the Quebec Nordiques.

"The issues in the arbitration will not be disclosed. The parties have agreed to use an independent arbitrator. A hearing will be held promptly, the exact time and location to be determined.

"In respect of the arbitration process, no comment beyond this statement will be made by the parties or by the National Hockey League."

■■■

"I get in at 6 a.m., and I can't sleep, anyway, because I'm scared shitless," Smith says, resuming his recollection. "This is the biggest deal of hockey history. This could be my whole career, right before my eyes. It goes against the grain of how a team should be built, and yet I know that this might be the greatest player to come along in my career, and this might be the only opportunity you get to trade for a player of that magnitude, EVER. And I'm going to be the one that does it.

"And yet, if he's a bust, I know there's no sense trying to blame anybody. It's going to be my ass. The Messier trade was easy to make compared to this one, and the Nicholls trade has completely disappeared — and at the time, that had been a monumental, huge thing. There was also an excitement level about Lindros that wasn't there for any other player we've dealt for, because there had been so much hype, SO much hype.

"I call Stanley Jaffe at 7 a.m. and say, 'We've got a deal, hockey-wise.' He had been kept abreast of the hockey components, and he had been in conversation with Marcel about how much money it would take if the hockey guys could reach their deal. Stanley had become involved because Marcel had come to me and said, 'We need X number of dollars.' And I said, 'Marcel, one thing I can say very happily is, I'm not involved with money. I'm a hockey person, I know hockey. I don't know the meaning of what dollars equate to in this. You have to talk to Stanley. He's going to make that decision and I don't want any part of it.'"

If there is one place where the Rangers might have lost the deal, one place where they may have tripped over being owned by a corporation, it was right there. Arguably, had Smith been empowered to reach agreement on the financial as well as the player aspect, he could have thrown his body in front of the door and not permitted the Quebec guys to leave until all details had been boxed and wrapped in a neat, air-tight package.

Except nowhere in pro hockey does one man have that much money, that much power and that much insight into the personnel aspect. And Jay Snider, president of the Flyers, was working under the same constraints as Smith was. His father, Ed, the team's majority owner, was working the purse strings.

Recalling a Friday conversation between Aubut and Ed Snider, Bertuzzi's paper stated, "It was left that Aubut should work with Jay Snider on the players and draft picks and Ed Snider would speak to Jay Snider regarding the money."

So it's a push. Had the Rangers won the arbitration, there would be no way to criticize the Flyers for not having acted quickly enough.

■■■

"Now, this is Saturday morning, and I'm very, very upset," Smith recalled. "I'm extremely upset that I haven't had my scouts meeting, where we make all our plans for how we're going to attack the draft the next day. Larry had been filling me in, but it wasn't the way it should be. You should sit in a room for four or five hours, talk about each one of these kids, hear the psychological report, the physical report, and really know that draft. So that when you walk in the next day as the head of the thing, you're fully prepared. You know which direction you're going in.

"I go over there (to the Nordiques' hotel), and Pierre leaves me sitting in that room again for about an hour. Now I'm mad. Because it's draft day and I'm nervous about the draft and it's 10 or 11 in the morning. I'm sitting there all that time, talking (on the phone) to Larry, talking to Stanley. Stanley says, 'I'm leaving the house in five minutes. If they haven't called to confirm this thing, we'll have to do it when I get into Montreal.'"

It was around that time Aubut and Snider made their agreement, according to the evidence Bertuzzi gathered. It was around this time Aubut provided Snider with Lindros' phone number, about the time Snider reached the Lindros family and set out procedural conditions for a contract.

"So now," Smith says, "I'm in that room at about 11:30 and I'm fucking furious."

The room sits to the side of the banks of elevators. If you turn left from the elevators, you bump into the armed security guard. Turn right and go into the first room, you find Neil Smith.

But Smith isn't sure whether anyone is supposed to see he's there. He opens the door a crack and peeks out — "like a hostage," he says — just to see if Page is coming down the hallway.

What Smith sees is all the Quebec scouts. They're waiting for the elevators, heading for the draft.

"I call Andre Savard (one of Quebec's assistant coaches) over and I say, 'Get Pierre Page in this room. I want to go to the draft. I don't want to sit in this room another minute.'

"Pierre comes in and I say, 'I'm leaving. I'm going to the draft. This is ludicrous. Maybe you're going to come back and say 'No deal.' He says, 'I'll see you at the draft and that's where we'll find out what's gone on between Stanley and Marcel.'

"So I take off and go to the draft. I'm tired. I'm pissed off. I'm ugly. I get to the draft. We're way back at the back corner table.

"I keep looking at Quebec's table, and nothing's going on. I'm predicting to Larry, 'I bet you they've made a deal with Philly and they're going to announce it.' I call over to their table after a few picks and I go, 'Pierre, are we doing this deal or are we not doing this deal?' He says, 'Hold on a minute.' Marcel gets on the phone and says, 'I got to call you right back.'

"Now I look over and I see Jay Snider talking to Marcel Aubut in the middle of the floor. And I say, 'Uh-oh, he (Lindros) is going to Philly,' and I'm waiting for the order of selection to come all the way back to us. I see Jay Snider coming over, and he signals me over. And he says to me, 'I just want to tell you, don't announce your deal.'

"I said, 'What deal?'

"He said, 'Your Lindros deal. You've traded for Lindros. But don't announce it, because we're going to take the whole thing to arbitration.'

"I said, 'What deal? I haven't made any deal with Quebec. As far as I'm concerned, you can take him and shove him up your ass. I don't want the fucking guy, I don't need the fucking guy. I've got a good fucking team.' At this stage, I'm just bitter at everybody, at the whole situation that made me miss my draft meeting, fucked me around, had me sitting alone in a room eating chips."

An instant later, the phone rang at the Rangers' table.

It was Aubut.

"I pick up the phone," Smith recalls, "He says, 'Neil, you know Stanley and I completed the deal this morning. The deal is done.'

"My response to Marcel was, 'Marcel, talk to Stanley when Stanley gets here.' I wouldn't acknowledge anything to Marcel, because by now, I don't know who's lying to me and who isn't.

"So all of a sudden Stanley gets on the scene. Ziegler's involved, (NHL general counsel) Gil Stein's involved. All these people are involved. We go into a back room. The Flyers are going to take us to arbitration.

"Stanley says to me, 'We had a deal. I confirmed it with Marcel Aubut before I left New York. Our deal was done.' I didn't find out, until Stanley arrived, that we had a deal for sure — that his part had been sewn up."

It was, but it wasn't.

"I sat through the whole arbitration, every minute of it, and it is completely mind-boggling to me that he (Bertuzzi) made the decision he made," Smith said. "To not have any signed document, to not have any FAX into the league, to not have any word given to the league that there had been a trade. There was no documentation. Nobody had called the league and said there was a deal. Nobody had counter-signed documents saying there was a deal."

Bertuzzi declared there had been one, though. That was all that mattered.

"The thing is, I can say Marcel screwed us, which he did," Neil Smith said. "But he screwed himself, too. His hockey people wanted our deal."

Aubut's hockey people ended up with goalie Ron Hextall, center Mike Ricci, defensemen Steve Duchesne and Kerry Huffman, left wing Chris Simon, the rights to center Peter Forsberg, plus first-round picks in 1993 and 1994. Quebec also received $15 million (U.S. funds), which would be paid, according to Bertuzzi's ruling, "in four equal annual installments with interest payable to 'actualize' it if Aubut wanted the cash over a longer period of time."

Smith ended up in a peculiar position on two fronts.

The first was, even if he had gotten Lindros, Smith could have faced criticism that he had gutted his team to do so. An extreme reactionary might even assert that after sacrificing so many players to acquire Lindros, the Rangers might finish last. In the end, Smith kept all the money and all the players and finished last, anyway.

"The other irony is," Smith added, "one of the premises I had operated under during the whole thing was, we had shown — again — that no matter how good a season we had, we were trying to do everything we possibly could to be the best team in the NHL and acquire the best players for the fans. Yes, we have high ticket prices, and yes, we haven't won the Cup in all those years, but we're making every concerted effort. Instead, it ended up seeming like a failure, a botched trade.

"I'll never forget Bertuzzi, obviously. And I'll never forget the Nordiques," Smith added, "and I will never, ever, EVER, trust Marcel Aubut."

■■■

In a delicious piece of scheduling, the Rangers would host the Flyers and Nordiques in consecutive games the final week of October, starting with Philadelphia's visit on the 26th.

The Flyers would come to the Garden for their skate that morning, and when it was done, Lindros, in all-black workout gear, left the ice by the doorway at center ice. He walked down the rubber mat that leads to the ice in a "T" formation. You turn left to reach the visitors' room, turn right to head the Rangers' way. Lindros was just about to make the left when a tall fellow, standing at the end of the mat, extended his hand.

"Hi, Eric. Neil Smith," Lindros' almost-boss said.

They chatted a few moments. Lindros admitted to being a passenger on the Toronto Blue Jays' bandwagon, Smith said the same. They talked about Mark Messier, about the Bentley automobile Messier bought from Wayne Gretzky a few years ago. They talked about Flyers coach Bill Dineen, who coached Detroit's AHL farm team in Glens Falls when Smith worked for the Red Wings.

Then Keith Acton, the veteran center, one of Lindros' father figures on the Flyers and a marvelous needler, came off the ice. He walked down the mat and waved Lindros toward the Philadelphia dressing room.

"Come on, kid," Acton said. "They didn't want you."

Acton winked at Smith, whose smile looked just a bit forced.

CHAPTER 6

GETTING STARTED

THOUGH THE GARDEN is their home rink and their corporate mailing address, the Rangers' real headquarters is the Ice Casino at Rye Playland, some 30 to 40 minutes north of the city. Nestled on a shore of Long Island Sound, the quaint Art Deco facility sits behind a miniature golf course, just inside the entrance to an amusement park.

The Rangers spend the end of training camp under the domed roof there. They practice there, even on the mornings of home games. Virtually all the equipment is delivered and stored there; it is brought in by van for the home games, is brought back to Rye immediately afterward.

Players get their injuries treated at Rye, get their messages, their massages and their mail there. The coaches have offices there. The satellite dish facilities are there, so other teams' games can be videotaped, edited and analyzed. The mirrored workout room is located there, so is the whirlpool and the sauna. They had a tanning bed at Playland the years Phil Esposito was boss; it's gone now.

Rye's clubhouse is more like a baseball clubhouse, where odds and ends accumulate in a player's locker because that is his real habitat. You can expect to find hockey cards somewhere in Darren Turcotte's stall, because Turcotte dabbles in collecting. You can expect to find a Clint Black baseball cap somewhere at Joe Kocur's dressing place, as the wing's musical tastes run enthusiastically toward country. From the corner, by the door to the video/meeting room, Tie Domi studies the weapons in his arsenal and sets his strategies; if he cannot wing a pillow-soft stuffed football at somebody, he at least will launch a caustic comment in someone's direction. Or he will leave himself available to be insulted.

Domi is an avowed enemy of silence, but, within limits, there is something appealing about that. The job description, after all, is hockey PLAYER. Hockey is a business, of course, and a sport. It requires dedicated labor. But it is forever and always a game.

And after all, they are at Playland — a place more than miles from a city where sadness grows every day. New York can be the best of the best, the worst of the worst, but the worst is running away with the race now. Every day is an episode of M*A*S*H; you patch up the wounded soldiers and send them back out to fight.

In a way, that makes the Rangers the perfect hockey team for New York. You can get kicked in the head all day by your job and the traffic and the dirt and the misery, and then, at night, and especially in the playoffs, you can get kicked in the heart by your heroes.

Ceil Saidel lives in the Bronx and she lives for the Rangers. Some nights they make her old, some nights they keep her young. She remembers the 1940 Cup, although it was the next season before she could persuade her father to take her to a game. Virtually ever since, she has loved the sport while hating how it has hurt her.

"We had good teams, better teams, worse teams, but the results were always the same," says the small woman with the willing smile. "Each year we hoped, but were never fulfilled. Frustration began to build.

"I only wish that once more I could experience the excitement I felt so long ago," Ceil says, "but the years have taught me that life conditions — wars, hunger, disease, crime, homelessness — these are the IMPORTANT things. Hockey is only a game, but it is the greatest game on earth, and the Rangers are my team.

"I sometimes feel if they did win the Cup, I wouldn't know what to do," she admits, "but I still root and I continue to wish, fervently, that they would. Is that what they mean by hope? That's what keeps me coming back."

It is what keeps bringing people back to the Garden, one of the things that brings the players back for another run up the mountain in 1992-93.

"We set a standard of excellence last year. Now, we've got to prove it was no fluke," Messier said. "I get a sense that having a good year isn't going to be enough for this team. We need to win it this year."

You didn't have to guess what 'it' was.

■■■

While Messier spent the summer in the eye of the storm he created, the Rangers' other trophy winner, Brian Leetch, spent his off-season just as he likes it: in relative privacy.

The defenseman stumbled into the spotlight briefly during training camp, however, when he signed a $19-million contract that had some jaws dropping. Having played out the final season of his contract, Leetch had achieved "free agent" status. Although under the Group II classification, which gave the Rangers the right to match any offer, there didn't seem to be much freedom involved, at all.

There was Leetch, a premier talent coming off an all-league season. And there were the rest of the teams in the league, terrified of having to come up with the dollars and draft choices it would cost to sign him. It is safe for you to assume the Rangers did not win a bidding war.

"I don't think we really explored it (creating a bidding war) to the fullest," said Jay Grossman, the defenseman's agent. "I can't even say we explored it all that well."

Leetch did not seem to mind.

"It isn't upsetting that more teams didn't bid," he said, "because I didn't want to leave. This is where I wanted to be."

Leetch entered the top half-dozen salaries in the league with the deal that started at $1.663 million and skyrockets to $3.5 million in 1998-99. The deal included provisions that would upgrade Leetch's salary after the fourth year, to keep pace with any dramatic inflations in salaries across the league. And should Leetch reach other high performance levels — another Norris Trophy, league MVP, first all-star team or top scorer among defensemen — he would join the league's top three or four salaries after the 1995-96 season.

So maybe there hadn't been a bidding war. But given the fact Leetch had made $250,000 in the final season of his prior contract, he had done quite well for himself, indeed.

"I don't even know what a million dollars is," said Leetch, who would be finding out soon enough.

■■■

As camp proceeds, a few players catch a lot of eyes. One is the Russian newcomer, Kovalev, who has gotten stronger in the year since Neil Smith drafted him. Kovalev's spectacular dipsy-doodling with the puck draws all kinds of oohs and aahs, produces any number of highlight-film goals in the scrimmages. Kovalev is living up to the stature of his selection and seems a sure bet to make the team better. Clearly, it would have been an immense sacrifice to trade him in the Lindros package.

Another attention-getter is goalie Corey Hirsch, one of the top prospects in the organization. Virtually since Richter joined Vanbiesbrouck to form the team's goaltending corps in 1989, there has been constant speculation about when one of them will be given the No. 1 job, which will be traded, and what type of compensation that goalie might bring on the trade market. All this was contingent, of course, on whether the 20-year-old was ready to handle NHL competition; this training camp would provide an indication how close Hirsch was to being ready — and, by extension, how close Richter or Vanbiesbrouck were to being traded.

Of course, Vanbiesbrouck has been traded once already, since he was in the package that was headed to Quebec for Lindros. So was Kovalev. So was Doug Weight, who kept a level head about being traded — but not being traded — after his eight-goal rookie season.

"It was a slap in the face. It wasn't an insult at all, but it makes you think, wakes you up," Weight said. "It's a weird feeling, but I can't be bitter. I didn't do enough last season to merit staying.

"I kind of feel lucky to still be here. Now, I've got a chance to do something to keep it that way," he added. "I feel like I belong here, and I'd like to stay."

Hirsch has a good camp, but the trade front freezes when Richter strains a groin muscle. A groin injury at Los Angeles in January had been the clear dividing line between the ups and downs of Richter's season in 1991-92, and there was too much at stake in this camp to rush any injuries. So trade thoughts were set aside, replaced instantly by concern.

"It just sends up a yellow flag," GM Neil Smith admitted. "We want to make sure it isn't something that's reoccurring. You get really concerned when a player gets a recurring injury."

Another commanding presence is the veteran Kocur, who had undergone surgery during the off-season to repair some of the damage done by years doing his job, bashing his bare hands on helmets, cheekbones and foreheads. It always has been tempting to spell Kocur's last name by capitalizing the second letter, too, making it a more appropriate KOcur, given the fact that he is the Rangers' acknowledged knockout king and the team's undisputed heavyweight champ.

Since Kocur had averaged almost 30 penalty minutes per goal in his career, the right wing's performance at training camp — scoring on breakaways, wheeling out of the corners and carrying people to the net for slam-dunks — had people wondering if the doctors had taken anything out of Kocur's hands or had transplanted a scoring touch into them. In a September 29 exhibition game against the Islanders at Nassau Coliseum, Kocur got some time on the power play and made the most of it, scoring three times in the customary 8-5 loss.

"I've come here to have the best camp of my career, to earn the respect of management and my teammates," the 27-year-old said. "I want to demonstrate that I can do more (than fight) to help this team, and if I'm successful, maybe I can earn a more important role."

Kocur's hands have made his living, but there is nothing wrong with his eyesight. He can see change is coming to the NHL, that fighting is becoming less a part of the game. And he can read a depth chart; Kocur knows one-dimensional skills will not earn him a job.

"This team is loaded with talent and depth, loaded on both wings. I've got to prove I can play on this team," Kocur said. "You never want to look back and say, 'If I'd had a good camp, I'd have been with the team that won the Stanley Cup.' You'd rather say, 'I had a good camp, made the team, and won the Stanley Cup.'

"It's obvious they (management) are going to have to make a trade pretty soon," he added. "You look around and there are surplus players, good ones, at every position."

The ice was crowded, indeed. So was the clubhouse once camp broke and the team returned to Rye to prepare for the start of the season. The mob scene became a defining issue of the early season, and Kocur's statement was the first sighting of the storm clouds that were gathering in the distance.

"A lot of players are going to have to suffer through not dressing every game," Neilson said, acknowledging the especially dense-packed situation on the right side. He had Gartner, Amonte, Kovalev, Domi, Kocur and Paul Broten.

Who would YOU sit?

If you have three right wings with offensive capabilities, your other one "should be a role player who's reliable defensively, like Broten, or a hitter or a tough guy," Neilson observed.

But how do you bench Domi after giving him three years at a total of $1.3 million? Do you sacrifice the speed and offensive power of Gartner and Amonte? Do you break Kovalev in gradually, when he is a spectacular talent for the four-on-four or three-on-three situations that figure to account for most of the playing time? Or do you plunder your depth in a trade, just because players are going to be sour if they sit for extended periods of time?

"It's too complicated to think about," Broten said. "We've got five good lines. If we have a healthy team this year, we're going to have extra players. If you get in the lineup, you've got to use a full tank of gas every night."

In a late-September body count, as the October 5 waiver draft draws near, Smith finds himself with two goalies, nine defensemen, and "16 forwards that legitimately have a shot at making our team." That's 27 players, and Smith says he's comfortable with around 24, "so it seems like three people have to go."

And it continues to seem that way for a very long time.

"In other years, most coaches would prefer to have 20 guys, and if you're short, bring somebody up from your farm team," Neilson said, throwing his two cents in. "But with 84 games in the season, three or four games a week, you almost need two extra forwards and one extra defenseman. I would imagine we're going to have 24 or 25 players — certainly not more than 25, hopefully 24."

Three days before the opener, there were so many forwards that Phil Bourque practiced on defense. Neilson placed Archibald on the left of Randy Gilhen and Tie Domi, forming what surely seemed to be the line that would watch the opener from the press box. He put Gartner on the right of Messier and Graves. The checking line of Kris King, Darren Turcotte and Broten was intact, while Jan Erixon teamed with Sergei Nemchinov and Kovalev while Kocur shifted to the left of Weight and Amonte.

The 1991-92 defense pairs (Hardy-Patrick, Leetch-Beukeboom, Cirella-Wells) remained in place, with Bourque, Djoos and Andersson forming a makeshift fourth pair.

"There are probably 25 to 30 guys here who could play in the NHL," Domi said. "So players are working for a spot here, or a job on another team."

With all those players around, though, there still are holes that need patching. They have a bunch of centers behind Messier, but no clear, defined, distinct No. 2. Despite his 30 goals, Nemchinov seemed better-suited for the No. 3 spot, but then again, so did Turcotte. If Gilhen was a perfect fit in the No. 4/defensive-zone-faceoff role, where did that leave Weight?

Also at issue: From the first week of 1991-92, when Bernie Nicholls was traded to Edmonton for Messier, the Rangers had been without the ingredient that had made their power play so effective. They lacked the right-handed shooting puck-handler who could set up plays to the goalmouth from the left-wing corner.

In coaching parlance, there was no "down-low option" in the area in front of the net—which left the attack without a vitally important weapon. Boxers punch hard to the body, trying to get an opponent to lower his hands and expose a few critical inches of chin. Football teams need penetration with the running game to buy the pass receivers some freedom. And hockey teams need that down-low option, to keep the opposition from overplaying the shooters from the point.

Without a down-low option, the Rangers' version of a play in the slot was camping Mike Gartner in front of the net, sacrificing him to murderous mayhem in the hope that some point man's slap shot might go in off his body. Nice strategy, huh? Eventually, there was no need to worry whether Gartner was there or not; all the penalty-killing forwards had to do was position themselves within eyeball distance of Leetch at the left point or Patrick or Turcotte at the right point.

What this did was take away the point as a play option, creating a different geometry to the rink, a different point of attack, and all but eliminating the advantage. With the opposition's two forwards out near the blue line with the two Ranger point men, the game was reduced to the three remaining Rangers and the three defenders (two defensemen, one goalie). Three-on-three is not a power play, especially in the now-smaller space between the tops of the faceoff circles and the endboards; the only thing that creates an advantage is puck possession, and possession isn't that great an advantage when the skaters aren't in motion and neither is the puck.

Mark Messier is an exceptional hockey player, and it was in proper deference to his skill that Messier was handed Nicholls' setup duties. But Messier, a left-hand shot, is most dangerous off the rush, when his speed provides one threat and his backhand provides another.

On two-on-one rushes, Messier always gravitates to the right side because he is among the most accurate backhand passers in the league. He also has one of the top backhand shots in the league. So he can hold the puck on the backhand, shield it with his body, force the goalie to commit to him, then pass at the last second. If the goalie anticipates the pass, cheats away from the near goalpost to brace for a shot from Messier's rush-mate, Messier's backhand is easily strong enough and accurate enough to score.

But once the power-play formation has set up in the attacking zone, however, speed no longer matters. Quick decisions matter. Quick puck movement matters. Good motion by the players who don't have the puck matters. Often, far too often, the Rangers would end up with none of these ingredients. Messier would position himself at the outer hashmarks of either faceoff circle, his backside along the boards. His first passing option, to the point, usually was closed off, so he had to check off to less-viable options.

Thus, more times than the organization would care to admit, Messier ended up holding the puck for what seemed like hours. Ultimately, all the opposing penalty killers had to do was hold their positions; Messier and the Rangers would take care of killing the clock.

Given the shockingly strict manner in which the referees enforced the rules during preseason games, it seemed clear 1992-93 would be a Special Teams Season in the NHL. When your power play gets a chance to snap a tie, or to create one, or to turn a one-goal lead into a two-goal lead, it had to produce. And it seemed certain that valuable points would be lost if the team spent even a single game night without a semblance of a down-low threat on the power play.

You think Eric Lindros might have changed those circumstances a bit?

"I'm confident we have the personnel. I'm sure it will come around," Neilson said. "If we get a goal a game on it, we won't be too disappointed."

■■■

Nonetheless, the day before the season begins, these were the facts of New York sports life: The Mets and Yankees were winding down disappointing seasons. There was a new football folly every week at the Meadowlands. And since the Nets and Knicks had not started yet, the Rangers clearly were the area's top team when they raised the curtain on the 1992-93 campaign.

They were coming off a fabulous regular season. They had a nice blend of youth and experience, finesse and power. They had all kinds of players whose games were tailor-made for all the four-on-four and three-on-three situations that seemed certain to arise because of new rules. They had enough offense to win shootouts, enough goaltending to win squeakers. They had all kinds of penalty killers, even if the power play was a question. They seemed nicely positioned to do something, they seemed almost impossible to screw up.

The day before the season began, practice was in full swing and the Rangers were in the middle of a drill when Axl Rose's voice began blaring from the speakers above the Rye Playland rink. The Guns 'N' Roses vocalist was knock, knock, knocking on heaven's door, and Messier decided Rose needed accompaniment; so he used his stick as an air guitar and lip-synched a little harmony as he glided back to a corner of the rink.

Later, when a U2 song came on the tape Colin Campbell prepared, Domi turned the knob of his stick into a microphone and tried to get Sergei Nemchinov to sing along as they stood by the benches. This activity was not a big hit with the Russian. Nemchinov took English lessons over the summer and made tremendous progress in his communication skills, but in this instance, non-verbal communication served the purpose: A steely look gave Domi the message.

"I tried to teach Sergei how to (play) golf the other day," the ever-helpful Domi explained. "And he was bopping to the Guns 'N' Roses song, so when U2 came on, I tried to teach him how to sing."

Don't get the idea Nemchinov is a humorless chap. He is serious, certainly. He is mature, dedicated to his game and committed to his teammates. He is like a big dog, and Domi is the kid who always pulls Nemchinov's ears or his tail. Nemchinov doesn't seem to like it much, but he never snaps.

"I just bug him, have fun with him, get him going," Domi admits. "I say, 'Sergei, what's up? What's UP?' And he'll go, 'Shut up, Tie.'

"We have this stuffed football," Domi continues, "and one time, I threw it as hard as I could. I didn't want to hit him in the face but I hit him right smack in the face. And he turned red as an apple. I bug him that he throws like a girl; he gets all pissed off.

"He calls me 'Crazy' all the time. He says, 'Tie, you're crazy. CRAZY.'"

Domi is always good for provocative quotes, except these words provoke Nemchinov, who, after the quote appears in print, seeks out the reporter who published them. At some airport, on the way toward the metal detector, Nemchinov says, "I NEVER said Tie is crazy." There seems to be some hurt in his eyes, as though concerned he had insulted Domi.

He should have known that was just about impossible.

■■■

Before the first puck of the season drops, everyone is a champion. Every team is filled with optimism that this will be the year.

Or at least it COULD be the year.

Or it better be.

Or we aren't far off.

Or we're rebuilding, but we'll give it a shot.

Or, there's a good draft coming up; we'll get a good pick.

Before the first puck drops, the schedule is a collage of boxes and blanks, potential glories, potential disasters.

There will be nights you will win and be utterly shocked so pitiable an effort can reap so great a reward in a professional league.

There will be nights your team will do everything right, but a screened shot will go in off the britches of a guy the other team just brought up and you will lose at home with 10 seconds to go.

There will be nights the points will sit right on the table and if you don't take them, the other guys will . . . but nobody does.

There will be nights the crowd is asleep and so is your bench, but your tough guy tries to stickhandle past three people instead of just killing somebody—which is why you sent him out in the first place.

There will be nights the damn ref picks your pocket, but you can't kick his door down because he gave you 10 power plays and your overpaid bums couldn't make a pass to save their ass — or your job.

There will be nights all a guy has to do is get the puck deep, which you've told him to do a thousand times, but he doesn't do it. The guy you've told a thousand times to dump the puck in the corner decides he needs to make the first drop pass of his career. Of course he leaves it for a guy who isn't ready, of course the other team goes down and scores, of course you lose a divisional game as a consequence. And two weeks later, when somebody asks why the guy isn't playing, you say, "His groin's a little sore."

There will be frozen nights the flight gets cancelled, nights the bus doesn't come.

There will be nights the rookies buy dinner and everybody orders four entrees.

There will be proud nights in Toronto or Calgary or Boston or Philly, when mom and dad and your brothers and sisters can come to the game, and when the proudest moment you've ever had is to skate in front of them in an NHL uniform.

There will be nights when you wish mom or dad or brother or sister could have lived to see how far you've come.

There will be nights the doctor says, "Let's get some X-rays of that," mornings the doctor says, "It looks like six to eight weeks."

There will be nights the fans scream, "You suck!" and you can't say a word because, in fact, they're absolutely right.

Before the first puck drops — when there hasn't been a bad break yet or a bad call or a bad goal or a bad loss or a bad trade — everyone's unbeaten. Everybody's tied for first.

On the other hand, you're also tied for last; 188 days ought to be enough for you to break that tie.

And it was.

The Rangers would have last place sewn up long before that last day.

■■■

Things always seem to happen in Washington. There was one afternoon game in 1991-92, for example, when the Rangers trailed 6-1 after the first period but won 8-6.

Not all the things that happen there are as pleasant. Late in the sixth game of the 1991 playoffs, in which the Capitals eliminated his Rangers, Neil Smith slammed the press box countertop with his hand. Afterward, he sat on a table in the hallway that connects the various rooms of the visitors' dressing quarters, ripped his underachieving team and vowed changes. The biggest change ended up being the arrival of Messier, one game into the subsequent season.

When the Rangers play at Capital Centre, which actually is in Landover, Maryland, either they get killed (fairly common) or they pretty much do the same thing to the Capitals. They don't seem to play squeakers there, and the opener of the 1992-93 season is no squeaker, either, despite the score. The Rangers beat the Capitals, 4-2, playing one of their best games of the campaign and grabbing early control of the nine-game season series.

"We played well," said Richter, who got the opening-night nod in goal. "We played — I don't know, is 'mature' the right word? No? Maybe 'composed' is."

You never really know which Washington team you're going to face in the black-ceilinged arena with the swaybacked roof. Some nights the Capitals come out banging and forcing and swarming, and on a lot of those nights, you just hope everyone gets on the bus in one piece after the loss. Other nights, the Capitals come out without passion but still play well enough to keep the game on the table.

This night is more the latter. The Capitals aren't really skating, aren't really pressing in that cavern on the Beltway. The Rangers limit the number of odd-man Washington rushes, deny chances at any rebounds Richter leaves available. They are quicker to the puck and a little stronger on the boards, they keep the slot clear, keep the crowd quiet. Despite their glorious record in 1991-92, the Rangers weren't great on the road in the Patrick Division until later in the season; to open 1992-93 with a Cap Centre victory as efficient as this one suggests the Rangers have come to this campaign ready to lead the race, wire to wire.

They outshoot the Capitals 17-8 in the first period, and, after the Capitals pull within 2-1, made it 3-1 on Phil Bourque's first Rangers goal. Tony Amonte takes Al Iafrate deep with a rush up the left side and hooks a pass past Michal Pivonka to Bourque, who one-times the puck from 30 feet from the left-wing circle. It gets close at 3-2, when Messier loses a faceoff in the defensive zone and Calle Johansson ends up with enough time to convert his own rebound, but the Rangers toughen and Adam Graves clinches it by handcuffing goalie Don Beaupre with a 20-footer at 17:22 of the third.

"When you beat a strong team like Washington on the road in the opening game, it's really encouraging," says coach Neilson, who selected a lineup that did not include Kovalev, Domi, Andersson, Gilhen, or Archibald.

The victory is complete enough that people start to get starry-eyed.

"We feel we've got some unfinished business," says Mike Gartner, who scored the 2-1 goal, "and this is the start of (finishing) that."

It also was a game that seemed to affirm some preseason speculation. Look around the Patrick Division, you see Pierre Turgeon on Long Island, Eric Lindros in Philadelphia, Messier at the Garden, Mario Lemieux, of course in Pittsburgh. The Patrick Division, clearly, is home to four of the top centers in the game.

There are six teams in the division. Only four will make the playoffs. It appears unmistakable that possession of a franchise center will be of immeasurable help to the four teams so blessed, and it will be of extensive harm to the Capitals and New Jersey Devils, the two teams short on "prime beef" in the middle.

Of course, the Capitals have the eternally under-rated Mike Ridley, the eternally dangerous Dale Hunter and the perpetually puzzling Michal Pivonka. But Ridley's offense historically has not been at the 100-point level, and any game-breaking he does is of a quieter nature. The Devils, meanwhile, were hoping to get another season out of Peter Stastny and were depending on Alexander Semak to fulfill his potential.

If the Capitals and Devils would be suffering from this shortage up the middle, the Rangers would be among the first to have those suspicions confirmed. Games against each of these teams were the first two on the Rangers' schedule. And while Pivonka sets up both of Washington's goals in the opener, Ridley does not get a shot and Hunter ends up minus-2. Messier, meanwhile, runs up three assists and the theory appears sound.

In New Jersey the next night, though, the lack of a franchise center does not hinder the Devils a whit. They win 4-2 at the Meadowlands, leaving the Rangers at .500 and leaving Gartner with some unfinished business of his own. He takes five shots, four in the second period, but shoots wide of the net during a three-on-one, thus failing to snap a 2-2 tie.

"The philosophy I have is never to miss the net. Always make the goalie make a save," Gartner said. "Missing the net bothers me."

Gartner is also turned back by some exceptional Craig Billington goaltending. Billington gets his stick on a 10-footer in the closing moments of the second period, gets his stick on Gartner's tip of a Messier centering pass, and gets lucky when Gartner misses the net a second time.

"There's a big difference between being frustrated and being angry," says Gartner, the first to admit a reputation as a streak scorer. "'Frustrated' connotes that you're getting tighter and tighter and trying too hard, and I'm not. It takes a lot of games before frustration sets in. Another night, maybe four of the five shots go in. That's the way it works with me."

Bobby Holik endures no such aggravation. The Devils forward scores three times on seven shots, one of them a blast over John Vanbiesbrouck's left shoulder from the right-wing circle. The goalie called the shot "a 'popper.' It popped the water bottle right off the net. That definitely goes in Volume I edition of 'Hard Shots in the League.'"

So instead of roaring into their home opener on the momentum of two divisional victories on the road, the Rangers arrive at the Garden pretty much at Ground Zero, at .500, following a victory with a loss. The power play is off to a 2-for-15 start and the Rangers — healthy, loaded with talent — are getting their first indications that neither the division, nor the season, is going to be any kind of cakewalk.

But last season pretty much had been, at least until the strike scrambled the eggs. The Rangers' 50 victories in 1991-92, despite 245 man-games lost to injury or illness, had set a team record and was five more than runner-up Washington could manage. Their 105 points had been seven more than the Capitals or Detroit Red Wings could amass.

So, before opening their home season, against Hartford October 12, the Rangers honor themselves by hanging two new banners from the Garden roof. One flag is for the regular season Patrick Division title, one is for the overall NHL points title. As the season progresses, the flags atop the Garden surface will serve an important function: To remind that only a season earlier, this Ranger team was atop the hockey world.

Their play in the home opener against Hartford at least suggests more banners might be forthcoming. Neilson puts Kovalev in the lineup for his season debut, and the 19-year-old responds with one of the plug-ugly goals of our lifetime — a three-inch shot that caps a four-goal second period in a 6-2 conquest of the Whalers.

Before and after, though, Kovalev gives glimpses of what might be expected of him. Just 2:04 into the contest, the Whalers' Doug Houda wants to welcome Kovalev to the league with a big hit, but it is the Hartford player who ends up on the seat of his britches. Later, Kovalev will split the defense with some fancy moves — only to get powdered along the right-wing boards by defenseman Jim Agnew.

It is 1-1 after one period, with Doug Weight having steamed past defenseman Eric Weinrich to score on a breakaway before the entire Ranger team watched Patrick Poulin bury an Andrew Cassels rebound. Weight, who had a fabulous training camp, may have been jump-started into the home season by a visit Michelle McLean, Miss Universe, paid to the hallway outside the dressing room before the game. Unmarried Rangers were solicited to take publicity photos with the beauty, so Graves, Amonte and Weight reluctantly agreed.

Tough job. Somebody's got to do it.

Weight scores in the first period and Amonte tallies twice in the second. McLean should have stayed around another 40 games or so.

"It was the first night (of the home season), and we all thought we were going to put on some tic-tac-toe plays and get the crowd really into it," Amonte observes. "But the ice really wasn't good for that, so after the first period, the consensus was, 'Let's get the puck to the net and grind it out.'"

Just 1:36 into the middle session, Gartner starts atoning for his Saturday miscues in New Jersey. Though he misses the net AGAIN during a three-on-one break in the first period, Gartner at last grabs a Brian Leetch rebound at the goalmouth, kicks the puck to his stick while moving to his right and sends it past a sprawling Sean Burke.

Then Gartner sentences himself to some remarkable punishment in front of the net, freeing Amonte for both his goals from Burke's left.

"He (Gartner) was getting beat like a dog out there and stood up to it," the sophomore wing marvels. "When I get crosschecked like that, I usually go down."

During a career that has spanned more than 1,000 games, more than 500 goals, more than 1,000 points, the 33-year-old Gartner has learned to plant his feet wide apart in the slot and lean on his stick, turning himself into a tripod and making it extremely difficult for a defenseman to knock him down. The weight on his stick also is useful for deflecting extra-hard shots from the blue line; Gartner has become expert at tips through his legs while his back is to the net. He camps just far enough outside the curl of the goal crease to allow an opposing defenseman to step between Gartner and the goalie; that way, if Gartner steps backward, he stays in legal territory outside the goal crease but the defenseman bangs into the netminder. If the goalie is jostled, there is a chance he will be distracted from the play; and if a defenseman is occupied with Gartner, there is going to be room available for some other Ranger.

In the home opener, that other Ranger is Amonte. Tired of waiting for Agnew to floss Gartner from the goalmouth during a Ranger power play, Burke decides to lay a crosscheck on Gartner. Amonte takes the cue, sprints to Burke's left and converts the pass Messier launches from Burke's right at 9:29 of the second period. Just 2:04 later, a Leetch point shot glances off Gartner — who was getting killed again, this time by Houda — and Amonte is free to score from the same place, using Houda's skate for his bank shot.

"I isolate on Mike a lot when I'm not playing," says Richter, who makes 37 saves. "He usually takes a beating, but he really got mauled tonight."

Richter nearly gets mauled, himself, in an extremely physical game that ends up with referee Rob Shick assessing 217 minutes in penalties — 125 to the visitors. Four of the more noteworthy minutes are assessed Kocur at 12:09 of the second period.

At that moment, Nemchinov works the puck into the goal crease, just out of Burke's reach. The disc is sitting on the line when Kovalev rushes in to knock it across with his first NHL "shot." Agnew elects, at that juncture, to crosscheck Kovalev and trigger a significant sequence.

Kocur steams right in for a conversation.

Kocur is a positively fearless fighter, most of the time as cold and calm as an assassin. If necessary, he is more than willing to accept two or three of the best shots you can throw, more than willing to let you wrestle with him for a while. But you know, while you're throwing, while you're tangling, that you better be lucky or remarkably accurate. Because Kocur does not simply want to win the fight; if he gets the right hand loose, Kocur wants to hurt you with it. When that right comes, it is coming hard and it is fueled by more focused fury than you've ever faced before or ever want to face again. If the front of your head is protected but the back of your head is exposed, it is all the same to Kocur. If you have a helmet on, he will punch the back of your helmet, will try to make it a permanent part of your skull. All he wants is one good shot, maybe two. Then it's over.

Kocur doesn't fight that much any more. And his scrap with Agnew is not deemed a fight by Shick, who assesses Agnew two minutes for roughing and Kocur four. The more significant issue is that Kocur, "Joey Kayo," has stood up for Kovalev and has made a statement by doing so. Kocur essentially has proclaimed to Kovalev, "You do anything you want. Anybody who wants a piece of you has to come through me." He says this to the rookie, to the Garden fans and anybody else who cares to listen. He already had said it once at training camp, running over Gartner like a freight train in a scrimmage after Gartner had tried to check the kid; Gartner was not the least amused by this, but there were no audible complaints from Kovalev.

"I know here (in North America) they don't just pat you on the head," Kovalev says.

Kocur is at the center of the storm again with 33 seconds left in the second period, when Brian Leetch gets run over by defenseman Steve Konroyd and hell starts breaking loose.

After Konroyd leaves the penalty box to steamroll Leetch, Weight goes after Houda and Kocur battles alternately with Agnew and Houda.

Eventually, Burke leaves his goal crease to enter the fray — which means Mike Richter has to join his counterpart. Burke enjoys a healthy advantage in height, reach, and weight, all of which he uses. Burke has his mask on and Richter had his mask on, but Burke wanted to change that; so he sticks his fingers through the bars of Richter's mask the way a beer-league bowler grabs a bowling ball on a Thursday night.

"I was thinking how short my parents are, and how, obviously, I wasn't adopted," Richter says, laughing at the absurdity of the moment and creating another one.

"He was playing exorcist a little bit," says Richter, alluding to the horror movie in which Linda Blair's head spun around.

Richter's head does not spin around. His mask does not come off, either. The goalie wrestling match is a comic highlight on a nasty evening.

"I've got 200 pounds of equipment on," Richter says. "I didn't think I'd get a real beating, but I didn't want to find out, either."

The Rangers are back over .500, they are impressively physical against a physical team. Kocur has done his thing, Kovalev has done his, Gartner has done his. Leetch has a goal and three assists. The Rangers have resumed their dominance at home. Things are looking pretty good.

CHAPTER 7

THE DANCER

IN THOUSANDS OF NEWSPAPERS across North America the morning after the Hartford game, Kovalev's goal was described with an assortment of names and numbers in tiny letters and figures — the summaries on the agate page. The line read: Kovalev 1 (Nemchinov, Kocur), PPG, 12:09.

That's 24 letters, five numbers, a colon, three commas, two parentheses, five spaces. While splendid in its simplicity, simultaneously telling you everything and nothing, the one line simply does not do justice to the time, money, thought, and effort that went into the play — specifically, the thousands of miles people travelled to scout Kovalev, the hours spent deciding to make him the first Russian player ever claimed in the first round of an NHL entry draft, the hours of negotiation involved in gaining his release from Moscow Dynamo, the hours of negotiation involved in getting him signed, the millions of dollars involved in transfer fees and contracts.

His goal was one of 7,311 that would be scored in an NHL season of 2,016 games. It boiled down to one tiny line among hundreds on a page of newsprint. Somewhere between the business pages and the comic strips, between the tears and the laughs of another day in world history, an exceptional moment sat there, available to millions of eyes — so few of which would pause to read it, to consider its significance.

Because it wasn't so long ago when places like British Columbia or Prince Edward Island were the ends of the hockey world. Now, here was the first NHL goal by the first Russian player picked in a first round.

Although there were instances when NHL teams simply signed an occasional player from overseas, there were no European players drafted until St. Louis chose a Finnish fellow named Tommi Salmelainen with the 66th pick overall in 1969 — a year the draft swelled to 84 selections from 24 the prior season. Per-Arne Alexandersson was the first of five Swedish players who in 1974 became the first claimed from their nation; he was taken 49th overall by Toronto. And in the next draft, June 3, 1975, the Flyers claimed the first Russian player, Viktor Khatulev, with the 160th pick of the 217 made that day in the NHL office in Montreal's Sun-Life Building. Fred Shero was Philadelphia's coach then; he had been to Russia for coaching seminars and had become an enthusiastic supporter of their teaching methods and philosophies — even if Shero's best player, Bobby Clarke, seemed to enjoy few things more than smacking Russian players whenever international competitions occurred.

"When we started (scouting Europe for the NHL in 1983), the European championship tournament for players under 18 years of age was held in southern Germany and there were five NHL scouts there. Neil Smith (then of Detroit) was one, Marshall Johnston (New Jersey) was one, Neil Armstrong from Montreal was one, Lars-Erik Sjoberg (then of the Rangers) was one, and myself," said Goran Stubb, the NHL director of scouting in Europe. "Eight years later, 55 scouts came to the tournament, and five Europeans were drafted in the first round."

The Olympics may have given you a slightly skewed sense of what European hockey is like. Sure, there are lots of pretty rinks in gorgeous settings, plenty of glamor players to watch for the scouts who get the plum assignments. There are other places, though, where the meat on your plate cannot be identified readily — and you get the idea it might be better not to know. And there are places like Usti, a place Stubb remembered from northern Czechoslovakia, back when there was a Czechoslovakia.

"It was an industrial town," Stubb said. "You couldn't see out the windows for the pollution."

The draft, now that it is a TV spectacle in parts of North America, may also have provided rather a glamorized version of things. You see the top players on draft day, in their new suits and shirts that still hold the original creases — having been freed of their pins and cardboard only minutes before the family left for the rink. But go to Russia, you see elbow pads peeking through the holes in game jerseys. You see shin guards through the unrepaired holes in the socks. You see goalies in chest protectors you wouldn't give a kid for ball hockey.

"When we started with this European scouting, most of the clubs were interested in the Swedes and Finns, because you could get them out (of their homelands) and there was no real big problem," Stubb added. "Then, with the Czechoslovakians, it was a kind of an adventure. It was a kind of a challenge to some of the clubs to try to get a Czechoslovakian to defect, and some of them did. There was really not much interest for Russians, because Russians didn't defect often, and to get them out was more or less impossible."

That changed as Communism began to dissolve. Russian teams used to get extensive financial support from the government. Once that support no longer existed, those Russian team leaders who saw the crisis coming realized they would need other sources of income. But while clubs in Finland or Sweden were able to raise money by selling small advertisements on the jerseys or pants of their uniforms, the Russian teams could not do that because there were no Russian companies per se; the government had been The Big Company.

Once things got desperate financially, about the time Kovalev was drafted, doors that had been closed and locked began to open for the NHL clubs. At least as important, Kovalev was drafted from Dynamo, the super-elite team in Russian hockey. Dynamo boss Alexander Steblin was one of the first club operators to realize how heavily dependent on Western dollars Russian teams would become.

Steblin created an exchange program, through which, for a certain consideration, Dynamo allows a few NHL players to come to Novogorsk for training. The summer of Smith's visit, the Winnipeg Jets sent rookie left wing Russ Romaniuk and veteran wing Pat Elynuik for a two-week stay.

To further the friendship bridge between the Russian and North American athletes, Elynuik and Romaniuk once took some teammates to Moscow's Pizza Hut.

"There were, say, seven of us, and we treated them to dinner, and they thought we were nuts for spending that much money on them. We had to coax them to come in," Romaniuk recalled. "The bill was $117 for seven of us to eat, pizza with the works. That's like, over 3,000 rubles. A hockey player here gets 500 rubles a month."

Neil Smith was one of the first NHL operators to "formalize relations" so to speak, with a Russian team. It is one thing to make a phone call or two, to see how the team and the player are doing; it is another to pack up and fly across the world to pay a courtesy call, to meet the kid on whom you risked a piece of your credibility, to give him the same ceremonial jersey the North American youngsters get when their names are called.

In August, 1991, that is just what Smith did.

"Not too many GMs go over to Russia, to talk to the teams there in a friendly way," Christer Rockstrom, the Rangers' European scout, observed at the time. "If other teams go over, it's because they want the player immediately. Neil went to build up a friendship for the future.

"The Russians do not trust all the teams in the NHL. That's what they told me," Rockstrom added then, "but all the Russian federation people are happy with the Rangers because they acted first class. You don't want to do it like, 'We are from New York, we rule the hockey world,' then come in and grab the kid when we want him."

Smith wanted the kid, all right, but wanted to show patient good faith as well. Was there a chance, at least, that Kovalev might come to training camp for a short visit that September?

Smith filled part of his luggage with clothing and most of it with gifts for the executives of Dynamo and the Soviet federation because that is the custom. The top of the pecking order gets the good stuff — a Ranger golf shirt, even a jacket. The lower levels might get a Ranger hat, a Ranger pennant, a Ranger towel. Everybody gets a Ranger pin or a keychain. It isn't so much bribery as tradition and plain good manners.

For Smith and his wife, Katia, there were gifts from Dynamo, as well; the one thing Smith wanted, though, he couldn't have: The white-and-light blue Dynamo T-shirts the players had were great-looking, but impossibly scarce. While licensed athletic apparel has proved an absolute gold mine in North America in the 1990s, the marketing craze had not reached the Russian league by the time Smith found his way to Novogorsk — the suburban training center that is Dynamo's answer to Rye.

Novogorsk means "new mountain." It sits in the country, some 30 minutes from the downtown Moscow streets where filthy children tug at your sleeve until you give them a coin. Novogorsk is some 30 minutes from the delicate blini and sumptuous pelmenyi you may savor at a splendid restaurant named Kropotkinskaya 36 — and for which you may pay with any currency that is not Russian. It is some 30 minutes from the Lenin monument in Red Square, "Red" translating to "beautiful" in the mother tongue.

At one rink in Novogorsk, the benches are so small that during scrimmages, the spare goalie sits on a padded lounge chair that is covered in tan vinyl. The benches are so small that a player or two must sit nearby on the stone walkway that runs the length of the rink on both sides.

It is from such a perch that Alexei Kovalev awaits his next shift in the swirling, skating turmoil that is this August night's exhibition game between Red Army and the Soviet National team. He wears a white sweater with the letters CCCP on the front and a silhouetted number 31 on the back.

Kovalev's name is missing from the back of the jersey, but that hardly matters, as most of the other sweaters bear names that mis-identify the people wearing them. One fellow's jersey shows number 12 on the back, and the name "Nemchinov" stretches across the shoulders. But the night of this game, the night before Neil Smith's arrival, Sergei Nemchinov is known to be in Rye, New York, settling his family into a home and preparing for his first season with the Rangers. And the Red Army's No. 6, proclaimed by his sweater to be Rangers draft choice Sergei Zubov, is none other than the Devils' Alexei Kasatonov.

There is no intention to defraud, and anyway, there is no way the misnomers are going to fool coach Viktor Tikhonov, who is watching from his tower some 20 feet above the end arena. Tikhonov sits on a stool and takes voluminous notes while a man with a video camera stands at his right shoulder, recording every move on the ice below.

Many of the moves that fill the viewfinder are dazzling, which is understandable, given the array of talent assembled. On defense skates a huge youngster whose shoulders and bulk strain the seams of his No. 4 CCCP sweater. That's the Islanders' kid, Vladimir Malakhov. You marvel at the strength in his stride, the power in his shot. Over there, with the puck, that's Pavel Bure, the Canucks' kid. What a skater! And over there, isn't that Alexander Semak, the Devils' kid?

Then there is Number 31, whose namelessness is compounded by a bad case of facelessness. While most of the other players wear a clear plastic half-shield through which they can see, and be seen, Kovalev's features are hidden by the bars of the facecage he may have worn in a recent tournament.

There is no masking the skill, however. Kovalev carries the trademark of an elite skater. He is always gliding, always moving toward the puck or toward open ice. He is always weaving, shifting his weight and using the edges of his skate blades for turns — keeping both feet on the ice for remarkable balance and strength, rather than lifting one foot to cross it over the other. His use of the edges is remarkable; he can lean over so far that, at full extension, it seems a good three yards between the tips of his toes and the puck on his stick. With that kind of reach, it is not surprising that for entire shifts, either the puck is around Kovalev or Kovalev is around the puck.

Next to his balance, Kovalev's creativity with the puck stands out. He drives up the left side, fakes a snap shot, freezes the defenseman, then slides a sweet little pass ahead to a teammate — who had stepped into the hole the defenseman left and who might have scored had he made a better fake on the sprawling Army goalie. Another time, Kovalev makes a 360-degree spin out of the corner, brings the puck to the net and scores.

"Kovalev is a funny guy, a marvelous talent," said Stubb, the NHL European scout. "He has the tools to become a star, definitely. This guy, in my opinion, was the best (1991 European) available. He dances on the ice."

That may owe to the fact that Kovalev's first steps on ice were taken in figure skates in his hometown of Toliatti. Located on the Volga River, a full-day's train ride from Moscow, the Russian city bears an Italian name because the Toliatti company built its automobile factory there and the city sprang up around it. The people who built the tiny, boxy Lada cars needed places to live, places to eat, places to exercise.

Viacheslav Kovalev works as an engineer in the sports arena there. Paulina Kovalev works in a food store. A career in hockey was not a high-priority item with either of Alexei's parents, so the selection of skates was limited when he started.

"My father was a wrestler and a weightlifter, and he wanted me to be a weightlifter, too," Kovalev said. "My mother didn't care if I wrestled or played hockey. Her main concern was that I should be busy and not spend too much time in the streets. It is, always and everywhere, possible to find boys who are up to no good. It does not matter where you live. She wanted me to be busy with something that would be my future."

The choice was made easily.

"I didn't like weightlifting very much. I preferred hockey because I like the kind of sports that are very fast, strong, with a lot of action," Kovalev said. "When I was seven years old, I decided definitely that I won't be a weightlifter, but a hockey player."

On Alexei Kovalev's seventh birthday, February 24, 1980, a remarkable event occurred. In Lake Placid, New York, the United States Olympic team defeated the Finnish Olympic team 4-2 to win the ice hockey gold medal. The Soviet Union team steamrolled Sweden 9-2 to take the silver two days after the blackest day of its hockey history, the 4-3 loss to the Americans.

"I watched the games," Kovalev recalled, "but I looked at them only like a boy, not like a professional athlete."

In the Russian hockey environment, young players are not exposed to all aspects of the game at once. The Russians take a very scientific, layered approach to the development of their athletes.

Across Russia, there are 30 specialized hockey "schools" which have 10 teams of every age, starting at age seven and continuing to age 18, at which point the very top prospects have reached the level of "The Second Team of Masters." The schools are run in several regions of Russia — for example, the Ural mountain region, Siberia, the Moscow Area, and the Volga region. Kovalev's hockey upbringing began with the Volga region school.

Those seven to 10 years of age practice six hours a week (about half of it on dry land) and do not play any games. Players 10 to 12 years old practice nine hours per week and play 20 games per season, with gradual increases up to age 17 or 18, when the best of them playing on "The Second Team of Masters" practice and play very regularly.

The first two years of teaching deal with speed, coordination, skating techniques, stickhandling, the basics of team and individual tactics in hockey and other sports. Special attention is paid to stickhandling, and one favored drill is to have a player bounce a rubber ball into the air repeatedly with the blade of his stick. The challenge of the simple drill is to keep the ball in the air, and off the ground, for as many bounces off the stick as possible; the result teaches touch with the puck, stick control, hand-eye coordination and wrist strength, among other things.

To be conducted, that drill requires only the player, a stick and a ball — which provides several benefits. First, it does not require ice; there is a dramatic shortage of artificial ice rinks in Russia. Second, it does not require a puck; there is a profound shortage of quality equipment in Russia, and a ball is less taxing on a stick than a puck.

Another favored practice drill is to have a player handle the puck while skating backwards. The good players make it look easy; it isn't. Russian coaches also like to cordon off a section of the ice and have the players scrimmage, three-on-three, in the confined area. This develops stick-handling skills, strength on the puck, and puck control in close quarters — all qualities Kovalev boasts in ample supply.

At age 12-13-14, work is aimed toward improving players' speed, endurance, techniques of making and receiving passes, and bodychecking. It is at this age that the player's coach decides what position the player will play. Also during this period, special attention is paid to athleticism. There is a lot of jumping, especially one-legged jumping, because there hasn't been a hockey player yet who strides with both feet.

Jumping develops the leg muscles, adds explosiveness to the first step, imparts strength to the stride. On land, players will "duck walk," usually while carrying weights (sometimes while stickhandling a ball), to develop the quadriceps muscles, the long muscles in the front of the thighs that help flex the legs.

The on-ice regimen is one of the smaller aspects of a player's program. At Dynamo, players jog three kilometers and play about 20 minutes of basketball before going on the ice. Then they will eat, rest, do another eight kilometers, hit the weight room and follow that with more jumps and hurdles. It is no surprise Russian players come to the NHL with exceptional leg strength.

Along with the physical aspect, Russia's rich hockey education often is visible in Kovalev's play. He will shoot off the front foot, as most players do, or off the back foot, adding an element of surprise through the quickness of release. This makes up for an admitted lack of speed or power to the shot.

"During training, in a friendship (non-league) game in 1988, I went to take a shot but something happened. I broke my left wrist," Kovalev said. "That's why I don't have a good shot."

Kovalev will go into traffic, will work along the boards, and often will come away with the puck. Physical play is not a problem for him.

"In our hockey, we had enough (contact)," Kovalev said. "When I was in Canada with the junior national team, I liked the smaller ice very much and I liked the way the game was played — at high speed.

"My way of playing is not just punching or beating someone up. I prefer to be smart on the ice and to win in other ways," he said. "Wayne Gretzky plays the way I want to play — very smart, very fast, with good techniques."

And there is no question about the impression he wants to make.

"From my childhood," Kovalev said, "I have wanted to be the best player — a superman — and not let anyone get in front of me."

It is this style, skill and ambition that made Kovalev the top European prospect in a year when all kinds of Europeans would be drafted. It is this package which brought Neil Smith from behind his desk at the Garden, to JFK for an evening flight, to Sheremetyevo Airport, and, ultimately, to Novogorsk.

■■■

In Moscow, in August of 1991, one American dollar buys you 32 Russian rubles, and Neil Smith knows it will cost a great, great deal more to get Kovalev's autograph on a contract. Mere months before, the Quebec Nordiques had signed Red Army captain Valeri Kamensky to a four-year contract that would surpass $4 million in value if the left wing achieved all his bonuses. Kamensky is tall and rangy and, at the time, 25 years old. At the moment Smith's flight touches down in Moscow, Kamensky has played as much NHL hockey as the guy flying Smith's plane.

Which is none.

But this is the way the hockey business is going, on both sides of the world. NHL general managers cry poverty all the time, then somehow find a few million here or there to sign a player.

In the Soviet Union hockey business, the cries of poverty are authentic. As a result, while Smith was being chauffeured to Hotel Metropol, about the finest in Moscow, Dynamo GM Igor Tuzik was trying to convince the manager of the downtown McDonald's that sponsoring his team would be the master stroke of a business genius.

■■■

In Novogorsk, at Dynamo's two-story residence and training facility, the hamburgers are tasteless, but they are free. In the weathered kitchen, plump women take sturdy plates and start the entree presentation with a bed of rice. The burgers go on top of the rice and an egg, sunny side up, goes on top of the burgers. Then the women hand the plates to the players.

At every table in the spartan dining hall, there are plates of butter and cheese, piles of firm, strong, doughy bread, and wrapped bricks of chocolate. At the far end of the room, near the tape player that serenades the athletes before and after practice, stands a giant samovar from which the players draw steamy minted tea into glasses that rest in metal holders.

On a plate at one table, there are fresh vegetables. On another plate, Dynamo's manager, the fellow who makes all the team's arrangements, proudly presents a treasure: A sliced pear.

Of course there is a different dining room for the team directorate, a sort of officer's mess. The wood panelling on the walls is nicely burnished and the menu is decidedly more varied, suited to more patrician standards. It is to this dining room that Smith and his wife are escorted after the historic first meeting with Steblin, coach Vladimir Yurzinov, a few other officials, and 18-year-old Alexei Kovalev.

On a normal draft day, a first-round-caliber player attends the event. He sits in the stands with family or friends or both and waits to hear his name called. Then, as tradition goes, the player accepts congratulations from his entourage and walks onto the draft floor to meet his prospective employers.

The day Kovalev's name was called, however, the player was on the other side of the world.

"Somebody from Dynamo told me," Kovalev recalled of becoming the Rangers' historic selection. "It is one thing to hear about something, another thing to understand what it means. When I heard about it the first time, it was only words to me."

So it wasn't until weeks later that the 1991 draft took more tangible form for Kovalev. In Room 225, the coach's lounge, in the Dynamo barracks, there are pennants on the pale blue walls, souvenirs of various competitions in which Dynamo has been involved. There are a few trophies in a glass case. There is a large color TV, a pair of sofas arranged at right angles. A high-backed armchair, Yurzinov's chair, sits in the corner by the window.

The conversation is introductory and cordial, and it becomes clear substantive negotiations would not begin right away.

It also becomes clear that no one in the room believes Kovalev is ready to play in the NHL. Not even Kovalev, who later, in an interview, declares "Two years" when asked how long it will be before he is ready. He says this, remember, in 1991; two years would turn 1993-94 into his rookie season.

"He has some qualities to be a good player, but not yet. He needs time," coach Yurzinov declares. "His passing is not very good. That's why he is not yet a good player. He needs to learn how to pass with the whole team."

This is not a lesson that is learned in a hurry. Some players are 18 going on 30; some players are 18 and they play like it. Kovalev, through no fault of his own, is part of that latter group.

Kovalev is like a thoroughbred: You know he has the speed and the spirit to win a Kentucky Derby some day, but he is young. Right now all he wants to do is frolic in the grass. The notion of the saddle and bridle are foreign to him, and the concept of someone being on his back all the time utterly fails to register.

■■■

On the lobby level of the Dynamo compound is a screening room with theater-style seats. It is in this room, during the summer of 1991, that the team psychologist, Dr. Andrei Romanin, conducts voluntary English classes for the Dynamo players.

Romanin is assisted ably by four volunteer instructors from Liverpool, England.

The music of the Beatles is popular in Russia, and it is more interesting to assimilate than a Berlitz tape. Romanin hands the players sheets on which the lyrics of the songs are typed in English. He reads them, in English, and translates them into Russian so the players can begin to understand the words' pronunciation and meaning. On occasion, if an English-speaking guest is visiting, Romanin asks the guest to address the English class, to engage the players in conversation.

"I explain to the players," Romanin says, "that English is part of your professional preparation if you want to go to the NHL."

It is important on other levels, as well.

"The English classes are not only so they can play in the NHL," coach Yurzinov explained, sitting in that high-backed chair by the window. "Maybe they will play some day in Europe, maybe in the NHL. It is given in order to make their level of education higher, so that they can communicate better.

"All our players should go to America prepared for it, in all ways," Yurzinov continued. "They must know that to play in the NHL is very difficult. They also should know they are representatives of their country and of the Dynamo club in the United States.

"That's why we want the best players to go to the States, to be the representatives of the country. When these players are finished, we want American fans to remember those players from the best side. And we are trying to work with our 'sons' in that direction. The players and specialists of the Dynamo club are very strong and very experienced, and this is our pride."

It is up to the player to uphold the tradition and the standards their mentors have set. One afternoon in the National team dormitory, a short walk from Dynamo's headquarters, Malakhov, the Islanders' kid, sat in a lounge area and looked ahead to his North American career.

"You should believe in yourself, and go (to the NHL) only when you are sure you can play well there," Malakhov said. "It's impossible to go just to play; you should know you are a GOOD player, so the face of Soviet hockey does not lose respect."

In 1991-92, Sergei Nemchinov was just such a player.

He had come to the Rangers from the Soviet Wings club under circumstances very different from those of Kovalev.

Nemchinov had been a 12th-round draft choice, 244th overall in 1990, and arrived in New York with virtually nothing expected of him. When he settled near Rye, early enough in the summer to get acclimated to his environment, Nemchinov was nine years older than Kovalev; he was married, a father. He was a more 'finished' player, more experienced, the former captain of his team and a proven product.

If Nemchinov would spend his first NHL season as a lake of calm, deep, steady water, Kovalev would spend his as racing rapids. There would be contention over his contract before the season, mixed periods of brilliance and doldrums during it, disagreement at the end of it.

Within days of Smith's 1991 trip to Moscow, tanks had patrolled the streets outside the Kremlin.

Maybe it was a sign.

■■■

Smith's respect for Kovalev's talent, and Dynamo's need for American currency, led to the negotiation of a relatively high $400,000 transfer fee from the Rangers to the Russian team. Dynamo thus cashed in a player the way we might cash in a bond at a bank, waiting for the asset to mature, then liquidating its value. Kovalev would be a Ranger, starting with the 1992-93 season, providing, of course, that the Rangers could sign him.

The contract figured to be a large one, for reasons both obvious and subtle. The obvious: Kovalev was a history-maker on which Smith had taken a risk. Using a first-round pick on a Russian player is a bold move, but unless he is under contract, it doesn't matter much whether the kid lives at Novogorsk or in the Garden lobby; he isn't going to be of much use to you. If Alexei Kovalev was worth a No. 1 pick, if he was worth a $400,000 payment to Dynamo, Smith hardly was going to get away with pinching pennies when contract negotiations began.

Nonetheless, Smith threw out an early note of caution.

"We do have a salary structure to worry about," he said, "and if a player doesn't fit in at some kind of a reasonable level, it's a problem — a big problem."

The fact was, Neil Smith needed Kovalev on his team. The Patrick Division was stacked in a way that you could not afford to be without an asset who could turn a game. Every point was going to matter every night, because the division was so closely bunched. You couldn't afford to fall a goal short too many times, and Kovalev was a scorer.

Here was Smith, manager of the defending Presidents' Trophy champions, coming off a 105-point season, with no reason whatever to be overconfident that he could get out of his division in the playoffs. It wasn't like that in any of the other three divisions. Hartford and expansion Ottawa would be giving away lots of points in the Adams, Tampa Bay could be counted on for some freebies in the Norris and San Jose was a patsy in the Smythe.

But the Rangers had no nights off in the Patrick. The only charity came in the form of a schedule that seemed simply too good to be true — barely a handful of back-to-back sequences, all kinds of games against tired teams that played the night before and then travelled to New York, plus neutral-site games against weak entries from San Jose and Tampa Bay, AND a month of March in which only four of 13 games would be played away from the Garden.

None of that would matter, though, if a point or a game was lost due to a shortage of goals. There will be nights when you've got to outcheck a team to win, other nights when you may have to outscore them; and in hockey, it always is easier to find checkers than scorers.

"We'd like to get him to the point where he is an adequate defensive player," coach Roger Neilson said during training camp. "Right now, he is looking for the offensive option all the time, forcing the play, and you can't do that all the time in the NHL. You can understand it, though, because the way he will make our team is to score goals and he probably knows that."

On the other side of the Grand Central Parkway, there were the Islanders, entering play with three 40-goal scorers — Pierre Turgeon, Ray Ferraro and Derek King — while Steve Thomas and Benoit Hogue settle for 30. The Flyers, the prior season's doormats, got Lindros but knew they still might finish last again. The Penguins had two Cup rings and they had Mario. The Devils added Bobby Holik, who looked like something. Smith knew a point a game would not guarantee a playoff spot. Hard as it was to accept, he came into the campaign knowing well that the teams who reached post-season would have earned it and the two who didn't would know they had their chance.

Smith also had Kovalev over a barrel as talks grew heated. The kid was asking for big money, but had some concerns of his own.

"In the NHL, if you say something about yourself, if you are proud of yourself, it's good," explained Romanin, the Dynamo psychologist. "In our country, it's somewhat different. We appreciate it very much if you don't talk too much about yourself. In our country, if somebody says, 'I am a great player,' then people are laughing at him, or someone will say, 'Shame on you,' even if he is a terrific player."

Kovalev had left his country as a hotshot No. 1 draft choice. What would it say about him if he was unable to make it in the world's best league?

"I'm concerned about what the reaction would be," he admitted the night of the Rangers' final preseason game. "I'm afraid of how they would react. There would be so many questions about why I came back."

It nearly reached that stage. The night of that final exhibition game, Kovalev declared he had bought a plane ticket back to Moscow, with the flight leaving the next day. Smith, pointing to the presence on his right side of a 40-goal scorer in Mike Gartner and a 30-goal scorer in Tony Amonte, suggested maybe another year with Dynamo would be good for the youngster.

It proved classic negotiation posturing. In a matter of days, not only did Kovalev agree to terms on a contract, he agreed to a deal that was WAY more favorable to the team than the player.

Kovalev signed a five-year deal that called for a $300,000 signing bonus, plus salaries of $300,000 in 1992-93, followed by $375,000; $450,000; $525,000 and $550,000 in the contract's final season, 1996-97.

In so doing, Kovalev handed over two critical pieces of leverage.

First, he would be making only $550,000 the final season of his contract. If Kovalev lives up to the projected level of a 40-goal scorer, he could end up the league's compelling salary bargain at $550,000 in that fifth year.

More significant, however, was the impact of the fifth season on Kovalev's free-agent status. Kovalev would have been

23 years old at the end of a four-year deal, which would qualify him as a "Group I" free agent. That status — as someone under the age of 24 and with fewer than five seasons' experience — would allow Kovalev to sign with another team and leave it to an arbitrator to determine what compensation the Rangers would receive. Smith had signed Adam Graves off the Edmonton roster under those circumstances, and had gotten away with it when the arbitrator awarded Troy Mallette to the Oilers. Graves is a franchise player with the Rangers; Mallette has washed out with Edmonton and New Jersey.

There was no way Smith wanted to risk losing Kovalev the same way. Of course it is possible a completely new set of free agency rules will be in place by the end of 1996-97, but Smith had to protect himself against the current setup. Remarkably, Kovalev agreed to the terms and rendered himself a "Group II" free agent, which gave the Rangers the right to keep Kovalev by matching any offer from another team.

Group II pretty much is another name for slavery, but that was Kovalev's problem. Smith's task was to get the player to New York and get him signed, which he did. Roger Neilson's task was to get the kid in the lineup, which he did. The night of the home opener, Neilson sent Kovalev out with Nemchinov in the middle and Kocur on left wing.

Then it happened.

Kovalev 1 (Nemchinov, Kocur), PPG, 12:09.

CHAPTER 8

I WANNA PLAY

IF THERE HAD BEEN ONE CONSTANT in the first three games, it was that Randy Gilhen didn't play and Tie Domi didn't play and Peter Andersson didn't play. The first few contests, at least, Neilson wanted to reward the bulk of the team that had driven to such success the prior campaign; Domi and Gilhen had been parts, as well, but with all the extra bodies around, somebody had to sit. Andersson was the more intriguing scratch, because it had taken him so long to reach New York in the first place.

"I wanted to play," he said after the home opener, "but I waited nine years, so I guess I can wait a little longer."

There is something about Andersson that is reminiscent of Denis Potvin. Now, don't drop this book and faint; it might be something about his build or the way he skates or the way he plays the point. It might just be that he wears No. 5, as Potvin did in his years of distinction with the Islanders.

Actually, Andersson made another No. 5 spring into Christer Rockstrom's mind.

"Peter is, in my opinion, the best defenseman in Sweden since Nicklas Lidstrom left for Detroit," the Rangers' European scout said, speaking of the player who wears No. 5 for the Red Wings. "Peter played the power play, killed penalties, did everything. Mostly, he will play a mature game for this team."

That is, if he ever gets the chance.

Andersson was claimed with the 73rd pick of the 1983 draft, back when Craig Patrick was general manager and Lars-Erik Sjoberg was Patrick's European scout.

"Sjoberg was keeping the Rangers ahead of all the NHL teams before anybody else was going to Sweden on a regular basis," Rockstrom said. "He's the one who got them (defenseman) Kjell Samuelsson and Tomas Sandstrom and Jan Erixon, among others, but when Lars-Erik died (of cancer in 1987), I don't know if the Rangers really followed up with Peter."

Andersson never received a sense that the Rangers wanted to bring him to America, so he signed a long-term deal with the Malmo team in Sweden. Once Rockstrom took over for Sjoberg, the lines of communication reopened, and Neil Smith conducted extensive negotiations to gain Andersson's release from the deal in 1992.

"He's always been a good player, but he's matured as a person over the last two or three years," Rockstrom observed. "He needs a little time to adjust, but he's a good skater and he's very dependable on defense. He's not physical, not aggressive; he tries to play the man but will never be a punishing defenseman.

"He's like a Leetch or a Ray Bourque in Swedish hockey," Rockstrom said, "but he's smart enough to know he can't play that way over here."

It is difficult to play any type of style if you can't get a sweater, but the first month or two in a season are a time when all kinds of roster experiments occur. There always will be a series of games when a veteran doesn't play when you expect him to play and it will be natural to wonder what the coach can be thinking.

Lots of times, a player doesn't play because the coach knows the kind of game that athlete will give him. There are no questions to be answered. The coach may have questions about the guy who is taking the player's place on a given night, or somebody might be getting showcased for a trade.

More to the point, in Andersson's case, the circumstances simply had not been favorable yet to play him. The first two games were divisional contests, in buildings that never have been easy places for the Rangers to play. The third game was the home opener, where the 1991-92 gang deserved to get one more ovation. Kovalev made his NHL debut in the home opener, but there had been so much ballyhoo about him; Andersson was a lower-round pick whose arrival had created far less of a stir.

Nonetheless, his performance in training camp won Andersson the Lars-Erik Sjoberg Award, which Phil Esposito had implemented after a newspaper guy got a bright idea. The prize would be presented annually to the player judged to have been the outstanding performer of his first NHL training camp, and Andersson, though hardly a rookie at age 27, had been a relatively clear-cut winner in the election.

"The strength, for him now, is he understands what he's got to do here," Rockstrom said. "He will be similar to Nemchinov in that way."

Andersson got a chance to show his stuff when the Devils came to the Garden October 14. Neilson scratched Joe Cirella and replaced him with Andersson on Wells' right. Patrick and Hardy started the contest, but when New Jersey's Janne Ojanen was called for holding Messier's stick 1:46 into the contest, Neilson sent Andersson out on the right point, with Leetch on the left.

Almost instantly, the puck went back to Andersson, whose shot was blocked in front of the net by Devils defenseman Scott Stevens. Seconds later, Andersson accepted a cross-ice pass from Leetch and attempted a one-time shot that sailed wide of Craig Billington's net. Later, Andersson would be paired with Beukeboom when Weight scored his second goal in two games, making it 4-1 from close range at 18:27 of the middle period. It wasn't a glamorous debut or a spectacularly memorable one, but when he skated off the Garden ice that night, Andersson had contributed to a 6-1 victory, against a divisional opponent, and had helped make up for the unspectacular showing the Rangers had offered at the Meadowlands those few nights earlier.

Darren Turcotte scored a shorthanded goal, Messier scored on a power play, and Nemchinov had tallied while the teams were at four skaters per side — giving the Rangers a goal in three different special-teams situations, giving them three goals from centers. By the time Nemchinov made it 3-0 at 15:25 of the first period, the Rangers had a 15-6 lead in shots on goal; by the time Bobby Holik drilled another shot past Vanbiesbrouck at 17:04 of the second period, the shots were 21 per team.

Weight restored the three-goal lead by scoring just 1:23 after Holik, squashing the Devils' thoughts about a comeback. The Rangers ended the evening with two short-handed goals and two power-play goals, plus Nemchinov's four-on-four score.

The Rangers also finished with a 42-28 advantage in shots, which means New Jersey was outshot 21-7 over the concluding 22:56.

So here were the Rangers, paying the Devils back for beating them. A good sign. Here they were with three victories, two of them in the division, in their first four games. In each of those triumphs, they had limited the opponent to two goals or fewer. They were in a first-place tie with the Penguins and Devils.

There were 80 games to play, 160 possible points available. Thus it was easy to overlook that 21-minute period when they got outshot 15-6, easy to overlook the fact that they had won a game by playing barely two-thirds of the 60 minutes.

With Kovalev having played against Hartford, with Andersson making the lineup against the Devils, only Gilhen or Domi awaited a seasonal debut. Gilhen, a veteran wise to the ways of early-season machinations, accepted the situation with a bigger picture in mind.

"It's something we do think about, but we can see that everyone will get his turn," said Gilhen, the voice of experience. "It's a problem a lot of teams would like to have."

Domi, 22, less-experienced, more hot-headed, had a tougher time with the concept.

Usually, by definition, a pro athlete's job is to play his sport for his team. There are times, however, when his job is NOT to play—when the needs of the team are suited better by not having him participate. This, of course, is a devastating blow to any ego; every player thinks he should dress for, and play regularly in, every game his team plays. Circumstances often cause this not to be the case, and it didn't take long for people to get cranky about it.

"I'm trying to be patient and not say anything that might distract the team or stir things up, but it's tough," Domi said. "I'm mad about not playing. I wouldn't be worth much if I wasn't."

The Rangers had decided Domi was worth more than $400,000 for each of the next three seasons, whether he played or not. Three seasons means 252 games, give or take exhibitions and playoffs, but Domi could not see much beyond the first handful of his first season as a wealthy athlete.

"If it (a regular spot in the lineup) doesn't open up in a reasonable amount of time, I'd have to ask for something (a trade)," Domi said. "People keep saying, 'You're only 22 (years old), but you're only young for a short period of time. It's time for me to be playing . . . somewhere."

Domi's words were symptomatic of the virus that would spread through the Rangers' dressing room. It was as though he was trying to blame the Rangers for putting a gun to his head and forcing him to accept a three-year contract. Rob Zamuner had been in a virtually identical free-agent situation and had chosen a full-time role with the new team in Tampa Bay over the bystander role he foresaw in New York; the same option was available for Domi and he chose not to take it. So the "trying to be patient" argument was flimsy at best. The Rangers had given Domi a contract and they had given him a job — stay out of the lineup until we need you — that he decided he did not want.

Neilson knew it would be difficult to keep control of the 24 lions in his cage. When there are only 20 stools, that means four lions are roaming, restless and growling.

"It is a problem," the coach said. "Guys go to the morning skate and they don't know if they're playing. Then they find out, so four guys go to the game unhappy. And the four guys they ride with say, 'You should be playing,' so there's eight guys unhappy. That's a third of your team. Some players, it might make (them) more determined. For other players, it's unsettling."

Bourque, who had come over from the defending champion Penguins, was scratched from the lineup for the second Devils game. Here was a guy trying to get some momentum going with a new team, only to find himself watching from the seats. Domi, in his defense, was trying to prove he was worth the salary the Rangers had given him — wanted to show he could do other things than fight.

It also would become increasingly difficult to get a fourth line on the ice because of the new 70-second delays that were implemented for television. While the TV people were running commercials, everybody on the bench was getting a rest. That meant a coach could use his top center for a full shift, take advantage of the long break, and send his top gun out again. If the fourth line was only getting a couple of minutes' ice-time per game in 1991-92, they would all but vanish as 1992-93 would proceed.

Getting everyone involved in a game is a noble aspiration, but one that was way out of whack with the new realities of NHL play.

Along with the change effected by television, it seemed that giant chunks of the season would be played in special-teams situations. When you're killing a lot of penalties, or when you spend a lot of the night on the power play, the line rotation gets jumbled because not everyone on your bench plays on the special units. After a power play or a penalty kill, a coach tries to regain the waltzing, 1-2-3 sequence of his lines, but sometimes there is another penalty before the third line gets back out there. When coaches say, "We couldn't get any flow going," or "We lost our rhythm," that is precisely what they are talking about.

If you can't get players into uniform, or into the games, trouble is bound to spring up.

"The best time for a coach is when the team is winning and they're happy and you can see it," Neilson once said. "The players are confident in their mates and themselves, and it's usually at those times that teams are together the most. They're thinking 'team.'

"I've had teams that have lost, but really lost gallantly, where we absolutely played our best and we couldn't quite do it, but they all gave everything and they all knew they gave everything and you can tell them you knew it," he added. "Those aren't bad times, either. As long as everybody performed to the very top of their ability, you know, as a coach, you have a right to be proud of them."

■ ■ ■

If there was to be one time the Rangers could send a message that this year would be different from the others, the night of October 17 would have been the time to do it. It was their first visit of the season to Nassau Coliseum, where they had lost eight and tied two in the prior 10 tries since October 28, 1989. No team is as good as the Rangers at finding ways to lose at Nassau; few teams are as good at finding ways to beat the Rangers than the Islanders are at Nassau.

"We haven't had a world of success there," Vanbiesbrouck admitted.

They certainly had no success in the fifth game of their season. Upper management of the Islanders had changed just before the season began, and a new publicity slogan was created to generate excitement. So a "New Ice Age" was proclaimed on Long Island.

To the Rangers, it looked exactly like the old one.

Just 4:19 into the contest, Leetch intercepts a Benoit Hogue centering pass and tries to clear it, but succeeds only in driving it past Richter's right foot.

"I just tried to push it to the far corner of the ice," Leetch observed sheepishly, "and I pushed it into the far corner of the net."

"My fault," Richter said dryly. "I gave Leetchie too much room on the far side."

It is one thing when the Islanders beat you, another thing when you beat yourself. To end a streak such as the Rangers have compiled at Nassau, it helps so much to have the lead; instead, they put themselves behind fewer than five minutes into the match.

You heard two sounds at Nassau Coliseum when that puck went in. You heard the Islander fans breaking into another chorus of "1940" and you heard the Ranger starting to unravel.

Just 38 seconds after Hogue's "goal," Beukeboom elbows Hogue and is penalized. The power play is 66 seconds old when Malakhov's shot from the right point is deflected past Richter — by Phil Bourque.

Now it's 2-0 Islanders, thanks more to the Rangers than anyone else. There are more than 53 minutes to play, and certainly the Rangers are good enough to wipe out a two-goal deficit, their chances of winning might improve considerably if they started putting pucks past the goalie at the other end.

Then David Volek just throws the puck to the net from the right-wing boards, and it looks as though that one goes in off Richter, making it 3-0 at 13:21. Replays show clearly the puck changes direction off Brian Mullen in front of the net, making him the first Islander of the evening to be responsible for an actual goal.

Three goals is an awful high hill to climb on Long Island, no matter who put the pucks in, and the only message the Rangers end up sending is that there is plenty of work to do. Even those few minutes when they were "in" the game, the Rangers had been sluggish through the neutral zone, they hadn't managed much penetration in the attacking zone and they certainly weren't sending many pucks to goalie Glenn Healy's doorstep.

The Islanders, meanwhile, were extremely crisp in their transition from defense to offense. They were winning races to the puck, winning battles for it in the corners and along the boards, then driving to the net for 'dirty' goals. Though Turcotte's one-timer pulls the Rangers within 3-1 at 6:14 of the second period, Steve Thomas restores the three-goal Islander lead at 11:44, and it's 6-1 before Kovalev and Gartner score in the last few minutes of garbage time.

"It was just an awful effort by us in the beginning of the game," Leetch says. "We've talked about what to expect from them. There's no mystery about it. But all the talk doesn't mean anything when we get on the ice."

Now, it looks like a trend is emerging. They follow a 20-minute lapse against New Jersey by going to the Island and registering a reckless, ragged, soft performance in the opener of a home-and-home series.

"We played a lousy game, lousy in every area," Neilson declared. "They got a couple of breaks early on deflected goals, but in the first 10 minutes, they certainly looked like the better team.

"I think," he added, "this game might wake us up."

It would not take long to find out. The next night, the Islanders were paying a return visit.

Maybe it was time to turn Domi loose.

■■■

As poorly as they have played on Long Island the last few years, the Rangers have fairly dominated the rivalry at the Garden, suffering just three defeats in the Islanders' prior 15 meetings entering the season.

In an effort to continue the trend, Neilson takes Andersson and Cirella out of the lineup and swings Bourque back to defense as a partner for Jay Wells. He fills the extra forward spot with Gilhen, and replaces Kocur with Domi.

Hey, Tie, where ya been?

"On the George Washington Bridge, ready to jump off," Domi replied. "A few times, I almost went off the handle. You wonder what you did wrong, why you're not playing. Growing up in Canada, as a kid, my dream was to play in the NHL — as a player, not just a fighter."

After the loss at Nassau Coliseum, Domi had a different dream.

"I dreamed about my (late) father," Domi said. "My mother says, 'Any time you dream about your father, something good is going to happen.' Sure enough, when I get to Playland, I find out I'm in the lineup."

Neilson starts a scrap metal line of Kris King, Gilhen, and Domi, making sure the game will begin with the crowd roaring.

There is a huge cheer when Domi's name is announced, and good hits by Wells and Messier keep the racket going. But Malakhov, who had banked his first NHL goal in off Bourque the night before, gets the fans quiet with a wrist shot off his back foot that seems to zip past Vanbiesbrouck off Adam Graves. So there were the Rangers all pumped up to do something, only to be deflated 2:03 into the contest.

You judge a team by its ability to focus, its ability to overcome adversity, to always feel there is enough time for a comeback and enough talent to mount one. That was an unmistakable trademark of the team that won 50 games in 1991-92. They were so together, so confident. They believed in each other, believed in themselves, simply KNEW they were better than the other guys — knew somebody would make the play to turn momentum back in their favor.

The guy who does it in this game is Gilhen, who is nothing if not well rested.

The Rangers receive 1:36 of a two-man advantage, after Rich Pilon hooks Weight at 3:59 and Bill Berg roughs Gartner at 4:23, and think they have tied the game at 5:58 when Leetch sidesteps defenseman Uwe Krupp at the blue line and sets up Gartner for a rocket under the crossbar. But referee Don Koharski rules Amonte was in the goal crease, interfering with Mark Fitzpatrick, and nullifies the goal.

So now the Rangers go from thinking they had tied the score to knowing they still are down a goal, which is another adversity to conquer. There is another hill to climb when Beukeboom is canned for hooking Steve Thomas at 8:10 and Messier is called for crosschecking Ray Ferraro at 9:15, giving the Islanders a two-man edge for 55 seconds. Gilhen helps kill the shortage, keeping the deficit at a goal. And later, while killing another penalty, Gilhen ties the score.

With Wells off for holding an Islander stick, Beukeboom zings the puck out of the zone — barely missing linesman Kevin Collins with his clearing pass. Gilhen is no speedster, but he outraces Krupp to the puck, making it a one-on-one with Fitzpatrick.

Fitzpatrick charges out to his right, then loses his balance and falls. Gilhen hits the empty net at 17:22, and the Rangers leave the ice tied at intermission instead of down a goal.

Coaches always talk about having "character" players, leaders who never lose their will to win, who know what it takes and who do what it takes when The Big Play is most needed. Gilhen's play qualifies as a character play, and it serves as a springboard for a 4-3 Ranger triumph.

"The experience of sitting is not something I'm used to," Gilhen said. "I've sat out before, but not five in a row."

"I knew, sooner or later, I'd get a chance to get in there," the 29-year-old added, "and I knew when I DID get a chance, I wouldn't try to do more than I'm capable of doing."

Of their four goals this night, the Rangers would score twice on the power play and get Gilhen's goal while shorthanded. They would get outshot 42-30, but would find a way to survive this educational squeaker.

There often had been games in 1991-92 when the goaltenders had been key performers in turning losses into ties, ties into victories, and Vanbiesbrouck's 39 saves in this game spark memories.

"Beezer stole us the two points," Leetch declared. "I don't think we played a very good game. In fact, I think we're all a little disappointed. The Islanders didn't play all that great, and they still got almost 50 shots."

The Islanders had gotten 40 the night before, even if two of them had gone in off Rangers. Eighty-two shots against in a home-and-home series is an awful lot to give up. Eighty-two shots in two games means you're depending on the goalies a lot more than you want to.

"If you take away the good goaltending we've had, I think you'd probably see we've played a lot more poorly than our record shows," Leetch said. "The only solid, consistent game we've played so far was the opener at Washington."

"It's difficult for those players who are coming in and out of the lineup," Leetch added, "but what's the excuse for the rest of us?"

CHAPTER 9

THE TEMPEST

IT WAS STARTING TO APPEAR by now that the Rangers were buying on credit. They were running quite a tab, and it was only a matter of time before the bills would start flooding the mail box.

They won a 2-1 tingler from the Capitals, Kovalev snapping a tie by roofing a Messier rebound with 4:04 to play. Still, your eye had to be drawn to the smaller numbers on the scoreboards.

The important number was the score, of course. But right underneath the "1" that represented the Washington goal total was the "41" that represented the Capitals' shot total on Richter. That was trouble.

Okay, Washington is a decent-to-good offensive team. And 16 of those shots had been by defensemen; the Capitals involve their defense in the offensive play more, perhaps, than any club in the league.

And hey, what about the 18 shots the Rangers had in the first period? It was 11-0 before the first Washington shot, 9:41 into the match.

But if you think about it, that means the Capitals ran up 41 shots in 50 minutes, 19 seconds. What the heck kind of defense is that?

It was the same kind of defense the Rangers would play two nights later against the Montreal Canadiens, the kind of defense that can turn a 3-1 lead into a not-unexpected 3-3 non-win.

Characteristically, coaches face a near-impossible task when they ask for 60 minutes from their team in the game following a divisional contest. The division is where your playoff bread is buttered, where your hatreds are more pitched and more sincere

— yet where your respect for your opponent is most profound. A division game is a life-and-death struggle, but you can't afford to be shorthanded because of penalties all night because a power-play goal-against can kill you. So the games are tough and hard and physical, but there isn't much stupid stuff.

The next game, against a team from another division, might properly be referred to as a Letdown Game, because the intensity rarely gets as high without artificial assistance. It shouldn't have been a surprise, for example, that the Hartford game was the only one of the Rangers' first seven to see a high total in penalty minutes. After all, it also was the only one the Rangers had played outside the Patrick Division.

The Rangers had more talent than Hartford; that was unarguable. They had less reason to be focused on Hartford, because the Whalers play in the Adams Division. They had less reason to fear Hartford. But the fact is, coaches feel MORE afraid of those games, the ones at home against so-called lesser foes, because those are the times your team can lose focus and an opponent can pick your pocket for a point or two.

Hartford never really threatened to do that, although it was 1-1 after 20 minutes, and the Rangers didn't build a two-goal lead until nearly half the game had been played. Sure, the Rangers had on their side the positive emotion of the home opener, of raising the banners, of facing the first pressure from the Garden fans. But the fact was, "lowly" Hartford ended up with 39 shots on the hot-shot Ranger defense, and that at even strength, the 6-2 "blowout" was really a 4-2 nailbiter.

Montreal was vastly superior to Hartford, which should have been ample motivation to the Rangers. But coming off six out of seven inside of the division, there didn't seem to be much left in the emotional gas tank. It was a fabulously entertaining track meet of a game, the teams sprinting back and forth like the head of a laser printer. There were some good hits and some splendid plays that demanded exceptional work by Vanbiesbrouck and Patrick Roy.

But a 3-1 Ranger lead midway through should have been enough for a victory and it wasn't. Neilson called the second period "our worst period of the year. We certainly fell asleep."

It shouldn't have been a surprise. Of course, the Rangers hadn't given Neilson anything resembling 60 minutes since opening night, so this problem was not unique to a Friday October evening against Montreal.

The start was good, Messier stealing from defenseman Kevin Haller and wristing a 30-footer past Roy at 14:35. Sergei Nemchinov gladly accepted one of several giveaways by defenseman J.J. Daigneault and fed Jan Erixon for the 10-foot backhand that would make it 2-0 at 17:17.

"Instead of coming out hard in the second period," Leetch observed, "we kind of waited and let them take it to us."

Leetch had first-hand evidence. At 5:45 of the session, Denis Savard sped to the corner to Vanbiesbrouck's right and chopped the puck off Jeff Beukeboom's stick. Gilbert Dionne beat Leetch back into the play from the sideboards and smacked in a short shot to start the Montreal comeback.

Gartner accepted another gift from Daigneault, a generous man this night, and buried a blast to Roy's short side at 9:11, which should have been an encouraging score. It was the Rangers' third goal of the contest to come off a quick transition from defense to offense, the third instance in which the Rangers made Montreal pay dearly for a mistake.

You get three goals in a game on Patrick Roy, you've accomplished something. Get three on Roy, you better win.

In 1991-92, three goals against Roy pretty much would have finished the Canadiens. Though they were an all-defense team under Pat Burns, they were almost a non-offense team, too; there still were a surprisingly high number of games in which they permitted only two or three goals and failed to win. With Jacques Demers at the helm, these Canadiens arrived at the Garden having scored eight in two of their prior three games.

"We've got new players and a new coach," Demers said, "and we're trying to add a little offense."

Savard was enough offense to get a point out of this game. James Patrick and Mark Hardy both whiffed at a bouncing puck, so Savard jitterbugged a pass to Todd Ewen, who from the left-wing circle would score his fourth goal of the season at 10:48. Then Savard would convert the only power play the Canadiens would receive; he would grab a puck in the corner, fake as though coming out from behind the net to Vanbiesbrouck's right, and stuff in the disc from Vanbiesbrouck's left.

Including overtime, there still were more than 31 minutes of playing time remaining, but the tie would not be broken. It would be one thing if this point was one of the very few the Rangers would squander at the Garden in 1992-93; the fact was, it was merely the first of many.

Still, as the Rangers left the Garden for their chartered flight to Ottawa, you wondered if the game just witnessed was some kind of playoff preview. With some offensive support and Roy, with Savard skating like a demon, the Canadiens looked pretty darn good.

And, despite it all, the Rangers were 5-2-1 without playing especially well.

What could go wrong?

■■■

As soon as one game ended, Neilson admitted, the composition of the next game's lineup was an issue.

"You try to be fair, you try to put out a lineup that will win," he said. "You try to reward players who are playing well."

Still, there are only so many spots. If you want to play but aren't playing, the only way you get a sweater is by way of an injury or by way of someone else's slump. But no "team player" would wish an injury or a slump on a teammate. You can't root against a teammate, but you want to play. All you can do is hope the coach won't forget you. Sometimes things work out, sometimes they don't.

On the team's first trip to Ottawa, things worked perfectly. After scratching him from the lineup for the Washington and Montreal games, Neilson dressed Phil Bourque. It was the team's third game in four nights, and weather problems prevented the charter flight from reaching Ottawa until after 3 a.m. Saturday morning. Neilson inserted Bourque for "fresh legs" and the free-agent addition ended up scoring the winning goal in overtime, ending a game that never should have been close. The Rangers blew a two-goal lead, and got outshot 11-2 in the second period; there wasn't much to recommend the performance, but the Rangers, on a bad night, HAD to be better than this Ottawa bunch.

There was a chartered flight waiting to take the team home, but all eyes were glued to a TV that rested on a shelf in the dressing room. The Braves and Blue Jays were playing the sixth game of the World Series, and since so many of the Rangers were from the Toronto area—Domi being the most vociferous—there was unmistakable partisanship in the clubhouse.

The U.S. citizens felt compelled to stand up for themselves, which made the Braves "America's team" in the Ranger clubhouse.

Every swing of the bat drew an ooh or an aah. Even Neilson stood among them in the middle of the smallish quarters. When things started looking bleak for the Blue Jays, Neilson started ushering the players toward the bus.

"Come on, Ricky," the Texas-born Leetch to the Philadelphia-born Richter. "The Canadians want to leave."

On the plane, the pilot had some fun. The baseball game had ended while the plane was on the runway, and the pilot came on the speaker system to announce the final score. First, he advised that the Braves had won, giving everybody a chance to ridicule Domi for his Blue Jays ardor. Lots of Rangers did the Braves' trademark tomahawk chop.

Domi was heartbroken, until the pilot reversed himself and gave the actual score, which made world's champions of the Blue Jays.

Domi was unbearable the rest of the trip.

■■■

The Garden fans got their first look at Lindros in the next game, but the way it looked, after the Rangers had won, 8-4, the home side had been better off keeping what it had.

"In the long run, we'd have had to replace all that depth," Neil Smith had observed when asked about the ill-fated trade attempt. "We were only taking one regular player (Amonte) out of our lineup from last year, and putting Lindros in. But now, we're ecstatic about our team and the way it's composed."

This encouraging early-season night, Vanbiesbrouck backstopped the triumph. Amonte had the winning goal in a four-goal third period that seemed to underscore how much defense the Flyers had lost by surrendering Steve Duchesne and Kerry Huffman, how much they had lost in goal by trading Ron Hextall.

Lindros had an uneven night. He was booed during the introductions — "Dave Brown told me, 'Go with the helmet in warmups, kid,'" Lindros said, laughing. But he won the game's first faceoff from Messier, his idol. He scored a goal and shared the team lead with six shots. But he also was minus-four.

"Circumstances change moment by moment," Smith said, "so the circumstances today are far different from June 20, and the components of our trade (offer) are somewhat different today as components than they were when we were offering them. So is Lindros. It would be very hard now to turn around and say I would do it (the trade again) or I wouldn't do it. In reality, that question will never come up, and we're happy about that."

If Lindros had come, Smith said, "Our fifth line would be our third line. The guy who'd be suffering is (Binghamton coach) Ron Smith."

Ron Smith would end up doing his share of suffering, but that would come later. And the excess of players would play an indirect role in an outburst that would start the dominoes tumbling.

"I'm not management, and I would never want to be management," Tie Domi said. "But you have to see that the writing's on the wall. They have to do something."

■ ■ ■

Having seen the front end of the deal, Lindros in the flesh, the Rangers got to see the rest of its ramifications two nights later when the Nordiques came to town. It was not a pretty sight. Neilson scratched his entire checking line (Broten, Turcotte and Kris King), only to see the high-powered Quebec offense rain 43 shots on Richter and drive to a 6-3 victory.

The absence of Turcotte was especially intriguing. Before the game, Turcotte's agent, Jay Grossman said, "We've received a statement or an opinion from the club that if Darren ends up on the high side of his salary arbitration, they're going to move (trade) him."

Smith denied having made the statement, but made clear he would not disrupt his salary structure to pay Turcotte $700,000 if the arbitrator ruled in the center's favor.

Then the team played a game without Turcotte in the picture. Without Turcotte, King and Broten disappeared as well.

The Nordiques got goals from Duchesne, Huffman, and Mike Ricci — three of the players obtained in the Lindros deal — and pretty much made mincemeat of the Rangers' team defense.

"We just had a team meeting (a few days earlier)," said Leetch, who had a goal, an assist, and limited himself to 11 shots on goal. "Mark (Messier) started off by saying, 'We're 7-2-1, guys, but we've got to change some things. We've got to take some pride in what we do.'

"So we had our meeting," a disgusted Leetch said. "We got it out in the open that we've been playing rotten, that our goalies have been saving us. And yet we come out with our flattest game.

"We better not accept this as (merely) a loss that's going to happen," Leetch said. "We can't get by like we have."

The Rangers certainly weren't fooling anybody else in the league, so it was time to stop fooling themselves.

"The last few games — the whole year actually — we've been struggling in our (defensive) end," Jay Wells said. "Instead of just doing our (individual) jobs, we're trying to do everyone else's."

Nobody got the job done in the early stages of the next game at Montreal. The only team ready to play at the start was the Canadiens, who powered to a 26-9 lead on the shot clock and a 4-0 lead on the scoreboard before the Rangers reported for work at the Forum.

"I thought we'd be ready tonight, after a bad (Quebec) game at home," Neilson said. "If we'd come out hitting from the start, it might have been a different game."

It was the same as too many of the others.

"They were driving to the net, criss-crossing, and we didn't read the plays very well," Wells said. "We were getting beat one-on-one, from the defensemen up to the forwards."

There was ragged play in the neutral zone. The offensive zone remained the site of a power play that underachieved chronically. There are only three zones in the rink, and none of them had been a scene of consistently productive effort. Without strong showings by Richter and Vanbiesbrouck, the record would have been closer to 4-7-1 than 7-4-1.

"You lose two games in a row, you're not happy," Neilson confirmed. "But I don't think there's reason to panic just yet."

Maybe panic was an improper word. Neilson was concerned enough to cancel the day off he had promised the team following that blah loss in Montreal. He knew two losses can turn into three, which can turn into five, if "there's plenty of time left" weeds into a team's mindset.

The Rangers knew they had enough talent to win games with less than their best performance; they had done it the year before, and this was supposed to be a better team. So they started cutting corners, started turning away from checks, started fishing for the puck instead of fighting for it. With so much of the game going to special teams, some players were being overused, others were getting underused, and some weren't dressing at all. Barely a month into a season in which great things had been predicted for it, the team did not seem as focused or as driven as when Messier first arrived.

Team cohesiveness was being tested, and what better time for it? Get the slump out of the way, build some togetherness and get the show rolling. The only way to pass the test was to start working harder — a price not every Ranger had been willing to pay through the first 12 games.

"If anything," Messier said, "we've learned it's going to be a long, hard-fought year."

It didn't get much better when the following game turned into a scoring slugfest. The Rangers needed a goal from Turcotte at 58 seconds of overtime to survive a 7-6 battle with the Buffalo Sabres.

Most nights, when you give up six goals, you lose. Most nights, when the power play GIVES UP two goals, you lose.

And they nearly did lose. Despite deficits of 2-0 and 4-2, the Rangers survived on a vintage Messier performance. He tied the game 5-5 in the third period, set up the Amonte goal that tied it with 32 seconds left — and the Rangers' net empty — then fed Turcotte for the winner.

"I don't know if it's overconfidence or what," Turcotte said. "We've been getting by playing lousy hockey. We've had a couple of meetings, and we realize we haven't played to our potential."

Richter, particularly, was off to an erratic start. He started against Buffalo but was hooked after surrendering three first-period goals and returned in the second only because Vanbiesbrouck got hurt. James Patrick tripped Wayne Presley into him, and Vanbiesbrouck strained a groin he initially injured at Montreal.

Richter redeemed himself in a 3-1 victory over the Flyers and a 2-2 tie at Boston, although the Bruins stole the point by scoring twice in the final 5:41 of the third period.

The next afternoon, as though they had nothing better to do, the Rangers conducted the team skills competition that would produce their candidates for the league skills competition, set for all-star weekend at Montreal in February. There was a puck control relay, a fastest skater contest, a rapid-fire drill, a shooting accuracy contest, a hardest shot competition and a breakaway relay.

Some of the events were dumb and irrelevant, others intriguing because they highlighted the revolution in the hockey equipment industry. Pretty much everyone on the team had some newfangled, space-age skate, but the stick rack now seems to have 57 varieties of rocket launcher.

For the hardest-shot battle, there were the aluminum-shafted sticks favored by Darren Turcotte and Randy Gilhen. There was Tony Amonte's carbon-aluminum alloy, Jay Wells' carbon-graphite, Mark Hardy's plain graphite. Then there were the three conservatives — Jeff Beukeboom, Tie Domi, and Mike Gartner — who used the good, old-fashioned wood sticks carried in more ancient times.

Obviously, there was no real reliability to the scientific aspect of this study, but each player got two shots. It would be interesting to learn which player's shot was measured as fastest, of course, but at least as intriguing to see whether, this day, good old wood could hold its own against composite competition.

The answer was no.

Amonte won with a shot measured at 94.6 miles per hour, up 1.3 mph from his first try. Turcotte was runner-up; his first try was clocked at 94.5, his second at 94.1. Hardy was next at 93.7, but the best shot by any of the woodsmen was Gartner's 93.1.

It would be left to Washington defenseman Al Iafrate to rescue wood's honor at the all-star competition.

This is a man who has a tattoo of the Indian chief Crazy Horse on his left bicep, a man who allows hockey games but few other things to interrupt his devotion to Marlboro Lights. This is a 6-3, 220-pound player who loves his Harley-Davidson motorcycle almost as much as the rock group Metallica and who sits in for an hour every Thursday as guest disc jockey on a heavy-metal radio station in the Washington area.

Iafrate uses wood, only wood.

"I don't like the way the puck feels on your stick with aluminum," he said. "As much as I weigh, I haven't found one (metal stick) yet strong enough for when I really lean into a shot. Usually, they break."

Nobody in Iafrate's conference came closer than Steve Thomas of the Islanders, whose second try was clocked at 97.9. Mike Modano, then of Minnesota, now of Dallas, was the best of the enemy at 101.0.

The title of NHL's hardest shooter was lost on Iafrate, who had other goals on his mind.

"I want to beat Mike Gartner in skating," he said. "That's my thing."

It wasn't going to happen. The 33-year-old Gartner skated a measured lap of the Forum in 13.51 seconds, trimming Iafrate's 13.852.

That Sunday in November, Gartner won team honors at the Garden with a lap of 12.829 seconds — more than a half-second faster than the 22-year-old Amonte's 13.443.

"That's one for the old guys," Gartner said, smiling.

While the sprint portion of the program went off without a hitch, there was a nerve-jangling moment in the final event, when it seemed for all the world that Richter had popped a tender groin while trying to stop one of Kovalev's slither-like-a-snake breakaway moves. Vanbiesbrouck was hobbling as it was, and now, here was Richter, flexing his right leg after Kovalev had dipsied and doodled.

Goalie coach Bob Froese skated to Richter's net, to see if all was well, so did Kris King.

"I definitely had groin thoughts," said Richter, wearing an ice bag on each thigh instead of just the usual one.

Roger Neilson had other thoughts, about the three-game unbeaten streak the team would be putting on the line against the little-known expansion team from Tampa Bay. The night before, the Lightning had stretched its own unbeaten streak to three games with an overtime 6-5 triumph over the Islanders at Nassau Coliseum.

Which meant that the Lightning, in the first Long Island visit of its history, had more Nassau Coliseum victories than the Rangers had in their past 11 (0-9-2).

"They won't sneak up on the coaching staff," Neilson said, speaking of the Lightning. "It's the players we're worried about."

■■■

The Lightning left the Garden with a 5-1 victory over a Rangers team that made it nice and easy for them by brushing away from checks instead of finishing them.

Tampa Bay did what an expansion team has to do on the road against a team with more talent. It stacked four players across its blue line and dared the Rangers to play the dump-and-chase game for which Messier had particular disdain. It limited the number of odd-man breaks the Rangers could create to maximize speed entering the attacking zone. And it buried the puck deep in the Rangers' defensive zone as often as possible. It was boring hockey, but effective hockey for a team that had to wait for its chances, convert them, and try to use defense to squeeze out a victory.

The Garden crowd started booing when ex-Ranger Chris Kontos made it 1-0 after 14:11. The crowd was jeering by the end of the second period, when it was 3-0. Folks were openly rooting for a Tampa shutout by the dying stages, chanting "dee-fense, dee-fense" as Knicks fans did for the NBA championship team Red Holzman coached. They jeered Turcotte when he scored with 3:30 to play.

The whole thing stunk like a month's worth of garbage. There was no getting around it. You don't let an expansion team come into your rink and take two points.

So November 9 became a memorable date on the Ranger calendar for three reasons: First, the team announced a contract extension for Neilson. Second, the team got embarrassed by Tampa in its home rink. And third, Messier took some paint off the walls — not only of the dressing room, but the front office — with a rambling speech.

The Rangers' Garden dressing room is rectangular in shape, and the main entrance to it is in the corner. As you stand in the doorway, a small bank of three lockers is to your right. Beyond that is the door to the shower room, on which there is a huge portrait poster of the Stanley Cup. When Messier makes his post-game remarks, it usually is about 10 feet in front of that poster. Sometimes, the bowl of the Cup will be visible in the background — a subliminal message, behind his head — if the TV cameras capture his remarks.

This night, Messier stepped through the doorway and issued what amounted to a three-part monologue. (The divisions are the author's).

PART ONE: The Introduction

"I don't know exactly what you want to title that, but we knew coming in here that Tampa Bay was playing well," he began. "We knew how tough it is to win on the Island, and they went in there and beat down on the Islanders, so I don't think there are any surprises from Tampa Bay.

"We just didn't do things, right from the top of the organization to the bottom of the organization, in order to win this particular game. I think it was a real group effort on this one.

"I don't think it's anyone's fault. I don't think, any time you lose, it's anyone's fault. I just think it was a combined group effort on everyone's part. It's just one of those games on an 84-game schedule where absolutely nothing was going right for us. No matter what we tried, we couldn't get on track. We had open nets and missed even open nets.

"I really didn't think we were that flat at the start. I thought we came out in the first couple of shifts and had some pretty good shifts and seemed to get flatter as the game went on. We go into every game with the idea of winning; we just didn't play well tonight. We didn't do anything well. We lost the game and I'm certainly not going to go home and forget about it that quickly.

"I think when you lose and you've played well and had a chance to win, it's a different story. But when you lose like this, I don't think it sits too well — with me, anyway."

PART TWO: Messier makes his point.

"To tell you the truth, I think it's been coming for a long time. We've had 24 guys, now, since the start of the season. Last year, we pretty well had the same lineup game in and game out, everybody knew their jobs and what they had to do, and accepted their roles and did them. You have 24 guys this year, and instead of having four players unhappy, we have 24 players unhappy and it's becoming a problem. It's BEEN becoming a problem for a long time now, and it's just starting to catch up with us. What's to be done about it, I don't know.

"There are guys in and out of the lineup for no unforeseen (sic) reasons. It's just not sitting well with anybody. Therefore, right now I think there's a lot of unsettlement on our team. I think it's catching up to us. We won a lot of games earlier in the year because of our talent, but talent is only going to take you so far if you don't have good feelings chemistry-wise, feelings-wise, in the dressing room, coming from everyone. To tell you the quite honest truth, we're a long ways away from that right now.

"There are 24 healthy bodies ready and willing to play. I don't blame any of the players at all for the way they feel. If they didn't want to play, if they didn't feel they should be on the ice, I think there would be something wrong. I think we're almost a quarter of the way through the season and I don't see us improving from the start of the season. So far, I don't think we've played anywhere near our potential. I think we've played some good games in spots, but . . . that's just not going to win the championships. It's not about naming any of the players or anybody, but the circumstances, the way they are, obviously, it's just not working.

"Ideally, you would like to have 24 healthy bodies worked up and all that, but that's what a farm club is for. On paper, it looks like a fantastic situation, but it's just not working. I think there is just not a good, positive feeling on the team right now, because everybody wants to be in the lineup and they can't all be there.

"I don't think we're winning on team efforts. We're winning on pure talent alone. That's going to end soon, and when that ends and we have an off-night like tonight, that's the end result."

PART THREE: Summary and conclusion.

"I'm in the dressing room. I'm here with the guys 24 hours a day. I have a finger on the pulse of the team. I don't think it's anyone's fault. I don't think it's Roger's fault. I don't think it's Neil's fault. I don't think it's the players' fault. I just think . . . it's a tremendous situation to have 24 able bodies ready and willing to play, but I don't think that realistically it can work. It has taken away a lot from the things we had going for us last year. I think we need to make a decision and go with it, one way or the other."

■■■

If you cut away the fat and the confusing stuff, Messier was saying the team played poorly in a game it never should have lost. He said the club had been living on its talent instead of its teamwork, that having people randomly in and out of the lineup was counterproductive. He challenged management to declare its top 20 players and get the rest playing at Binghamton, so the players could know where they stood, because uncertainty over job status was affecting team harmony.

Each of those things was a core issue far better handled behind the scenes, but Messier now had brought the issues in front of the scenes, had hung the laundry on the line for all to see, had drawn a line in the sand and challenged management to step across it.

Messier's statement vaporized the pretense of peace between him and Neilson, ended the cease-fire. It shot a dart
toward Neil Smith, who, Paramount has taken great pains to
point out, qualifies as "the top of the organization."

Messier did a good thing in speaking up for the downtrod-
den non-players. But he compromised the segment of the team
that 1) was playing regularly and 2) liked Neilson. It takes brass
for one player to ask another to choose between captain and
coach.

This was Messier's first negative comment in his time with
the team. He'd made negative non-comments by not acknowledging Neilson over the summer, but this was his first overtly
defiant expression.

The gauntlet had been thrown at Neilson's feet, and he
declined to pick it up. This could have been Reggie Jackson and
Billy Martin, and that might have been healthy, if volatile.

Instead, the sore was left to fester. Messier's soliloquy
brought the Rangers to the edge of a cliff, though it might
properly be asserted that they were headed there, anyway. The
question to be answered was whether they would step back from
it or fall off.

CHAPTER 10

AFTERSHOCK

MESSIER'S REMARKS SQUEEZED Neil Smith between a bigger rock and a harder place.

Just two days earlier, Smith had spoken at length about how much trade talk was in progress around the league and how actively he was pursuing a deal. Now, though, even if he made a move or two as the earth continued to tremble from Messier's statements, the appearance still would be, "Messier speaks and Smith jumps," which is not the way the business is run. Players play, coaches coach and managers manage. When players are perceived as managers, you've got big problems unless order is restored emphatically.

Also problematic: When this type of cat squirms out of the bag, and every GM reads that Messier is snarling publicly about too many players in the dressing room, the price of a deal goes up. In a buyer's market, there's no way Smith is going to get value.

Yet if he doesn't act, Smith allows a destructive situation to continue to fester in the public eye, which makes him look bad.

There is a pressure attendant to Smith's job that is unique among the managers in the league, because no NHL team has gone longer than his without a championship. San Jose can lose 50 games and it doesn't matter. Ottawa can lose 50 games and it doesn't matter. They're new to the league; they can go another 50 years without a title before facing the pressure Smith faced from the minute he took the job. Even Chicago's drought is a mere three decades — just a blink compared to the Blackhawks' baseball brethren, the Cubs, or the Bruins' friends from Fenway, the Red Sox.

So it isn't simply that Smith hasn't made a deal to eliminate the problem. It's always, "Smith, WHOSE STRUGGLING TEAM HASN'T WON IN MORE THAN 50 YEARS, hasn't made a deal to eliminate the problem." The fact was, he made the deal, but Larry Bertuzzi reversed it.

Ironically, the 50-year thing was precisely what motivated Smith to obtain Messier, the five-time champion, billed as the ultimate leader and winner, in the first place. If he chastises Messier for speaking his mind, he indirectly admits a mistake in having brought Messier to New York, and that would be most catastrophic of all.

At the same time, if you bring a guy in to be your leader and winner, and he leads and wins as he did the year before, then exhibits the Type A personality which you brought him here to be, you can't hold it against him for stirring the pot. He merely is being himself, fulfilling a job description and a life description. You can't buy a chocolate bar and get annoyed that it doesn't taste like strawberry.

Aside from that, if anybody else in the too-crowded dressing room had said the same words, it wouldn't have caused the same stir. Kris King was one of Neilson's favorite players; he was scratched twice in the first 11 games, but who would have listened or cared if he had made that speech? Tie Domi signed for more than $400,000, played two of the first nine and watched the team go 4-2-1 in the other seven. He complained and most of the world said, "Shut up, Tie." Phil Bourque got the hook in three of the first eight; the team didn't lose once. It wasn't as though Neilson was pulling Messier's sweater, or Leetch's, or Gartner's.

Still, the last thing you want to do is start a hockey player thinking. And when a player is unsure of his place on the team, he is adrift.

"With the schedule now, you need more than 21 or 22 players on a roster. I'm convinced of that," Messier would say in a subsequent conversation. "You need guys around who are a part of the team who may not be playing at the time but who can step in.

"And that's hard," he added. "Probably the hardest part of being an athlete is being around a team and not feeling that you're contributing, but still being able to hold your chin up and work hard and keep yourself in shape while you're waiting for your chance to show you're the guy for the job. That's where you need great character people.

"But I don't think you can put a player in or out of the lineup just for the sake of taking him in or out of the lineup," he said. "A tough guy is a part of your team whether you're playing a tough team or a team that's not a threat physically. He's part of your team, so he's in the lineup. And just because you're playing a team where he might not be challenged doesn't mean you take him out of the lineup. Because then, pretty soon, he feels, 'I'm here just to fight. I'm not really part of the team; they're just using me, and I'll never get a chance to score a goal.' That creates bad feelings.

"I just don't think it's a healthy environment to play under," Messier said. "I don't think there's any incentive to play that way. If I'm not one of the top 10 players, if I'm in the 10-20 area and in my mind I had a helluva game — maybe I didn't get a goal or an assist, but I checked and worked and created — I need to be rewarded for that. Otherwise, where's the incentive to go out and do the little extra or go down and block a shot in the dying seconds or go out and mix it up or stick up for a teammate? It becomes an unhealthy environment.

"I think you need to establish who your team is. If there's injuries, someone comes in and plays. If for a 10-game stretch, a guy is not pulling his weight and there are five or six guys around who are working hard in practice, then one of them gets a shot and it's his job to win or lose. But there can't be a time when a player can play a great game and then, all of a sudden, be out of the lineup. Because then there's no incentive, no motivation to play hard, work hard."

Except for his salary, of course. It is an intriguing thing when someone pays you to NOT work.

"It's impossible to play 84 great games; if you have a bad game, it's up to you to bounce back over the next two or three," Messier said. "If you're a goal scorer and you're not scoring, at least don't hurt the team defensively. After that (if the slump continues), it's up to the coaching staff, if they need to get a guy's attention.

"But to change the lineup for no rhyme or reason doesn't work for the competitiveness," he said. "It's not a bad sign if a guy's pissed off that he's not playing, as long as it's not hindering the team. You have to establish who your 20 best are, and you go with them. If someone's having trouble, or struggling, as long as he's working hard and not hurting the team, you can go with him.

"You build your team so that your team can play on any night, whether you're playing Pittsburgh or you're playing Anaheim," he added. "You don't look at Pittsburgh and say,

'Well, I can't use this guy tonight. He's not fast enough.' You build your team so that you can play against anybody. You don't build a team where you have to interchange players. You change them if they're not producing or they're not playing well or they're not working hard enough. But you don't change a perfectly healthy guy from your original 20 because you're playing a team that has talent or skates fast. You've got to think of the kind of team you want, and then you go with it — if it's a fast team or a tough team or a team that can combine a little bit of everything."

There are places where Messier's argument is full of holes, however.

NUMBER ONE: The 105-point team Messier led was a fast team and a tough team and a team that could combine a little bit of everything, and nothing which occurred over the summer made it slower, less tough, less capable of combining a little bit of everything.

NUMBER TWO: There hasn't been a Stanley Cup yet that's been won in November. With the additions Neil Smith made, how is 16 games enough time for concrete opinions to be reached on what type of team (i.e., skating, banging, tough, finesse) the Rangers are going to be? What is the urgency to judge players before even one-fourth of the season is complete?

NUMBER THREE: While it is critical to an athlete to have a job description, there is no way it can be implied that any Ranger who isn't playing every night has an awful life. The team has a huge payroll. It may have the easiest road schedule in the league, because of its proximity to half the league. The Rangers take charter flights back from many of their road games, bus back from many others. They get back from some road games earlier than they get home from some home games.

NUMBER FOUR: Despite the mixing and matching, the team was four victories above .500, had lost just five of 16 games, was in second place by a relatively comfortable four points with 68 games to play. And Neilson merely was being true to the promise he made on breakup day after the Pittsburgh series. He said he would be doing a lot more mixing and matching, to avoid having his line combinations become predictable.

Look who Neilson scratched for the Tampa game: Randy Gilhen, Jan Erixon, Joe Kocur. Who were the big minuses in the Tampa game? Leetch and Gartner were minus-3. Tied at minus-2: Peter Andersson, Joe Cirella, Darren Turcotte, Sergei Nemchinov, Alexei Kovalev, Tony Amonte, Doug Weight.

Some pretty good players there. They must have been upset that Gilhen, Kocur, and Erixon weren't in the lineup.

Neilson had been consistent in his awareness of and concern over the number of players around; it is one thing to stick your head in the sand and ignore a problem, another to do the best you can under adverse circumstances while your boss seeks an optimal solution.

"I think Neil's well aware of the situation," Neilson said, immediately after Messier spoke his piece that November night. "At some point, I'm sure if there's an opportunity to use our depth to improve our team, we'll do it. But I wouldn't think we're going to do it for the sake of doing it."

That would be changing the lineup for no rhyme or reason.

"We've got 24 players. Lots of teams are carrying more than that," Neilson said. "They (the players) are paid to play, and if they don't feel they're getting enough ice time, they should ask for a trade. Otherwise, they should just do their business here and play hard when they get out there so they can stay in the lineup.

"This is what we've got to do for now," Neilson said. "They've got to live with it. That's life."

From the fast lane, Messier disagreed.

"We gave it a quarter of a season, to see if it would work," he said. "I think everybody would be in agreement that it's not working. So we go to Plan B."

■■■

Smith had to come up with a defense, so he tried a novel one: Temporary sanity.

"I don't make those (lineup) decisions, and neither does Mark," Smith said, with just enough firmness, just the right touch. "The decisions are made by the coach.

"I was instrumental in getting us to this 24- or 25-player number because I wanted to improve the quality of our depth, in order to be in a position to improve the team by using some of those 'chips' to obtain another high-quality player or two."

That didn't mean other teams were throwing players at him, and it didn't mean he would rush a deal just because Messier vented some steam.

"It would be foolish to simply get rid of your depth because it is causing some disgruntlement," he said.

"Mark's comments were clearly out of frustration," Smith added. "He's the captain of a team that's expected to go 84-0, and we lost, 5-1, to Tampa in our own building, where we're supposed to be a powerhouse. In my mind, there's not any controversy. Mark wants to win worse than anybody in this city. When we don't win, it's very hard for him to hide it.

"I don't like the appearance that anyone is second-guessing my coach," Smith added, "and I don't think he (Messier) is."

Nonetheless, Smith supported his coach.

"I think he's doing the best he possibly can," the GM said, sending the troops onward to a meeting with Washington.

"The Capitals are either going to be very fortunate to catch us when we're in this situation," Smith said, "or they're going to be very, very sorry that they caught us after something like this."

The Capitals were overjoyed.

You know who sat the next game?

Kovalev, who was replaced by Gilhen for a 7-4 loss to Washington.

Remember that game, for several reasons:

— It was a divisional game.

— It was at the Garden.

—The Rangers led 4-2 after 16:59 and led 4-3 after 45 minutes.

— The Caps had 45 shots and enough scoring chances to win 10 games. The mighty scorers who undid the mighty Rangers were Keith Jones, Steve Konowalchuk, Todd Krygier, and, into an empty net, Kelly Miller.

It was not a great night for hockey, but to blame it on the aftershock of Messier's monologue would be to give the Rangers an excuse they didn't deserve. It wasn't their fringe guys who got outplayed or victimized; Beukeboom was minus-four, while Messier, Leetch, Graves, Gartner, and Amonte were minus-2. Richter made 38 stops and still had a bad night.

■■■

To reach Quebec for their next game, the Rangers chartered a plane — as they usually do, for the sake of convenience or expeditiousness.

Your travel is dictated by the schedule of the league, and, unless you charter, that travel also is dictated by the schedule of the airlines. So you've got the league schedule telling you where to go and you've got the airlines' schedule telling you when you can get there. That means the team's internal schedule, the most important one to the people involved, can come in no better than third if left to the mercies of regularly scheduled airlines.

This is a competitive business, of course, and the idea is to improve your situation in any way possible. Charters become cost-efficient. Look at a typical New York-Quebec run on a commercial line: The widest selection of flights from the New York area require a stop in Montreal. So you would have to get the whole team on the first plane, get it — and the equipment — off the plane in Montreal, take it through customs, get to another gate and get on another plane for the short hop to Quebec City.

You take a charter, you leave when you want, you don't stop in Montreal, customs zips you through and that's the end of it. Presto. It's like having your own plane.

In fact, the plane the Rangers charter to Quebec belongs to the NBA's Minnesota Timberwolves — which delights the tallest Ranger, Jeff Beukeboom. Either the roof has been raised or the floor dropped, but the 6-foot-5 Beukeboom, conditioned to ducking as he boards an aircraft, smiles in relief at the comfort of standing fully, naturally upright. He looks like someone who just has removed tight shoes.

"This was built for me," he says.

There are Timberwolves pennants everywhere, including the bathroom. There is a little rug on the floor that is a replica of a basketball court. A Timberwolf crest sits in the middle of the center circle, awaiting a jump ball.

A small, magnetized Nerf basketball hoop has been attached to one of the stereo speakers on the customized bulkhead, into which two TV monitors have been built. From his seat in the front row, on the left of the two monitors, Neilson flips one of the honey-roasted peanuts that had been waiting, in little foil packets, on a panel between the seats. Neilson's shot goes off the rim and out.

Neil Smith picks up the peanut, tries a slam dunk and ends up pulling the basket and the backboard from its moorings.

Not much of a touch.

All 70 seats are first-class sized, but some have been removed from the middle of the aircraft to accommodate a table on one side and a sofa on the other. Vanbiesbrouck and Richter grabbed the couch and resumed reading their hard-covered books. There was a buffet set out on the table: fresh vegetables, fruit, little cubes of cheese, crackers.

John Davidson, the TV analyst, and Sal Messina, the radio analyst, prepare for the next night's game by using a contraption Davidson has secured in his travels. It is a portable videocassette player with a pop-up, three-inch diagonal screen. They start watching the tape of a recent Penguins-Nordiques game to see how Quebec played, who played on defense and on the forward lines, and to note any compelling events that might make interesting listening the following night. They see the Nordiques' Mats Sundin lengthen his season-long scoring streak to 17 games and file away the data: Sundin has 14 goals, 13 assists. He leads the league with three shorthanded goals, shares the league lead with four game-winners.

The game the next night is just 6:06 old when Sundin beats Vanbiesbrouck through the five-hole from the right-wing circle, extending his streak. And at 15:17, Sundin breaks in with a clean giveaway by Cirella, setting up the Scott Young goal which snaps the second, and final, tie of the evening. The Nordiques breeze, 6-3.

"The team right now is in a little bit of a slump, offensively and defensively," Neilson deadpanned. "We're not scoring too many, and we're not stopping too many, either."

As a consequence, the Rangers' slide has reached three losses plus the come-from-ahead tie in Boston that started it.

The team chartered home from Quebec right after the game. Neilson doesn't make much public show of his emotions. He tends to look the same when his team is ahead by three goals as when it is behind by three goals. But he seemed to make a show of his displeasure on the bus to the airport that night.

Neilson always is the last off the team conveyance, be it bus or plane. He sits in his seat at the front of the vehicle, everyone files past him and he either nods or comments or stares. This time, as the bus emptied, Neilson stared dead ahead. There was no eye contact and no chit-chat, and that seemed to say everything Neilson did not say.

Still, he gave the team Sunday off, and that night, the Rangers had a theme party at Joe Cirella's house. The theme was the 1960s, so Phil Bourque wore bell-bottomed pants and hippie-style glasses and a fake moustache. Randy Gilhen had on fake sideburns and glasses, too.

"Adam Graves and I were going as Sonny and Cher," Tie Domi said, "but we couldn't find lingerie to fit Adam."

What a shame. It would have been quite a sight. It would have been the equal of any of the bizarre things the Rangers would show in the weeks and months that lay ahead.

- CHAPTER 11 -

THROWING THUNDER

AS TIME PASSED, Tie Domi's status in the Ranger community became a matter of question. Domi had arrived at training camp wanting to show he could play the game as well as fight, could prove himself worth the exorbitant salary free agency had earned him; but after being scratched for the first five games — seven of the first nine, then three of the next eight — it was difficult to tell where he stood in the platoon setup with Kocur. Basically, when Kocur played, Domi didn't, and vice versa; in the first 18 games, they would be in the same lineup only twice, for home games against Washington October 21 and Quebec eight nights later.

This was due partly to the fact the season still was young and the referees still had some interest in applying rules against holding the stick and crease interference. The officials always call the infractions closely at the start of the season to plant the notion in the players' minds that these rules must be followed. Eventually, the players get the point; even if they don't, the calls stop getting made.

Nonetheless, a lot of the early play was handled by the special teams, and with the new 70-second commercial breaks being implemented for TV, coaches simply were not using their fourth lines that much. That kept Domi pretty much nailed to the bench.

During an exhibition game in Toronto, his hometown, Domi barely played, but was assessed two misconduct penalties. Referee Richard Trottier called so many penalties that when the penalty killers weren't skating, the power players were. So one time, when Trottier was near the bench, Domi offered his gloves and stick.

"Here," Domi said. "You have more use for these than I will."

Trottier decided, thereupon, that perhaps Domi would like a seat on the other side of the Maple Leaf Gardens ice surface. It afforded a lovely view of the player benches.

"I knew the situation I was getting into when I signed back here as a free agent. My loyalties were here and my teammates, the fans . . . I took a chance on it, and so far it just has not been meant to be. You've got to just keep plugging away," he said. "I got an opportunity to play in preseason and I got four goals and a couple of assists, and then the season started and I never played the first five games. That's the disappointing part of it, because . . . I had one goal when I came back here: I wanted to be a regular. And I didn't achieve my goal. Now, my goal is to get back in there and prove they did something wrong.

"The ultimate goal is to play," Domi added. "It doesn't matter how much money you make. Money's not happiness. Happiness is achieving what you want to achieve, and what I want to achieve is becoming a regular and help this team win. I know I can do it, if I get my confidence. It's just a matter of time and the right opportunity. And it seems right now, the opportunity's just not there.

"I don't want to be made out to be just a goon. I hate that word, 'goon,' and I don't want to be made out that way," Domi continued. "My last two years of junior (hockey), I was the No. 1 right winger, playing with Mike Ricci. I know I can do it here; if I didn't have the confidence in myself, then nobody's going to have it. My father always told me, before he died, 'Strive for something, and you'll get it.' And I strived to get in the NHL and I got it, and was fortunate Neil Smith had confidence in me.

"(When Smith was working) in Detroit, he was going to draft me. And he traded for me," Domi said. "My mother didn't want me to sign anywhere else, because of Neil. Neil came to my father's funeral, and that meant a lot to my family."

When the team travelled to Philadelphia November 19 for their 19th game of the season, Domi made only his ninth appearance. The Flyers aren't a scary team, but they have muscle and spirit, and they have Eric Lindros, who has ample supplies of both qualities. They also have Dave Brown — not what he was as a fighter, but still a major force with which to be reckoned.

True enough, Brown was placed on the right of Keith Acton and left wing Claude Boivin — a big kid with some smarts, some potential and an attitude of "What are you going to do about it?" Neilson put Domi on the right of two lines: with Graves in the middle and Kocur on the left, with Weight and Kris King.

In the second period, Boivin ran over one of the Rangers during a chase for a loose puck and Domi did what Domi does: He spoiled for a scrap. Boivin was ready to go when Brown gently shouldered his teammate aside, as though saying, "I'll handle this."

Brown is a student of the fight science and has no problem incorporating into his repertoire any nuance that might maximize his stay in the game. At 6-5, nature gifted him with an enormous reach, and tricks of the trade have granted him the constant element of surprise.

During the exhibition season, for example, the Flyers were playing Washington at the Spectrum when Brown squared off with a Capitals defenseman named Bob Babcock. Babcock dropped his gloves in challenge and put up his dukes, but he was kept waiting in puzzlement while Brown dropped his gloves — then removed his helmet and stripped off his jersey! Getting a good handhold on an opponent's jersey is a major component of success in a hockey fight; the absence of a jersey leaves you trying to grab skin, which is more slippery and less fighter-friendly.

Brown and Babcock would square off again in the second period, at the center circle, and this time BOTH would strip for action. They would try to go a third time, later, but the linesmen got sick of waiting for them to undress and broke things up before they got very far.

In his scrap with Domi, Brown apparently saw no need to remove any more apparel than his gloves. He allowed Domi a good handful of jersey, then pulled his arm out of the sweater's sleeve and started punching his way to a clear decision. It was not the most eventful fight of Domi's season but it was, unmistakably, a good warm-up bout. Brown was about the same size as Detroit's feared puncher, Bob Probert. The Red Wings were coming to the Garden in less than two weeks (December 2), and there was no question Domi wanted a piece of him.

Domi had fought Probert in February, 1992, and the Detroit slugger had left the bout with a cut on his cheek. Domi, meanwhile, had skated toward the penalty box while making hand motions across his waist, as though strapping a boxing champion's belt on himself.

Later, Probert slightly mispronounced Domi's name.

Called him Dummy.

The Rangers and Red Wings met again, at Detroit March 20, but a knee injury kept Domi away from a much-awaited rematch.

There was little doubt Probert would delight in beating the stuffing out of his far smaller antagonist, but Probert kept his mouth shut. Domi, a Toronto native, felt obliged to declare his intentions to *Toronto Sun* sports editor Scott Morrison the day before the Flyers game.

"You know how much I've been looking forward to this one?" Domi asked, speaking of the upcoming renewal of the Probert challenge. "I knew before the start of the season what day the (Detroit) game was."

Domi knew one other thing:

"There'll be no instigator in this fight."

Domi went on to make other expressions, about how the league directorate wrongly was trying to take fighting out of the game.

"All the new rules (limiting fighting) have done is given guts to guys who never had them before," Domi said. "Now, everyone's chirping, everyone's a prima donna. It's a joke. I can't wait to play an ESPN game. I'm going to fight, and I'm going to dedicate it to people who cry when we fight on TV."

Domi already had said most of these things. During a training camp interview with Mark Everson of the *New York Post*, Domi had expressed concern that hockey was becoming a sissy sport.

"The next thing they'll want to do is take out checking," Domi had said. "I can envision the game with guys wearing figure skates — wearing skirts out there. It would be like the Ice Capades.

"Face it: hockey is hitting and grinding and, yeah, fighting," he had said. "How many fights were there in the playoffs? One stinkin' brawl, (between) us and the Devils. Baseball and basketball have a brawl every week, and nothing's said about that. Instead, it's 'Hockey's too violent.' Well, it's all bull. Wait until the marquee players start getting hurt because there's no one there to protect them."

In the same breath, Domi could talk about the need for fighting in hockey, then try to distance himself from it.

"I want to get rid of this image of just being a fighter. I want to play," he said. "Mind you, I'm not going to forget what got me here. I'm shooting for 15 goals. And I'm looking forward to December 2 at the Garden."

He made that remark, the first of several about Probert, September 21. And if NHL president Gil Stein had any official reaction, at that time, it was kept private. But when Domi spoke up a second time about his plans and his promise, Stein made a statement of his own during a national conference call with the media.

"I believe people have the right to defy the law if they wish," he said, "as long as they understand they'll pay an appropriate penalty if they do."

NHL law declares fighting a penalty, punishable by two or five minutes in the penalty box. It declares instigation of a fight punishable by a penalty and ejection, and that is that. The referee is in charge of administering the law on the ice; the league office becomes involved in anything that goes beyond.

So here's Domi, virtually promising a fight with Probert. And here's Stein, virtually promising trouble if one occurs. The interesting thing there was, during the same conference call, Stein provided a statistical comparison of 1992-93 to 1991-92. He said fighting major penalties had dropped from 461 to 201, that instigator penalties had dropped from 66 to 16. Would he have anyone believe that 185 fights started spontaneously? Could he prove the 16 fights which led to instigator penalties were or were not the result of premeditation?

No way in the world.

Still, Stein expressed himself as follows: "If he [Domi] is stating he's going to take a particular action at a particular time, I have two choices: I can sit back and let him do it and deal with it afterward, or give him an appropriate sense of how the league would view that kind of an action before he does it."

Acting on what he believed was his obligation to the game, Stein had been a driving force behind the implementation of a new policy on supplementary discipline. Any suspension assessed a player for malevolent conduct, such as causing an injury with a stick, would be served on non-game, non-travel days. The player would miss no actual playing time, but would be punished through the loss of salary and practice. Stein reasoned that getting a message across to the player through his wallet would be a deterrent to further misconduct; taking him out of the lineup would be unfair to the fans who were paying top dollar to see him play.

Pointing to the fact that only six players had been subject to supplementary discipline in 1992-93, compared to 10 over the same span the prior season, Stein supposed, "Perhaps the new system IS a deterrent."

Perhaps not. Domi hardly acted terrified when advised of Stein's scrutiny.

"What am I going to do? Get suspended and not be allowed to practice?" he asked sarcastically.

"I never premeditated a fight or anything," Domi said. "I was asked a question and I answered it. If I can't answer a question, there's a problem."

America being a free country, Domi got to answer a lot more questions. He may like to fight, but Domi LOVES to talk, and, he's a funny chap — either by intention, by accident, or simply be being himself.

There was a time the year before, when the Rangers played an exhibition game against the Los Angeles Kings on an outdoor rink at Caesars Palace in Las Vegas. Domi got a breakaway, but tripped over a grasshopper and muffed the chance.

Of course, the players never let him forget that one.

Another time, on the way to the penalty box during an exhibition game against the Islanders, Domi flapped his arms like a chicken in the direction of Mick Vukota.

"I had his shirt over his head both times. He was lucky the linesmen got in or I would have put him out of his misery," Domi said. "He's probably my most hated (rival)."

Probert merely was his most-anticipated.

"I answered questions that I was asked, and it was made out to be that I was premeditating a fight — which is absolutely out of this world," he said one day, standing at that corner locker at Rye and explaining the chat he had had with Morrison. "It makes it look like I'm thinking only of myself fighting Bob Probert and I'm not thinking of the New York Rangers.

"The game is between the New York Rangers and the Detroit Red Wings, not between Bob Probert and Tie Domi," he added. "I'm going into the game thinking, 'It's another game. I've got to think of playing the game and helping the team win.' If I go into the game thinking just of fighting Bob Probert, that's totally out of this world.

"Ultimately, my job is my job," Domi said. "If anybody runs one of my teammates, that (fighting Probert) is my job. That's how we fought last year. He ran a few of my teammates, he ran Leetchie, and then, the next faceoff I was out there, and I knew my job.

"What's going to be said if Tie Domi scores a goal? What's going to be said if I draw two or three penalties? Nothing," he said. "The whole focus is going to be around Tie Domi and Bob Probert fighting. And that's wrong. I don't care if I fight, I don't care if I win or lose. I just want to win the hockey game. If we don't fight, who cares? If we do, we do. Great. The bottom line is winning the hockey game.

"I didn't get to play that game (the prior March) in Detroit," Domi added. "There was so much hype over our rematch, and I hurt my knee. Then I got a phone call a couple of weeks ago from a reporter in Toronto. He asked me a few questions and I answered them. And it turned out looking like I called HIM and was trying to premeditate a fight. I never premeditated any fight. I never said anything about Gil Stein.

"My job is to produce on the ice. That's what I get paid for," he said. "I'm not trying to be a PR guy, a reporter, or a publicity man. That's not my job. My job is to play the game. If I get asked questions, I'm going to answer them.

"I never knew one article in a Toronto paper would be all over North America. Now I know, and I learned my lesson for the rest of my career," he said. "But hey: I've got to stand behind what I said and I'm not going to change a line of it. I can back up anything I said. If guys want to call me 'chicken' or whatever, more power to them. Everybody's entitled to their own opinion. But let's get something straight. I'm not scared of anybody — on or off the ice."

■■■

The Flyers game of November 19 ended up being noteworthy for a few reasons. There was the scrap between Brown and Domi, and the beginning of the flap with Stein.

There was the fact that Garden boss Bob Gutkowski came down to the game, which set off little flickering flashers about Neilson's job status.

And there was the game itself. After hard, up-tempo practices Monday, Tuesday and Wednesday, the Rangers had arrived in Philadelphia optimistic a reversal of fortunes was in order.

The optimism lasted less than a minute.

It was 4-0 Flyers before the Rangers even had taken 10 shots on Philadelphia goalie Dominic Roussel. The visitors crept within 4-3 during a five-minute power play after the Flyers' Kevin Dineen, clearing the puck, inadvertently smacked Phil Bourque in the face with his stick on the followthrough. Goals by Messier sandwiched one by Doug Weight, and the worry, as this rally progressed, was that one would enter the dressing room later to hear excited remarks about how "We showed character by coming back the way we did."

You never want to hear that, because you never hear the flip side. You never hear a player say, "We showed NO character by falling behind before a minute had gone off the clock."

But that's what happened: Mark Recchi used James Patrick for a semiscreen off a shot from the left-wing circle 57 seconds into the contest. Richter hadn't done a great job of playing the shot — leaving simply too much room on the short side to his right — and the Rangers, already wobbling, were reeling early.

Lindros made it 2-0 at 16:02 with a far more impressive performance. Lindros bore in on Mark Hardy, then weaved a bit to his left, into the right-wing circle. While still moving, Lindros loosed a rising wrist shot from near the dot. The velocity on it was shocking. It seemed to catch Richter flat-footed and zoomed into a tiny window of space at the juncture of the crossbar and the goalpost to Richter's left.

It was a spectacular play by Lindros, and a perfect shot, more than it was a foulup by Richter. Nonetheless, it was another boost to the Flyers and another blow to the Rangers, whose freefall continued. At least the goal was scored by a respected talent; the striking thing about the Rangers' swoon was the number of goals they were surrendering to people who had shown no prior evidence of scoring skill. After the Rangers had come within 4-3, the guy who put them out of the game was the world-famous scoring machine Doug Evans, who had been claimed from Boston in the waiver draft.

In the loss at Quebec, that vaunted scorer Bill Lindsay had collected his first tally of the season. Before that, in the loss to Washington, the Rangers were undone by that Keith Jones/Steve Konowalchuk parlay, and that STILL wasn't as bad as the 4-3 loss to the Canadiens at the Forum, when Mario Roberge provided the winning score and swelled his career goal total to three. Roberge was set up on the play by Todd Ewen, the enforcer who illustrated his own, yet-to-be-published children's book and who studied art and criminology before turning to pro hockey.

The Rangers were unraveling. The club's winless streak had reached five games, the losing streak four, with that rotten performance at the Spectrum. The Flyers had won their fifth straight to creep within a point of third-place New York.

Sometimes you have to hit rock bottom. You have to reach a point where you can't play any worse, can't lose any more, and you just win because there is nothing else to do. The Rangers might have thought they had reached it during that loss in Quebec, but this one showed the fall was still in progress.

Lindros, who had been minus-four in his Garden debut October 26, was plus-four this time as the Flyers became only the latest Ranger opponent to wear out the shot clock. Philadelphia's margin at the end was 45-25. In the first period, three players took the five shots the Rangers were able to muster: Amonte and Turcotte had two each, Adam Graves got one.

It didn't get much better after that. For the first time all season — actually, the first time since October 20, 1991 — the Rangers would leave the rink having given up more goals (72) than they had scored (70).

"You know what it's like when you're in a slump," Neilson said. "We'll work our way out of it."

Doug Weight didn't sound convinced.

"We're playing bad in our (defensive) zone," he said. "I don't know if it's rock bottom, but I think we're at the bottom right now."

James Patrick, on-ice for four Flyers goals, echoed that concern.

"Every loss, it gets worse and worse," he said. "It's just disappointing, when we worked on what we were doing wrong for four days, then continued to make the same mistakes.

"I would say we're not the most confident group right now."

Leetch, having contributed a fragrant minus-three, said, "If I had an excuse, I'd use it.

"We're just not playing good hockey, right from our defense to our forwards," the defenseman said. "That's one of the best seven-goal performances by a goalie (Richter) that I've ever seen."

Time and again, the players were asked about the need for a trade, the problem of having extra people around. As always, Leetch cut through the bullshit, got to the point, better than anybody in the organization: "We've got a good team and good players. What we've got to do now is play well," he said. "We don't need more players or different players to play good hockey."

Leetch joined the team when he was a baby, barely 20. Now 24, you can see little strawberry-blond whiskers sprouting when he hasn't shaved, and those bristles were evident after the loss to the Flyers.

It is a long walk from the dressing room to the ice at the Spectrum. You turn left out the dressing room door and head down a long hallway that curls around the building. If the Spectrum were a clock, the visitors' entrance to the ice is 12 o'clock and the dressing-room door is about 9:30. The pathway slopes gently downhill as you walk toward the ice, uphill, of course, as you trudge from it — which makes the long walk back seem even longer and more difficult after a loss.

Give the interior decorators credit, though. Painted on the cinderblock wall, at eye level to your left as you head toward the ice (to your right as you walk from it), are foot-high hockey pucks — each decorated with the crest of an NHL team.

Long after the loss, Leetch walked down the hallway to the bus. He had not shaved. He did not smile. There was no reason, really, for either. He walked down the incline, past the pucks, and bitched at himself.

"It's my job, personally, to help get us out of this — to have a big hand in positive play. I don't know what the answer is," he said. "I feel every negative emotion you can feel. The longer this goes, the more I've taken it personally."

He reached the bottom of the incline. Had he been heading toward the ice, Leetch would have turned right at that point — under the little red shed that protects visiting players (and the officials, who also use that entranceway) from thrown objects.

Mike Richter's struggles landed him in Binghamton with the Rangers' American League affiliate in January.

Dependable Sergio Nemchinov was the team's fifth leading scorer with 54 points and, with a plus-15, its top-rated defensive forward.

Speedster Darren Turcotte became the third player in team history to score 25 or more goals in each of his first four Rangers seasons.

The December acquisition of veteran Kevin Lowe helped the Rangers survive a devastating string of injuries on the defense.

Injuries limited defenseman James Patrick to 60 of the team's 84 games, and ultimately required off-season back surgery.

Superstar Brian Leetch signed a seven-year, multimillion-dollar contract during training camp, but spent most of the 1992-93 season recovering from injuries to his neck and ankle—depriving the team of its foremost puck carrier on defense.

■■■

A sight seen all too rarely during the season: Rangers fans celebrate Mike Gartner's goal in a comeback victory over Boston.

Mike Gartner, the NHL's fastest skater, became the first player in league history to score 30 or more goals in 14 consecutive seasons.

Left wing Ed Olczyk was obtained in the December trade that sent Kris King and Tie Domi to Winnepeg in a deal that added Olczyk's scoring touch, but removed the grit provided by King and Domi.

Russian prospect Alexei Kovalev endured a perplexing rookie season, but still managed 20 goals in 65 games.

Mike Keenan brings his fiery personality and his hard-nosed coaching to the Rangers for the new season.

■■■

While superstar Mark Messier feuded with Ranger coach Roger Neilson off the ice, he continued to shine with his all-star play on the ice.

Leetch, however, was headed toward the bus; so he turned left and walked toward the cold and the empty night.

■■■

The next morning, Mark Everson used the "F word" for the first time of the 1992-93 season. Everson began his game story in the *Post* with three sentences: "The race is on. Neil Smith will have to decide whether to make a trade or fire Roger Neilson. His other options are vanishing."

One of Smith's options was the subject of a rumor that hit, hard, the next day: That on his way to Winnipeg, Smith had "bumped into" Mike Keenan in Chicago. Keenan and the Blackhawks had parted ways two weeks earlier, the team calling a news conference at Chicago Stadium to divulge the development. The SportsChannel station in Chicago was johnny-on-the-spot and covered the event live. Neilson somehow got word of it, had the satellite dish oriented to the proper coordinates, and watched the whole thing on the TV in his office at Rye.

Keenan was acquainted with Blockbuster executive Wayne Huizenga, owner of the expansion team that would be located in Miami. He also was on the short list for the GM-coach job with the other expansion franchise, the one in Anaheim, but was believed to be angling for a similar job with an established team — one that was closer to a title.

Hmm . . .

But wait a minute: The Rangers have a coach, albeit one whose team is doing chin-ups on the .500 mark. And they have a GM in Neil Smith.

And anyway, Keenan has a reputation for whipping teams to death, then leaving them flat as pancakes after a few seasons. Look backward for a second: What kind of condition were the Flyers in when Keenan left? What did he leave the Blackhawks, even if he got them to the Finals the year before?

What if he did the same thing with the Rangers?

What's the difference? If they haven't won in a few seasons, he AND the GM will be gone, anyway. If he wins, Keenan can write his own ticket. You wanna be GM, Mike? No sweat. We'll make the announcement right after the parade.

Hmm . . .

Neilson's options were dwindling, as well, so after the team travelled from Philadelphia to Winnipeg, he used two of them.

First, he scheduled individual meetings with several players — one exception being Richter, who took it as a vote of no-confidence by Neilson.

"Roger held individual meetings. Every player had one and not me," he told Jennifer Frey of the *New York Times*. "You need support in this game. I mean, you expect the fans to boo you sometimes and you deal with that, but you need the support of your coaches and your teammates. And I'm not sure I had that any more."

Second, Neilson went back to basics and reunited the lines that had been so successful in 1991-92. When the Rangers played the Jets, Adam Graves was on the left of Messier and Amonte. Joe Kocur was on the left of Sergei Nemchinov and Mike Gartner because Jan Erixon, who had been the port wing on that combination, was hurt. And Darren Turcotte went back between Kris King and Paul Broten, recreating the checking line that had been a mainstay of the 105-point team.

And it worked. Broten scored a goal and set up Randy Gilhen's game-winner. Vanbiesbrouck faced only 25 shots — a night off, the way the Rangers had been playing defense — and the Rangers won, 5-4.

Afterward, Broten was seated on a stool, in front of a TV camera and some lights. He was waiting for an interview to begin, because with the goal, the assist, and other sacrifices for the cause, Broten had been named a star of the game.

Turcotte, carrying a green paper cup, walked to the doorway of the spare dressing room that served as the TV studio.

He said, "Hey Brots, you need some water?"

Broten nodded. Turcotte gave Broten the water. Except Turcotte neglected to let go of the cup. He sent the water flying about 10 feet across the room and doused his buddy, his linemate.

Hang around Broten, Turcotte, and King long enough, you learn to expect this type of behavior. But anyway, Broten was having too good a day to have his spirits, uh, dampened.

First, the Rangers had ended their five-game winless streak.

Second, Broten had scored his first goal since October 10, scored it in front of his folks, who had made the six-hour drive from Roseau, Minnesota.

Third, the goal had won him $100.

Before the game, Broten had been doing some carpentry work on the sticks he was going to use when Neil Smith stopped by and jokingly wondered what difference the custom work would make.

"I've got a goal in this stick," the right wing insisted. Smith remained skeptical and put his money where his doubt was, offering 10-to-1 odds on $10.

At 14:07 of the second period, Broten was a winner. From the right of goalie Rick Tabaracci, he fired a shot that glanced into the net off defenseman Igor Ulanov. After the game, Smith walked into the dressing room and forked over a $100 bill.

This was dramatic because Smith NEVER goes in the dressing room. The morning of the game, Smith admitted that as the losses stacked, he was considering a dressing room appearance for the first in-season lecture of his tenure. But Broten's goal helped avert that prospect for a while. Broten grabbed the money, made a fist, then walked over to King and punched the left wing hard in his left shoulder.

"We're going for steak — you, me, and Turc (Turcotte)," he said, showing King the $100 and flashing a smile that looked like a million.

King also had cause for his elation: A point, his first of the season, after 17 scoreless efforts.

"When the goalie's got more points than you, and you're at the bottom, you feel you're not getting the job done," King said. "The last seven weeks haven't been fun."

■ ■ ■

The fun lasted until Pittsburgh came to visit. They would not leave until Mario Lemieux had two rally-killing goals and an important assist to go with seven shots at a pair of Ranger goalies. Richter faced the first 21 shots, the last of which was a weak Lemieux wrist shot that sailed cleanly between his legs for a 3-1 Penguins lead. Neilson reached for the hook and waved Vanbiesbrouck off the end of the bench.

Although statistics don't always tell you everything, Messier scored a shorthanded goal and still was minus-3, Graves and Patrick both were minus-4. The Penguins won, 5-2, and it seemed likely they would win again when the clubs played in Pittsburgh two nights later — the Rangers' first game at Civic Arena since the playoffs.

The return to Pittsburgh brought with it a lot of memories. The furor over the Graves-Lemieux incident never really died. Graves was obliterated in the media. There was concern for his safety. Neilson also was roasted, Lemieux declaring Graves had performed a "contract hit" on him.

So emotions were high for the Rangers when they arrived.

And emotions positively soared when Graves had a career game: two assists and three third-period goals. Messier got a goal and four assists. The Rangers won 11-3, blew goalie Tom Barrasso and the rest of the Penguins right out of the building, ending Pittsburgh's season-long home unbeaten streak at 9-0-2.

"Tonight," Neil Smith said, "we looked like the Harlem Globetrotters, instead of looking like the kids from Ice Hockey in Harlem."

For a team having such trouble winning, there was a natural peak of joy over the outcome. But to a man, the greatest joy was felt for Graves, who showed all kinds of heart doing what he did in so angry a place.

Sure, it was 5-3 Rangers after two periods, and the Graves goals were the third, fourth and last of a six-goal Ranger eruption. But hey, there had been enough times in the past when a two-goal lead entering the third period would not be enough for the Rangers to protect. And there would be similar times in the future.

When you get a chance to blow out the Penguins, you do it. When you get a chance to show you're not a killer, you're a hockey player, as Graves did, you do that, too.

During training camp, Graves downplayed the effect of the Lemieux thing, but that November night, virtually the entire team said even if it hadn't affected Graves, they felt for him through the ordeal.

"I think it's a bigger problem in a lot of other minds than mine," Graves had said during training camp. "I don't pass judgment on people and I don't think people who don't know me should pass judgment on me. I'm not going to worry about what people in Pittsburgh think. The only thing I regret is that I may have disrupted the flow for our team."

"I went, in one fell swoop, from being nobody to being the biggest goon in the league," he said. "I felt bad about it; you never want to hurt anyone. But I don't think I have to defend myself. Will I be any less aggressive? Just watch and see.

"I did hit him too hard, but he was back in four games," Graves said. "When it happened, it was a 'career-ending' injury, but he won the Conn Smythe (Trophy as playoff MVP). I'll play as hard as I can because if I'm not playing as hard as I can, I'm letting down my teammates. It's 1992-93. Last season is over."

This game made Graves' point and added an exclamation point.

For good measure, or bad, depending on how you look at it, Neilson ordered the dressing room closed to all but the New York media. And he turned Domi, who had not dressed for the game, into the sergeant-at-arms, in charge of booting out anyone not approved for entry.

Domi loved the job, of course. And he loved heaving little darts from his perch in the peanut gallery. Before an earlier game, the Penguins' Rick Tocchet had made some pointed remarks about the wisdom of the rough-house game plan Neilson had employed during the playoffs. As luck would have it, Tocchet was in the penalty box for the last three Ranger goals — leaving Domi delirious.

"Go ask Rick Tocchet who looks stupid tonight," he said, his arms crossed and his voice shrill as he guarded the threshold to the Rangers' clubhouse. "Hey, Kinger! He (Tocchet) is SMART. He's not stupid. He's the best. He plays with MAR-i-o."

From there, the Rangers went to Minnesota, for their last game ever at the Met Center in Bloomington. They tied it, 4-4, with a two-goal rally in the third period, running their road unbeaten streak to three.

They rallied in very strange fashion. Joe Kocur went to hit Minnesota defenseman Derian Hatcher, but Kocur's stick glanced off somebody, came up and hit him in the head. Kocur reeled from the force of the blow, and referee Denis Morel figured Hatcher must have administered it. So he ejected Hatcher for the stick foul, when Kocur actually had high-sticked himself. The Rangers scored twice on the power play and stole the point.

Meanwhile, it is announced, Messier has had a magnetic resonance image taken of his back, which has been giving him trouble.

When did you first notice the pain?

"Oh, about a week back," Messier said, making a hundred-year-old pun. "Must be some back-teria in there."

■■■

They lost the next game, 4-2 to the Stars in the rematch at the Garden. It was their fourth straight loss at home — they hadn't lost that many consecutively at the Garden since January 16-30, 1983 — but it was like the Dave Brown fight in Philadelphia. Just a warmup.

The matter at hand was the matter of fist. Domi and Probert. It's showtime.

There was some flimsy charade that Domi might not even be dressed for the game, but the thing had taken on a life of its own now. If the Rangers didn't dress Domi, then his courage would be questioned; everyone would say he had the knee injury last season and couldn't even get a sweater this time — that he wasn't even worth fighting.

And anyway, you know Joe Kocur, Probert's former teammate, isn't going to fight him. If you aren't going to dress Domi for that purpose, if the need arises, you might as well just release him.

Neil Smith didn't seem overjoyed that Domi was the center ring in the circus that had evolved over this event, but the fact was, Stein's over-reaction was the gasoline on the fire.

At any rate, Smith said he hadn't approved of Domi's original remarks, "and I told him about it."

And who's kidding who? Neilson loves this stuff.

"Our home record is not too good lately," Neilson said. "It's possible we need somebody like Tie to get us going."

It wasn't possible. It was positively definite.

An analysis in the December 2 *New York Daily News* put it this way:

"Teams coming here now are treated very politely by their hosts, are invited graciously to take all the points they want, to a maximum of two. 'Please beat us,' the Rangers say, while Paramount pays Tie Domi not to play. 'No reason to fear coming here. Make the world's greatest showcase your playpen.'

"The Rangers have lost four straight, five this season, at the Garden. They lost precisely eight times there in 1991-92, back when there was a visible commitment on the part of every Ranger to making the opposition regret having wasted the money on the trip to New York.

"Too many nights this season, too many Rangers have played as though afraid they might sprain their wallets. The Rangers lose at home and Domi sits when emotion is a mandate. He creates emotion and energy, he doesn't get a sweater, and the Rangers wonder why they don't win.

"Players are yammering about trade rumors, but can you name more than a few Rangers who are playing like they want to stay here?

"No team ever won anything feeling sorry for itself or taking the easy way out. So far, the Rangers have completely misread the value of the regular season. Sure, it's a tuneup for the playoffs, and where you finish after 84 games isn't as important as how you do in the tournament. But the work ethic still has to be there, because the Garden doesn't charge $20 for December tickets and $80 for April tickets. If people are paying a price to see you, you better pay the price for them.

"And the Rangers haven't paid a price in more than a few games all season. They're kidding themselves if they think otherwise."

■ ■ ■

Tie Domi's forecast was correct. There was no instigator penalty assessed, although that was simply because referee Bill McCreary blew the call after a fight that was memorable for its intensity, for its length, for the sheer number of punches thrown. Every blow was meant to hurt, to hammer a knockout end on a ferocious 10-rounder of fistic thunder.

Ranger and Red Wing. Toe to toe. The fight they wanted, the fight the Garden wanted, the fight 18,200 people came to see. Probert won an unarguable decision, because of the number of lightning bolts he threw and landed, because he dictated the pace and tempo. Probert threw nearly 50 punches, about twice Domi's total. It was a decision not even an Olympic judge could blow.

The Rangers won the game, though. They made a way to win in the third period. They got Sergei Nemchinov's goal on a semi-breakaway at 8:23 and ended that four-game Garden losing streak with a 5-3 victory over a bigger, stronger team.

Nemchinov's goal was an afterthought, of course. So was Mike Richter's goaltending. The post-game talk was about the fight, because so much of the pre-game talk was about it.

"I did my talking on the ice. That's all I'm going to say," was all Probert would offer. "We didn't win the game; that's what counts."

Had the contest been determined on the number of punches Probert landed, by the number of purply scrapes and blotches on Domi's face afterward, the Red Wings would have run away with it. As it was, they had to counterpunch three times to wipe out Ranger leads. They took 21 shots in the second period, and Richter was equal to every one but the one Steve Yzerman sent out — from behind his net for 2-2.

But enough about the game. There are 84 of those and there hasn't, in a very long time, been a fight like the one Domi and Probert had.

It started after just 37 seconds. A Ranger offside created a faceoff outside the Detroit blue line, right in front of the Red Wings' bench. Probert took his position on the left wing, then looked up to see Domi.

The linesman dropped the puck and Probert went right to Domi. He crosschecked Domi twice, across the chest.

That, Gil, is instigation.

Domi finally dropped his gloves and Probert landed eight right-hands or forearms before Domi threw his first.

Domi clearly was willing to take a few to land The Big One. And he got in some big lefts. But Probert got in more — many, many more — and dropped his opponent with a short, strongarm right hand at the end.

"Probie annihilated him," said Detroit's Sheldon Kennedy, who scored the 1-1 goal. "That guy tried to fire it up by saying things, then Probie goes in and beats the snot out of that guy."

There was lots of other yapping — by guys who weren't throwing, or receiving, the bombs those guys were throwing.

"Great fight," Neilson said. "Let's face it: People going home tonight, one of the things they're going to be talking about is that fight."

They sure wouldn't be talking about Nemchinov's winner or Richter's goaltending, although Richter, after watching three straight games, stopped 20 shots in the second period and the usual 39 in the contest.

"We all saw the result," said Red Wings left wing Gerard Gallant. "I don't think Bob Probert has to fight guys like that."

Probert obviously felt the need. Domi felt the need, too.

"When I jumped on the ice, the whole building started cringing," Domi said. "I could feel it. My adrenaline started pumping."

So did Probert's fists.

"I said I'd show up," Domi said. "I guess I showed up."

Gil Stein would make his presence felt the next day, declaring he wanted to review the incident.

Neil Smith said he received a call from Jim Gregory, the league's vice president of hockey operations, and was advised Stein wanted to see Smith, Domi, and Neilson.

"But we're not sure yet whether that (meeting) will take place or not," said Smith at the Capital Centre, where the team was preparing for a game. "There's nothing to review. Two tough guys had a fight. That should be the end of the story."

It wasn't.

"It sounds like Gil Stein wants to get fighting out of the game, and he's using this particular incident to further his crusade," Neilson said sharply after practice. "Eventually, fighting may be out of the game. But right now, it isn't; and while it's in there, there couldn't possibly be anything wrong with that fight. Two guys who have fought before dropped their gloves and fought again. They got their five minutes and the game went on. I really can't see what this meeting would be all about.

"We had told Tie very clearly that with all the hype there had been about it, we didn't think he should be the instigator," Neilson said, "and he made sure he wasn't the instigator."

And Domi wasn't adding any gasoline to this fire, either.

"The fight's not hurting the game. It's all the criticism that's circulating around it," Domi said. "The fight happened. The game went on. Let it alone. Don't let it disrupt the New York Rangers or the Detroit Red Wings. Let us go on with our year. We have enough problems."

- CHAPTER 12 -

SHAKEUP

AFTER PLAYING SO WELL against Detroit, Richter clearly earned the start in the next game, at Washington. The goaltender, wobbling so much of the year, seemed to have gotten at least one foot on solid ground.

"Your peers mean so much to you," Richter explained after the Red Wings had been beaten. "You want them to have some confidence that you're going to go out there and do a job for them."

He wanted the coaching staff, which just had scratched him three games in a row, to have that same confidence.

"No one likes to NOT be called upon in a time of need," the goalie said, "and when you've been told in a roundabout way that, 'We're not going to rely on you right now, because we don't think you're going to pull through,' there is something to prove.

"You want to prove everyone wrong," he continued. "I certainly wanted to make a statement (against Detroit), if anybody would listen."

Neilson made his statement in Washington, pulling Richter for the second time in three starts after three goals in the first 15:05.

The first was a long shot by defenseman Paul Cavallini which went in off Richter's equipment after just 2:24 had been played. The Rangers were down two men due to penalties when Sylvain Cote's 45-footer slithered through a Beukeboom screen at 14:42. But when Dmitri Khristich beat Richter from behind the goal line, Neilson reached again for the hook. And as you watched him summon Richter to the bench that Friday night in

Landover, you wondered if Neilson just had lost his last molecule of trust in Richter or whether the goalie had just lost his last ounce of trust in the coach.

After all, the shots were 14-2 in Washington's favor when Neilson sent Vanbiesbrouck into the goal. Clearly, there was a need for a change in momentum and a goalie change can affect such things. But when he sent Vanbiesbrouck over the boards, even as the goalies tapped each other on the pads as they passed on the ice — one heading toward the net, one away from it — the assumption was that Neilson would send Richter to the bench, give him a deep breath, then send him back in.

"When Beezer tapped me on the pads, he said, 'Be ready, because you don't know what he's going to do.' It just didn't work out that way," Richter recalled. "Whether it was in his (Neilson's) mind or not, I don't know. I think sometimes he waits to see how things go before he makes a final choice.

"I waited for a little bit, kept my lid (helmet) on for a little bit," Richter added. "He (Neilson) didn't say much, so I took it off. I changed sticks and got ready in case he would send me back in, but he didn't. John came in, made some saves, and he (Neilson) was hoping, I'm sure, it would change the complexion of the game."

If it did, it didn't change the complexion for long.

The Capitals were a team that had been playing poorly at home, had won precisely two Patrick Division games, and had been all but handed a huge lead. They barely had to work for their goals.

The Capitals won, 8-4. The Washington defense contributed six goals in the landslide; in 26 games, with a healthy Leetch, the Rangers' entire defense had totalled eight.

It was 6-1 after two periods, utterly over, and it was peculiar to see Messier — who everyone knew was playing despite a bad back — still playing in the third. The Rangers had come back from a 6-1 deficit to beat Washington 8-6 in a game the season before, when everything was going right, but they had a lot more time in which to do it than the 20 minutes that remained this awful, awful night.

At long last, the game ended and the sorry group skated off the ice. When they reached the exit door at the corner of the rink, the athletes on skates towered over their coach, who never has looked physically smaller than when he walked among his players on their plastic stilts. Neilson strode the long length of the black rubber mat with his eyes studying every groove on its surface; before him and behind him, all you heard was the tramping of the players' skates and the squish-squoosh of their nylon pants as they walked back to the dressing room, lopsided losers again.

"Maybe a goalie can come up and just steal one game and that will be enough to turn everything around," Richter said. "It hasn't happened yet. Hope is not lost, but it's damn disappointing. It doesn't make coming to work very much fun."

When he came to work the next game, against Toronto at the Garden, December 6, Richter found Corey Hirsch's equipment in his locker.

Things had reached that point. The Rangers hadn't won consecutive games since the first week of November. They had gone 3-7-1 in the 11 games since, were merely five points ahead of the last-place Islanders.

Neilson had had enough.

"I'm not happy," Neilson said in a rare public display of strong emotion.

Neil Smith had had enough, as well.

So four players — Hirsch, Kovalev, right wing Steven King and defenseman Sergei Zubov were summoned from Binghamton and dropped right into the lineup. The additions swelled the parent-club roster to 27, so seven had to be scratched: Jan Erixon was healing an injury, but the six healthy deletions were Richter, Joe Cirella, Mark Hardy, Kris King, Domi and Phil Bourque.

"This is simply a lack of performance," Smith said during a news conference in the press work room at the Garden. "Our players have not played up to the level that we have a right to expect of them, based on how we've seen them perform in the past. And there's only a few things management can do before they step in and move people around and make trades, and this is one of the avenues we could address. I don't think this is anything new, to call people up and to sit other people out. This is done by a lot of different teams.

"What you're trying to do is you're trying to give wakeup calls to the team. It's one of the last steps (before a major deal), and even if this works, that doesn't mean there won't be a trade," Smith said. "But it means there won't be a massive trade if this works.

"This wasn't in the plans — to call up four guys at this point," he added. "We're looking to make changes, because of the way the team has performed. It would be nice if we could make some changes from within the organization without going out and taking from our strengths to fill in for our weaknesses. We know we're going to have to make trades at some point to strengthen areas that are weak. But before we go and make rash decisions on trades, it would be nice to see how Zubov and Kovalev and King and these people can perform."

After all: Smith had seen the others perform, and it hardly was a beauty to behold. The idea was to bring in people at each position, so that the goalies didn't feel it was a goalie thing, the defensemen didn't think they were the specific targets, and the forwards didn't feel likewise. This was a fairly democratic process, where everybody was expected to hear a message.

"What you saw in the Washington game and what you've been seeing lately is some pretty poor play on the parts of a lot of our players," Smith said. "The players we've called up have played very well. We hadn't thought the timing would be that we would bring these guys up that quickly, but we let our players on our team make that call. And after we saw that game in Washington, they just made it an earlier call for us.

"They may play a lot of games," Smith said of the newcomers. "It'll all depend on how they play and how the team responds to them being here. But that's a coaches' call.

"I don't think we played tremendously against Detroit, and we won that game. Then we went into Washington and, I thought, had just an awful game," he continued. "There's only so many rabbits you can pull out of your hat. You hope you don't get to the stage where you have to make a huge trade to shock everybody into playing better. If this doesn't work, then maybe that's the answer; but we hope not.

"We've always said that we're happy with the team and we like the way it's composed, but it seems like this year, our games have been not good enough and they're proving us wrong on being happy with the team."

Then, Richter's name came up.

"There's a message from the coaching staff, obviously, to Mike Richter," Smith said. "Certainly, he hasn't played up to his own expectations, I'm sure, and certainly not up to ours. I think it's just a move to try to motivate him."

Why not let him work through his struggle?

"And keep LOSING?" Smith snapped.

"Goaltenders are part of the team, and that part of the team hasn't performed well — just as other parts of the team haven't performed well. So when that part doesn't perform well, you get it out of there and get something else in there.

"We're not down on Mike Richter. We're not going to send him to the minors or go and trade him tomorrow," the GM said. "I mean, we believe in Mike Richter. We believe in John Vanbiesbrouck. We believe in all the players here. But after a while, we've got to say to ourselves, 'Hey. Make some changes. Get things going.'

"I've been at (almost) every game, and some of the goals that have gone in should not have gone in — by Mike's own submission, by our submission," Smith said. "And there's got to be a reason why he has had trouble this year with some things — just as some of the forwards and some of the defensemen have had trouble."

Smith didn't say it at the time, but Richter's move from a large house in Rye to an apartment in Manhattan was at least a small factor in their thinking. Smith worries about everything that is Ranger, and he admitted to friends the Manhattan thing was an issue. For some reason, Smith seemed less edgy about Messier and Leetch, each of whom is a Manhattan resident. But he had a problem that Richter had moved to Manhattan, to Leetch's building, in an Upper West Side high-rise that looks out on Broadway.

They form an interesting pair, these refugees from the 1988 Olympic team.

Leetch is the reclusive Ranger, which is unfortunate, because his comments always are straightforward, intelligently expressed and unsparingly honest. Interviews matter much more to the media than they do to him. He does what he is obliged to do, volunteers a lot of time to charity but calls no attention to it unless it will help the cause. The only time he barked to a newspaper about management was after the Ice Hockey in Harlem golf tournament the prior August. He was ticked they wouldn't let him practice without a contract.

Richter, meanwhile, is the most talkative player on the team. He is one of the main reasons several print reporters on the Rangers beat carry tape recorders and others consider it; because one question — although not always necessary — often guarantees a filibuster of an answer. A chat with Richter is like word golf: The first question brings a long answer, in sentences and paragraphs, like a drive off the tee. Sometimes, he lands in the rough, and spends the next few answers chopping his way back to the fairway, toward the green. Sometimes, he lands right in the fairway. Later questions see him hunched over a putt of a response, thinking, thinking some more, then plopping his reply in the cup.

Shakeup night was like that. Vanbiesbrouck made the customary 40 saves and shut out Toronto, 6-0. The team seemingly responded to the jolt the team's administration administered, and Richter made sure to be available to the media after the game — not to drop any kind of bomb, but to face the horde he knew would be seeking his reaction.

OFF THE TEE:

"You always want to be as much a part of the team as possible, but Roger said he was going to shake some things up, and he did. He's doing whatever he can to get the team going," Richter began, the response similar to the one he had provided after getting pulled — only from the game, not from the lineup — two nights earlier. "This team's been in situations before where it's struggled. He's doing whatever he can to get guys going, to get the message across he's not pleased with the performance of the team in general and specific individuals. There hasn't been an explanation given. He concerned himself with the game, made the lineup and concerned himself with that.

"As an athlete, you want to be part of your profession and you don't want to be sat out. But somebody's going to have to be sat out," he said. "I'm not pleased with my performance; I shouldn't look farther than that.

NINE IRON TO THE GREEN:

"That's the nature of the sport and the position. There's going to be some tough times, up and down. I know how I'm approaching it," Richter added. "I've had worse times in my career . . . when I was sent to Flint (in 1989), it was very difficult for me. Things can get awfully tough, but you have to maintain your focus and continue on. It's your approach that's going to pull you through, and I'll pull through fine.

"It's a matter of discipline in your thoughts. Do you become obsessed with yourself? Do you point fingers? I know I can play better, so I better concern myself with that and little else.

FIVE FOOTER FOR BIRDIE:

"You practice every day and work hard, so that you gain the confidence that you lose in whatever circumstances you're in. It may not happen over night. I wish it would happen quicker than

it has, but you just keep going. Hey: It's a tough situation right now. I can't complain until I play well."
RIGHT IN THE HOLE.

■■■

There was one other interested observer at the Garden on Shakeup Night.

Barely two weeks after Gutkowski had made a surprise appearance in Philadelphia, Binghamton coach Ron Smith made what seemed to be a surprise appearance at the Toronto game. As a coach in the Rangers' organization, specifically the coach of four people who would dress for the contest, it should not have been a strange sighting. In view of subsequent events, however, the visit was noteworthy.

Noting Binghamton had a week-long window in its schedule and would not be playing again until the following Friday, Smith declared, "My trip was planned a month ago."

A return visit — more permanent, more spontaneous — was less than a month away.

■■■

Later in his remarks regarding The Shakeup, Neil Smith addressed the prospect of obtaining veteran defenseman Kevin Lowe.

Lowe had played with distinction for Edmonton's entire NHL history. He was their first draft choice. He scored their first NHL goal. But now, he was holding out for big money, which Edmonton GM Glen Sather, seeking to reduce his budget, hadn't the slightest interest in paying.

Smith's team had the money, and need of defensive help, but Lowe's status as a Group III free agent meant Edmonton could keep Lowe by matching any offer New York made. The whole world knew the Oilers weren't going to match, but the mere possibility made it better business to trade for Lowe's rights after ascertaining Lowe wanted to play in New York.

Obtaining Lowe's rights meant giving up something. Sather, no dummy, reasoned that if the Rangers were willing to pay Lowe the roughly $1 million he was seeking — and remember, this would be $1 million in U.S. currency — they should be willing to give Edmonton a high-quality player to secure him, as well.

"Until I can sign Kevin, or know he will be signing, I'm not going to relinquish assets to the Oilers," Smith said.

Other teams were interested. Montreal and Quebec were believed to be waging a provincial war to secure his services, so Smith was under at least moderate pressure to get his deal done first. As his bargaining chip, Smith used the fact the Rangers were something of an Edmonton alumni association, anyway.

"He (Lowe) has said publicly he'd like to play with Mark and the Rangers," Smith said, claiming contract negotiations were "close," yet admitting the money and length of the pact were stumbling blocks.

"He (Lowe) would alleviate a lot of things with his intangibles," Smith said. "He's going to come in with a fresh start in a new city, with very much a winning attitude. And I think we saw it last year when Jeff Beukeboom and Mark Messier came here and Adam Graves came here (all from Edmonton). They brought with them a fresh attitude and a real spark, and I would think Kevin Lowe would infect the rest of our organization with that. And right now, during a down time, if he came in, Kevin is that kind of charismatic person who could infect others."

Still, 33 is old, when your defense already includes Jay Wells (33), Mark Hardy (33), and Joe Cirella (29).

"Obviously, we can't go along with an average age of 31.5 on our defense," Smith admitted. "But I think Kevin brings to the table more than just his age and his experience as a defenseman. I think his off-ice ingredients would really help our team right now.

"But I am concerned, yes, about the fact that Wells, Hardy, Cirella, and Lowe would all be elder statesmen, and I don't intend to go along with all of them playing at once and trying to win the Stanley Cup with that kind of defensive age."

Lowe would agree to terms late that week. He would be obtained from Edmonton for a third-round draft choice and an unsigned 10th-round choice from the 1989 draft, a right wing named Roman Oksyuta.

It turned out, because of a technicality, that Oksyuta would not be permitted to play in the NHL until 1993-94. It turned out, because of fate, that Lowe was obtained in the nick of time. The deal was done December 11; six days later, Leetch suffered the nerve injury that would keep him out of the next 34 games and all but guarantee utter disaster for the team.

Following the shutout of Toronto on Shakeup Day, the Rangers headed south for their first regular-season visit to Florida. They would play and defeat the Lightning twice — first in a neutral-site game at Miami Arena, next at Tampa's temporary home at Expo Hall. They would record a 10-5 victory over Montreal, running their winning streak to four games.

It was their longest, and only, such streak of the season. They would win as many as three in a row just once over the last 54 games.

The Miami game was played at the basketball home of the NBA Heat and the collegiate Hurricanes.

"I had a tough time reaching the shower heads," said Jay Wells, who at 6-1 wouldn't qualify as a small forward for either team.

The Hurricanes' dressing room became the studio MSG Network used for its interviews, and among the guests was defenseman Mike Hurlbut, who had been summoned from Binghamton a month earlier and had been relatively impressive. In the hallway before the game, the soft-spoken 26-year-old from Massena, New York fairly bubbled with excitement.

"They can always change their minds later on," he said, "but they told me to get a place to live."

Hurlbut had been claimed in the 1988 supplemental draft, Steven King (no relation to the novelist) during the supplemental draft in 1991. It is rare for even one supplemental pick to make the NHL roster — if they had been talented enough, some team would have grabbed them in the regular draft. For a team to dress two players from that grab bag virtually never occurs.

"Mike battled against all the odds," assistant coach Colin Campbell said. "He came from a small college (St. Lawrence), and he wasn't drafted until the supplemental draft, which is like a hiccup after the real draft. Ron Smith said he had an NHL shot."

So he got a shot at the NHL.

"It's not like he's 21, a young guy where maybe you missed something (and that's why he plays in the minors)," Campbell said. "We might as well give him a real good look."

Hurlbut made his NHL debut in that 7-3 horror at Philadelphia November 19, took his first shot in Winnipeg, picked up his first NHL point with a power-play goal in the blowout win at Pittsburgh. Steven King took care of all that business in the same game, his debut, against Toronto.

"He's a guy the puck really comes to," Ron Smith observed, speaking of King. "The big thing is, when it's not working for him, he's still in there — hacking and whacking and doing the things he does well. Whether he can do it here (in the NHL or not), we'll find out."

King gave evidence he could by scoring the winners in each of the Tampa games, going to the net each time to score goals you have to "get your nose dirty" to produce.

When they embarrassed Montreal and scored 10 goals at the Garden for the first time in almost seven years, there was a fleeting sense that things were coming together. Richter was allowed not only to dress for a game and to start a game but to finish it, and it was almost impossible to determine which of those circumstances was more surprising.

"I figured I'd get back in at some point," said Richter, who had been scratched from the lineup for the three prior contests, "but lots of things go through your mind — like, 'Am I going to get traded?'

"In the back of my mind, I said, 'Whenever I do get my chance, I better play as well as I can, because who knows how many chances I'm going to get,'" Richter said. "I'm very glad I started, I'm very glad I finished. I'm very glad I was part of a win."

Granted, the Canadiens, coming off a divisional game against Boston the night before, had sent second-stringer Andre Racicot into their net. Still, four victories were eight points swept off the table, even if they left you with a decision to make.

The Rangers had won the four games, but in the three after the shutout had surrendered five, four, and five goals. It tells you something when you can give up four or five goals and still win, but common sense tells you not even truly great teams score enough to win that way every night.

After a practice following the Canadiens game, Neilson had mused, "Maybe some time in the future, we'll have a three-goals-against game."

The man was a prophet.

The very next contest, the Calgary Flames brought the Rangers back to earth, walking into the Garden and stifling the hotshots, 3-0. Mike Vernon handled all the first shots and the Flames made sure no Ranger forward got near a rebound. Though two of Calgary's top defensemen, Al MacInnis and Michel Petit, were injured, Vernon still stretched his personal shutout streak to 153 minutes, 46 seconds.

Richter wasn't quite as lucky in Lowe's Ranger debut.

"I was happy I wasn't pulled," the goalie said.

CHAPTER 13

TAKING THE FALL

THAT THEY SCORED 10 GOALS one game and no goals the next game was one of the perfect examples of the Rangers' wildly inconsistent year. They were just all over the place, in every manner imaginable. Good defense followed by awful defense, good goaltending followed by awful goaltending. They became a team of extremes, superlatives, like the prior year's entry; but as many good things happened in 1991-92, bad things would happen in 1992-93.

And probably none of the bad things was worse than the loss of Leetch, which turned a routine trip to St. Louis into a months-long tale of unfolding horror as the defenseman's injury turned from a bruise to a concern to a full-fledged crisis.

In his Rangers debut, Lowe was placed on the left of James Patrick, Hurlbut played on the left of Wells and Leetch was in his accustomed spot on the left of Beukeboom. For the St. Louis game, Neilson decided to change things around. He put Lowe with Beukeboom, an all-Edmonton tandem. He put Wells on the left of Patrick, so he had a banger on one side and a skater on the other. Fine, no problem.

Then, 5:31 into the contest, he put Leetch on the right of Hurlbut and jaws dropped in the press box.

"He's very effective coming from that side," Neilson told Walt MacPeek of the *Newark Star-Ledger*. "We thought we'd give Leetchie a new look."

BIG mistake.

Leetch was having a tough enough time with the old look. He was just starting to put a few "plus" games together after being "minus" for five straight and seven out of eight in one recent plunge. He had scored only once in 14 games, but was picking up assists and putting some electric current back in the power play. If you want a full-time left defenseman to shift to the right, let it be Hurlbut, for heaven's sake; moving Leetch over is painting curls on Mona Lisa's hair.

One of the few givens you have when you sit down with a lineup card is that Brian Leetch is your best left defenseman. End of story. There's no way you win by turning one of your few strengths into a weakness. Leetch confided to a teammate that he was completely out-of-sorts over the shift to the off-side.

You may imagine that defense is defense; if you can play the left, you can play the right. But that's absurd. It's more like imagining that if you can throw a baseball with your left hand you can throw just as accurately, just as far, with your right.

Some guys can do it with relative ease, some guys may even claim to enjoy it. But how many games are you going to win with a left defense of Lowe, Wells, and Hurlbut?

Actually, the Rangers would get a chance to find out.

At 12:36 of the first period, Leetch went to bodycheck a Blues left wing named Philippe Bozon, who played for France in the prior Olympics. Now the mere fact Leetch tried to hit a guy tells you how moving out of position had become an out-of-body proposition. Leetch NEVER hits. He bumps, he gets in a fellow's way, seals a guy off so he can't move any more. But this was a bona-fide attempted hit.

It went horribly wrong.

Leetch, going east-to-west, misjudged the speed of Bozon, who was going north-south. He misjudged the space to the boards, as well. They ended up clipping legs, and Leetch sailed into the heavy barrier.

Head-first.

Leetch was moving too fast to cushion much of the blow. The way he ended up making contact, Leetch's left ear reached over to the cup of his left shoulder pad, compressing, then stretching nerves in the Brachial Plexus — which no lay Ranger fan EVER heard of before 12:36 of the first period in St. Louis, December 17, 1992.

Leetch went into the boards so hard, you figured they could get his head out of the wood if two players grabbed an ankle each and pulled. He lay on the ice, near the Rangers' blue line — THE RIGHT SIDE of the Rangers' blue line — and everybody in St.

Louis Arena thought about that gruesome collision that caused New York Jets lineman Dennis Byrd to suffer a broken neck. Leetch stirred after a while, left the ice woozy, but self-sustaining.

Late in the first period, Barry Watkins came up to the press box from the dressing room and announced a left-shoulder injury that "doesn't look too bad." Later, it is announced Leetch will not return to the game, which the Rangers win, 4-3.

Later, his status becomes "day to day." After a few of those, it becomes "indefinite," because, simply, there is no way of knowing when Leetch might return.

"I saw him the following day. He had a rather profound paralysis. He couldn't lift his arm," Dr. Barton Nisonson, the Rangers' physician and orthopedic surgeon would say several weeks later. "The nerves that go from the neck to the shoulder were significantly injured.

"Part of the nerves were not badly injured; part of the nerve did have an injury that requires the nerve to regenerate," Dr. Nisonson added. "The area where Brian had his injury is an area where almost always it does regenerate. The problem is time. You cannot predict how long this injury will take."

It took 34 games and 82 days. The nerve that was affected will never regenerate beyond 90 percent or so, but that is not as bad as it sounds.

"If you look at the whole gamut of brachial plexus injuries, I would say almost every one will get a return of at least 90 percent of his strength," Dr. Nisonson said. "The 10 percent difference, if he does have a deficit, will not affect his playing ability and will not affect his strength, because he's going to be on a very stringent strengthening program. So I don't see this being anything that will hamper his career or his success and his ability to perform in his position."

It did affect Neilson's career and the team's success and its ability to perform. In the absence of Leetch, it became a darn lucky thing that Smith had gone to the trouble of signing Zubov during the off-season. It became a darn lucky thing Smith had obtained Lowe. It became a lucky thing Per Djoos had made his odd decision to return to the team.

"You don't replace him (Leetch)," Neil Smith said, "you substitute someone for his position."

If Leetch plays 30 minutes a game, which he often seems to do, that means you give 10 extra minutes each to three guys or 15 extra minutes each to two guys. One of those players ended up being Kevin Lowe, who was only in his second game of the season, trying, at age 33, to keep up with younger, stronger players who had been at it, hard, since September. In an instant, a player who would be the perfect fifth or sixth or seventh defenseman would end up being with the responsibilities of a key member of the top four — playing minutes way beyond his capabilities, generally against the opposition's best forwards.

Lowe did his best, so did everyone else who tried to be a patch big enough to cover the hole Leetch left. But it became a catastrophe.

The Rangers would tie 4-4 at Hartford, giving up the first goal 3:17 into the match when Hurlbut, shifted to the right, got toasted as Paul Gillis scored his first since the 1990-91 season. The Rangers would waste one chance to win by giving up a goal to Pat Verbeek with 41 seconds left in the third period. They would waste another with 23.2 seconds left in overtime when Graves and Gartner broke in against Sean Burke; Burke got his so-very-long left leg on Gartner's shot and the Rangers went home with one point instead of the two that were available.

Vanbiesbrouck added a 3-0 shutout of the Devils in New Jersey, and the logical conclusion was that Leetch's injury had caused the Rangers to close up the ranks — that they would concentrate on the defense they had ignored for so long when he was healthy, and would do the things necessary to win with the absence of the player judged, in 1991-92, to have been the NHL defenseman most valuable to his team.

"The disturbing reality is, we were losing earlier in the year, (when Leetch was healthy)," Mike Richter said. "You think of him in a flashy way, of scoring and all that, but there's also a sense of confidence when he's around, and the fact he just has the puck so damn much of the time that the other team doesn't have it. He might not do anything specifically flashy, like scoring a goal or making a great move, but he's just controlling it.

"It (Leetch's absence) shouldn't put the pressure, like, 'Brian's hurt, so we're done.' We still had to play better than we did."

Of the next six games, they would lose five, and four of those defeats would come at the hands of divisional foes.

They turned an early 3-1 lead into a 5-4 overtime loss to New Jersey, a game that left Neilson seething in his Garden interview area.

"We have a lot of forwards that just aren't doing the job defensively. That's the problem," he said after the Rangers had permitted a mere 47 New Jersey shots. "We just looked completely out of position in terms of defensive play . . . We didn't deserve to win this game by any stretch of the imagination."

They then went to Long Island, where they always lose, and convinced Neil Smith to change some travel plans.

Smith had planned to be in Sweden for the start of the World Junior Championships, at which four Ranger prospects were competing. Peter and Chris Ferraro, his prize picks of 1992, were playing on Team USA with Yale's Dan Brierly, a ninth-round pick in the same draft. Defenseman Darcy Werenka, a second-rounder in 1991, was playing for Team Canada.

The trip got pushed back a day, however, when Smith watched another evening of defensive slapstick in a 6-4 loss at Nassau Coliseum. It was the team's 36th game of the season, the 21st time in which they permitted at least four goals.

"I'm concerned about the way we're playing," Messier said. "We're not playing well."

The Islanders moved the puck better, moved their legs better. They seemed to work harder and more productively. They got the late man involved in the play better. They made it another night of misery for Richter, scoring five of their goals from within 10 feet of the cage and never taking longer than six minutes to score a goal of their own after a Ranger tally.

If this was the best the Rangers could do in an important divisional game, a game they wanted to win just so people would stop asking about a Nassau winless streak that now spanned two ties and 10 defeats, there were many more miserable nights in store.

"We would like to be playing a much better brand of hockey than we are," Neilson admitted. "The last couple of games, we just haven't been able to get it done."

The Rangers were outplayed in the first period and lucky to reach intermission tied 2-2, thanks to some questionable decisions by Islanders goalie Glenn Healy.

Given only a brief instant to decide whether Jay Wells' left-point shot was heading wide or heading toward his net, Healy determined — wrongly, the replays showed — the shot was too close to ignore. He thrust out his right skate, but did not get the puck cleanly; it squibbed into the crease and Kovalev ushered it in with a backhand for the only Ranger lead of the evening.

The Islanders counterpunched almost immediately. As Pierre Turgeon's shot from the left flank arrived at the net, Broten checked Steve Thomas directly into the puck — and into Richter, who was knocked sprawling as the disc went under him at 4:57. Brian Mullen converted a rebound at 6:24 and the Islanders were ahead until Healy made Fateful Decision No. 2.

That was when Sergei Nemchinov reached way back for the puck and got exceptional rotation on the wrist shot he slung toward Healy from behind the right-wing faceoff circle. The puck sped upward, either off the stick of defenseman Gary Nylund or from the power with which Nemchinov launched it. Given an instant to decide if it was headed under the crossbar or over the net, Healy decided to err on the side of caution.

"We don't have the benefit of super-slow-mo," he said.

Nemchinov's shot glanced off the webbing of his catching glove and nestled in the back of the net, tying the score at 14:01. Healy redeemed himself with a reflex left-pad stop on a Patrick 10-footer during a four-on-four with 1:30 left in the session, however, preserving a deadlock Patrick Flatley would undo just 25 seconds into the middle period.

As this was going on, Smith sat in the second row of the Nassau press box, watching the Islanders create good scoring opportunities time and again. Leetch was out. Lowe, who had a stomach virus, was out. Beukeboom was returning from a wrenched right knee. Cirella and Hardy were hitting the conditioning wall that comes with long absences from the lineup. Hurlbut was okay, but the Rangers needed him to be Doug Harvey.

After the first period, Smith sat with Sal Messina, prepared to be interviewed on WFAN radio. Somebody asked Smith if he still planned to leave the team and head for the junior tournament; in the press room before the game, he had waffled somewhat, and after the opening session, Smith said he still planned to go.

On the air, during the interview, Smith seemed less certain. And by the next morning, with the Bruins roaring into New York on the heels of a 9-4 stampede over Hartford, Smith's trip had been pushed back a day, Zubov had been invited back from Binghamton, and Erixon, at long last, was back in the lineup. The Rangers had gone 7-3-2 with Erixon in the lineup, but the loss at Nassau had left the team 11-11-2 without him.

With Zubov, with Erixon, with Lowe a possibility, the Rangers had to feel their chances of winning were better. But the postponement of Smith's trip was a sword of Damocles over every Ranger head.

Smith already had tried making trades, and he and Neilson had presided over the December 6 shakeup. The team was not moving forward, and there weren't many alternatives available. On December 26, 1991, the Rangers had wiped out a 6-1 deficit and had beaten Washington 8-6, improving their record to 24-12-1; on December 26, 1992, the Rangers stood at 18-14-4, nine points short of the prior year's team statistically but light years removed from it in terms of performance.

"We've got the toughest part of our schedule coming up," Neilson said, observing that 17 of the next 27 games were on the road, "and we're going to have to play a lot better defensively to get through it in good shape."

Smith left for Sweden thinking the team might play a bit more relaxed if he was far away from them, far away from seeing anything that might make his big-trade trigger finger any itchier.

A 6-5 Garden victory over Boston the next night eased the pressure slightly, as the Rangers played 53 mostly rotten minutes, then scored four times in the closing 6:41. Kovalev the unpredictable completed his hat trick with 36 seconds remaining to win it, and the Rangers were back at five victories over .500 . . . for the last time until their March 11 victory at Chicago.

The Boston game also was the 11th straight in which Domi was scratched from the lineup. Kris King, who had no goals in 45 games, was deleted as well.

The next day, the Rangers announced both had been traded to Winnipeg for Ed Olczyk.

And the remainder of hell began to break loose.

Though he was under absolutely no obligation to do so, Barry Watkins arranged a conference call between members of the New York media and the city's newest ex-Ranger, Domi. If the Rangers do not lead the NHL in conference calls, they certainly must come close; such calls save the player or executive involved from having to return 20 or 30 calls, and it saves some reporter from the wait involved in being 30th on the list. Everybody gets the same quotes, which is a drag, but everybody gets pretty much the same quotes some nights in the dressing room, too.

And the Domi quotes were vintage.

Having been frustrated over playing in just 12 of the team's

37 games, troubled all the more by Stein's illogical prosecution of the fight with Probert, Domi had a lot on his mind. Before he put Domi on the phone, Watkins had urged him to use his head when he spoke.

Domi did not use his head. His circuits overloaded. He essentially blamed all the team's troubles for the season on assistant coach Colin Campbell.

"There are some things here that have to be straightened out," Domi said. "It's not the GM, it's not the coach. It's one individual person. He's hurt my career. Maybe I speak too much, but Colin Campbell hasn't been supporting me much lately. He was always in my corner, then he turned on me and everything went on the down side for me.

"It seems like he's always negative about everything that happens around here, and that's unfortunate," Domi continued. "Every time I do something, it's wrong, and if someone else does it, it's great.

"Colin Campbell really had a lot to do with getting me traded," Domi said. "I can guarantee it. He turned on me. The same thing happened with Mike Richter, and the same thing happened with Phil Bourque. I think Colin Campbell had a lot to do with it. I don't think an assistant coach should have the influence of a coach or a general manager. That's very unfortunate. That has to be settled down. One thing he has to realize is, he's just a coach and he has to have good relationships with the players. An assistant coach's job is to be nice to everybody."

The unfortunate thing was, Domi had the wrong man. The guy who got him out of there was Neilson, who later would admit as much. And if they had problems with Campbell, neither Richter nor Bourque was prepared to admit it.

When a team has two assistant coaches, one is usually the good guy and one is usually the bad guy. The good guy is the one who listens to the problems, all the bitching; the bad guy is the one who skates the spare players until they puke. Campbell ended up with a lot of bad-guy time, because Domi almost never played.

"I came down hard on him at times," a stunned Campbell admitted, "but I almost treated him like a son — whacking him, treating him hard. But if I'm the guy he strikes out at, fine. I'm very disappointed, but if that's the way he feels . . .

"He had spunk and fire on the ice. He'd say stuff and then go out and back it up," Campbell said. "It's nice to have a guy like that."

Winnipeg was overjoyed. Jets coach John Paddock, who had coached in the Rangers' organization, needed protection for his premier rookie from Finland, Teemu Selanne. Domi was more than up to that job description and so, if need be, was King. The Jets had a whopping number of European players, needed some muscle to go with their finesse, and were more than willing to part with Olczyk, who was going to be a salary arbitration headache, anyway.

The Rangers traded two guys with a total of two goals — both Domi's, believe it or not — and received a guy who could bolster the left-wing scoring behind Adam Graves.

"I did not pursue Ed Olczyk; they pursued our two players," Neil Smith said. "When you've got something someone else wants, you've got the upper hand."

The trade of King, a Neilson favorite, seemed to send that upper hand across the face of the Ranger coach.

"It was like cutting my heart out when Kinger got traded," Neilson said. "I think I took this one tougher than Kris."

King went out with considerably more restraint.

"We weren't winning games we should, and the pressure was on the coaches to make changes," King said. "The checking line (with him, Broten and Turcotte) played well. I can't explain why it was taken away, but it hurt my confidence and my game after being used for three years as a regular."

An illness in the family prevented Olczyk from joining his fourth NHL team right away. He got to Capital Centre in time to watch the Rangers blow a 3-1 lead in the concluding 14 minutes, lose in overtime and drop to third place. That made three trips to Washington for the season and three noteworthy events:

— October 9 was one of the season's best showings, a 4-2 victory.

— December 4 was one of the season's worst, an 8-4 loss.

— December 29 was one of the season's most painful, two points torched by a third-period collapse against a division rival.

Peter Bondra tied the game with 2:33 left in regulation. Michal Pivonka won a faceoff from Nemchinov in the circle to John Vanbiesbrouck's right and Bondra ripped a wicked shot past the goalie's left glove before anybody could move. It was one of 21 third-period shots by the Capitals to just six for the Rangers.

"In the first two periods, we played the best defense we've played all year," said Adam Graves, noting the Capitals totalled

10 shots in the first 40 minutes. "In the third, we sat back too much and played Kitty Bar the Door."

In overtime, Pivonka's centering pass from the left-wing corner glanced off Vanbiesbrouck's stick, then off Darren Turcotte's stick and into the net, handing the visitors their seventh defeat in the past nine division games.

It was just an overall bad trip. The Rangers were to have taken a shuttle flight to Washington from LaGuardia Airport, but shifted to rail service once fog started causing plane cancellations. There is a train station a few miles from the Capital Centre, but the train the Rangers were on was not scheduled to stop there. Amtrak agreed to make a special stop, allowing the team to disembark.

The equipment couldn't make it on the train, because there wasn't room on the baggage car. Trainer Joe Murphy and assistant trainer Tim Paris had escorted the equipment to LaGuardia in a van that dropped them off, then went back to Rye. They had to rent a van nearer the airport and drive to Cap Centre. They arrived at 5:55 p.m. for the 7:30 start, which qualified as cutting things a bit short.

It wasn't worth it.

"As well as we played, as much as we deserved to win, you can say, 'Well, did we really?' because we didn't do what we needed to do in the third period," Messier said. "You can't play 20 minutes in your own zone. It's just as simple as that. To me, that's not defense. That's sitting back, waiting to get beat.

"We sat back, didn't create anything defensively, didn't move up and forecheck, get the puck deep and cycle 'down low' and try to hem them in their zone," Messier said. "And you need to do that. I don't care if you're in the 38th game of the year or the seventh game of a sudden-death final in the playoffs. (If you don't do it), you put so much pressure on yourself and the goalie and everybody else that it becomes just a matter of time before you lose. And that's what happened."

Goals by Darren Turcotte, Doug Weight, and Adam Graves — the last at 19:05 of the second period — represented the Rangers' offense. They got 20 shots the whole contest, gave up 21 in one period.

Turcotte scored from the right point on a power play 43 seconds into the game, Weight canned Alexei Kovalev's rebound at 13:17 of the second. Then Graves steamed up the left side and drove a shot past Don Beaupre's left glove for 3-1 at 19:05 of the second.

In the remaining 22:53, the Capitals outshot the Rangers 24-6.

"We got off our game. We tried to go into a shell," Graves said. "Time is on the side of the offensive team."

It was NOT on the side of the losing team, in the hours before the game or the several days after it. From Washington, the team would fly to Buffalo and ring out the old year with a game against the Sabres.

For Richter, 1992 could not end soon enough. He stood in the locker room in Buffalo and looked forward to a new page on the calendar.

"Things will just be fine," said Richter, who finished the calendar year with a regular-season record of 18-15-3 while Vanbiesbrouck was 26-12-5. "They haven't told me to find another city to live in yet, and until they do, I'm going to work hard as I can. I think this year (1993) can be a great, great year for me."

Richter expressed nothing but admiration for Vanbiesbrouck, with whom he had jousted for the Ranger top spot since his full-time arrival two-plus seasons earlier.

"He's an outstanding goalie and he's been nothing but supportive," Richter said. "I have so much respect for him as a person and a player, he's been playing well, and I think he's a great, great goalie. I really do. If they want me around, I'm very happy to work myself up to the point where I feel I'm playing my best hockey, and then I'll be in great shape to start any game. I think I'm a good-enough goalie to win the job back."

As much as the situation troubled him, Richter said he had not asked to be traded.

"My work isn't done here. It's a tough situation, but I don't want to run away from it at all. I'm not going to do that," the goaltender said. "I just want to work through it. I feel good support from Neil Smith, and that provides a huge light at the end of the tunnel. As long as I know they have some support for me, I'll get through anything."

Richter had been loose and relaxed at the morning practice. He skated freely, made all kinds of acrobatic saves. He even seemed to have — dare we say it? — some fun.

"If that's the best way to get yourself to play well, you have to do it," he said. "You've got to be your own support, you know? It's always the way it is and it's always the way it's going to be.

Sometimes, if it's an effort to enjoy yourself, well, that's the way it goes. You've got to find a way to have fun. There just comes a point where you say, 'The heck with the situation. The heck with everybody else,' and I don't mean anybody in this room, I mean anybody trying to detract from you reaching your goals.

"People talk about salaries or a zillion things, but players just like to play, and there's no way you're going to be happy when you're not playing," Richter said. "What gives me the most satisfaction in my life is performing, and when you're not, it's very hard. The thing that gives you the most satisfaction is now the thing that gives you the most pain."

The game that night would be a whopping pain to the entire organization. The Rangers got pulverized, 11-6, in a game which didn't seem all that different from the 8-4 loss in Washington or the 7-3 loss in Philadelphia or even the 5-1 loss to Tampa Bay. There was not enough effort, not enough focus, not enough cohesion.

It didn't look like the Rangers were a badly-coached team.

It looked like they didn't even HAVE a coach.

They were pathetic.

Either Neilson had lost the team or the team had lost Neilson, but the connection simply was not there. Messier had one of the worst games of his life (one shot, minus-five). Amonte was right there with him (three shots, minus-four). Graves also was in the mix at two shots, minus-three.

By now, enough had to have been enough. Neilson rarely displays much emotion in his remarks to the media — his "I'm not happy" remark before The Shakeup Game was a veritable tirade — but this was a night for yelling and screaming, for ripping the team and the lack of self-respect it showed.

He went as far as to say, "Yeah, it was embarrassing," but not much beyond that.

"It wasn't like they were outplaying us," he said, "their shots were going in, one way or another."

Kevin Lowe came a bit closer to the point.

"You can't afford to throw games away at this time of the year," he said. "If you're going to go down, you've got to go down battling."

There wasn't much evidence of a battle, though Joe Kocur fought Gord Donnelly and Mark Hardy went with Brad May. Otherwise, Vanbiesbrouck and Richter just spent the evening sweeping pucks out of their net, accompanied by the deafening noise from Memorial Auditorium's boat horn.

"Tonight's game," Messier summarized, "was pretty disappointing for everybody."

Wasn't anybody ANGRY about this? Wasn't anybody going to SAY something after 11 goals-against?

"Some time," Messier said, cryptically, "at the right time and the right place, I will."

■ ■ ■

Neilson did his talking the next day, New Year's Day. Welcome to 1993.

Practice was scheduled for 10:45 at The Aud, but for nine minutes past that time, the ice surface was empty and waiting. At last, Randy Gilhen, wearing the red jersey assigned his line with Phil Bourque and Paul Broten, squeezed through the narrow doorway at the end of the rink.

You didn't need to be a brain surgeon to know the team just had been aired out, yelled at. You could see in their faces as they emerged and stepped onto the ice. They took small strides, scooped wrist shots into the net and off the glass, but there was no chatter. You heard the scraping of their skates on the surface, you heard the plop of the pucks as they flipped into the air, then fell to the ice.

And you almost could hear the players thinking about whatever it was Neilson had said to them.

"Roger doesn't exactly yell, and I've never heard him swear," one veteran said, "but he said 'crap' a lot."

It was a long time, 11:05, before the coaches shouldered through the doorway. First Colin Campbell, now the center of his own controversy, thanks to Domi, then Dan Maloney.

Neilson was a long while behind them.

In fact, if you hadn't seen him at the hotel and you hadn't gotten to the rink before the meeting began, you might even start to wonder if Neilson was there.

Had he been fired?

Eventually, Neilson stepped onto the ice to coach his millionaires, answering the question.

He ran them through five-on-0 drills, which, to the goalies, must have seemed just like an actual game. He ran them through two-on-nones and two-on-ones and three-on-twos and three-on-nones and one-on-nones. He ran them through breakout plays from behind the net, with the players working three-on-two on the return rush.

Then, after an hour of that, the whistle concert began.

The players sprinted for 15 seconds, coasted for 15 seconds, Neilson's whistle bleating on cue from his stop watch. On and on it went, until the Auditorium's ice looked like a snowy beach.

After the final sprint, Neilson charged off the ice and stormed through the exitway. You wondered if he would even bother to take off his skates, or if he'd just keep going, right down the ramp, out into the cold and back to the hotel.

But he stayed for a moment, answered some questions.

"Our back-checking was atrocious, our defense and goaltending not much better," said Neilson, coach of a team that had lost four times in five starts. "Some players played hard the whole game, hit the whole game and worked to the end. Others didn't seem to be into it."

He seemed to mean Messier.

"I've played the last month and a half trying to get healthy," the Rangers' captain said. "I'm certainly not happy with the way I've played the last month and a half. I don't think I've played to my potential."

If there was one lesson taught by the ultra-ugly defeat, it was that as the Rangers changed their calendars to 1993, they also should reset their clocks.

"We've got to be ticked off at game time — not after the game," Turcotte said. "You have to think, before games to come, how we felt after the Buffalo game and (compare it to) how we feel after we win. We're approaching the halfway mark of the season. It's time to start turning things around."

Otherwise, disaster loomed. This already was well on its way to becoming the road trip from hell, what with the late loss in Washington and the debacle in Buffalo. The Penguins were next on the tour, that 11-3 loss in the Rangers' prior visit fairly fresh in their minds.

■■■

To an observer, at least, it seemed all-important that Neil Smith's face be the first the team saw when it got to Pittsburgh.

It is fine to be off in Sweden, watching the players who will be your future, but it is more important to be on-hand for your team's thoroughly awful present.

Smith's players were fishing for the puck more than they were knocking people off it. The goalies' best usually wasn't good enough. The power play was more or less a joke. The defense in front of the net was ragged, at best. Neilson's popularity in the dressing room was sliding. The Rangers were facing a crisis, possibly the most profound one of Smith's tenure.

The same could be true of Neilson, who did what he felt had to be done. Feeling Messier had abandoned the leadership role he had performed with such flair in 1991-92, Neilson travelled a different path.

"In Pittsburgh, we called a meeting with Mike Gartner, Kevin Lowe and Adam Graves," he would recall later. "I told them, 'Mess just isn't leading us, and you guys are going to have to do that job. And once we get the team going, I think Mark's competitive spirit will bring him back to take charge again.'"

It was a compliment to the respect accorded Lowe that he could be with the team barely three weeks and yet be included in so astonishing a conference on so sensitive a topic. It was an insult to Lowe's intelligence, however, to imagine he wouldn't tell his longtime friend and current roommate, Messier, about what had transpired.

They lost to Pittsburgh, 5-2. Joe Mullen used a Lowe screen to score 2:20 into the game, and during a power play fewer than two minutes later, Messier turned the puck over to the Penguins' Ron Francis. Francis relayed to Mario Lemieux, who had Messier, Zubov, and Turcotte as escorts for his shorthanded goal. Errey made it 3-0 just 23 seconds into the middle period — the Rangers weren't ready to play, AGAIN — and though Gartner got them close with goals 46 seconds apart, the Rangers would come no closer.

"You look around this locker room," Vanbiesbrouck said, "and you see all this talent here, and it's pretty frustrating to be losing like this and giving up so many goals."

Neil Smith had been frustrated about those same things for a long time. The days in Sweden gave him time to think about what he had to do, but the conclusion he reached there was one he could have reached on a spaceship in orbit.

Sunday night, as Smith's plane headed toward New York, the phone rang in Vanbiesbrouck's suburban home.

It was Neilson.

Vanbiesbrouck learned he would be starting the next night at the Garden against the Devils.

"We really need a big one from you, John," Vanbiesbrouck heard Neilson say on Neilson's last night as the Rangers' coach.

CHAPTER 14

GUILLOTINE

NEILSON WAS FIRED the morning of January 4 and replaced for the rest of the season by Binghamton coach Ron Smith, a longtime associate of Neilson's. Colin Campbell was given Smith's duties behind the Binghamton bench.

The day King was traded to Winnipeg, Neilson claimed to have been hit harder by the news. The day he went to Rye and fired Neilson, Neil Smith seemed to make a similar assertion.

"I was completely devastated, just devastatingly sad. I could hardly pick my head up to tell him," Smith recalled. "I hated myself for it. I didn't want it to happen.

"Then I went into the other room to ask Colin to go to Binghamton, and I went from there to talk to the players," the team president continued. "I said, 'Now you've made me go and do this. I want to be paid back.' I was really angry. 'Fuck' was probably used 30 times in a minute. I stared at all of them. A lot of them put their heads down.

"We made a couple of callups, we sat some people out, we threatened some people, we made some trades — albeit not big trades," Smith said. "But if these players aren't the right players for the New York Rangers, then I guess that's the next step — to make big trades and get in a different group of players. And that's why they'll have to perform now, because their jobs are on the line."

It was a graduation of sorts. Neil Smith had fired all kinds of people in his three-plus years steering the Ranger ship, had handled coaching changes at the minor-league level. But never had he fired someone to whom he felt he owed so much. Smith flashed back over years of acquaintance, friendship, thousands of phone calls, hundreds of decisions made together, millions of laughs. It was a wrenching moment, one that dwarfed both of them, then passed.

"It didn't last long," Smith said. "I knew, when I turned and walked into the other room, that I had to do it. The whole season was going to slip away if I didn't do something."

As a season progresses, the natural expectation is that a team's play will improve. As this season had continued, the Rangers' play had deteriorated. Sure, they were 19-17-4 after 40 games. Sure, there was plenty of time for them to get healthy again, get in shape again, get happy again and start working toward a common goal. While Pittsburgh had run away with the division lead, the Rangers were within range of second place, and a second-place finish would serve two purposes: It would give the Rangers the home-ice advantage in the first round of the playoffs, and it would give some other team the opportunity to upset the Penguins.

At that moment, though, none of those prospects seemed particularly bright and there was no guarantee the Rangers even would make the playoffs. Unable to find a team that could lose to them, the Rangers were dead in the water. The goaltenders were buckling from nightly strafings. Defensemen, trying to do too much, were sprawling and sliding all over the ice — which served only to screen the goalies or tip shots past them. The forwards could not score enough goals at one end to make up for their inattention at the other.

When they had the lead, the Rangers would squander it. When they fell behind, in most cases the Rangers did not catch up. Morale appeared poor. Cohesiveness seemed sporadic at best. And there was something ugly about that January 2 loss at Pittsburgh, when seven skaters in their lineup were 30 years old or more.

The team never had defined itself. If it couldn't check well enough to be a defensive team, couldn't score well enough to be an offensive team, didn't hit enough to be a grinding team, didn't scrap enough to be a brawling team, then what kind of team was it?

It was a team four points out of second and four points ahead of the fifth-place Islanders, who tend to beat them a lot. It was a team adrift. When they skated off the ice in Pittsburgh, the only reason they hadn't lost six straight was because of the seven-minute rally that got Kovalev his hat trick and the Rangers a victory against a Boston team still living the high from its triumph in Montreal the night before.

There were other issues:

— By never publicly telling Messier to shut the hell up, Neilson bailed out on a dispute he should have controlled forcefully if he hoped to hold onto the team. If the lion tamer gets clawed during a performance, he damn well better shoot the lion before any of the other beasts smell fear or taste blood in the cage.

— Though Kris King had no goals and just 23 shots in 30 games, Neilson continually played him over Bourque, for whom he obviously had no use. It is one thing if a player doesn't score but helps in other ways, another thing if he doesn't do much of anything but still gets a sweater every night while a capable player watches from the stands.

Neilson persisted with King despite the fact the Rangers had enough scrap for the left side but little speed and, outside of Graves, very little scoring there. Bourque may be limited, but he can skate and he can find the net once in a while. With all due respect to King's grit and the other important things he brought to the Rangers, the addition of Olczyk's scoring touch and the chance to get Bourque more work would compensate amply for King's departure.

— Neilson lost several power brokers in the clubhouse.

Certainly, Messier was anti-Neilson. Leetch was not overtly anti-Roger, but he is unequivocally pro-Ranger. Those were the team's two marquee guys. They were the cover of the Ranger yearbook. Where they went, several would follow.

But there were players Neilson lost on his own.

"Senior guys are influenced when they're in and out of the lineup, and they definitely influence other senior guys," Vanbiesbrouck said. "When you become a veteran, you want to help guys as much as you can; but, all of a sudden, you come to a point where you have to become a survivor yourself. You're in the lineup one night, out the next. You're treading water."

Richter declared his personal confidence problems worsened when Neilson met with players in Winnipeg but excluded him. Neilson ignored Bourque and had his doubts about Kovalev. Even Gartner, the distinguished elder, started making comments about the team's seeming lack of direction and morale. Kocur's splendid training camp had become a mere memory.

That didn't leave Neilson many important allies.

The team was "having problems" before his shoulder injury, Leetch said, analyzing the demise of the coach. "We weren't happy.

"We were winning, but we wouldn't play that well or we would just get by. We'd lose some games we should have won and I thought I could be playing better. Mess's line (with Graves and Amonte) and myself and Jeff Beukeboom were big minuses at the beginning of the year, and we were trying to battle our way out of that. It just seemed nothing ever got untracked, and instead of turning it around and having a turning point to start up, I think we just continued to decline all season long.

"Roger was going to stick with what he believed in, anyway, and to be honest, I don't know if that would have got us the Stanley Cup," Leetch said. "I think sometimes you have to be willing to change certain things, especially against a team like Pittsburgh, which had beaten us the year before and was having success again. If what you're doing is not working, you've got to come up with something new.

"I think Roger listened a lot; he listened to people's input and I'm sure he listened to his assistant coaches and what they thought," Leetch added, "but he believed strongly that if the guys just executed what he said, we'd be successful and we could win the Stanley Cup. And you can't fault him for that.

"If you were going to make a change, it probably would have been better to make it when we did, so if a new coach came in, he had time to change the way things were going to go," the defenseman said. "But if we had been winning, I know Neil was happy with Roger and wanted to keep him. I'm sure he'd still be here if we were winning."

The Rangers were winning, but only on occasion.

"The fact was that we weren't playing well, and that's why Roger got fired," Leetch said. "Mess had his differences with Roger during the previous season, when we were playing well. Management listened to that, but when we're winning, management does what it thinks best for the team, and they thought Roger was the best guy there. And Neil made clear he still thought that was the case, but we weren't playing well, and he thought that (firing Neilson) would change the way things were going.

"We had a lot of players," Leetch said. "Neil went out and

got a lot of different new players, but we had a lot that could do the same job and were interchangeable, and that caused a problem; but there was really nothing in the locker room that you could say led to as poor a performance as we played. It just started to slip away, and I don't know the reason for that."

Few people did. But most fingers were pointed at Messier, including Neilson's, now that it was too late to change anything.

"I don't think Mark liked the way I coached, and this year, I didn't always like the way he played. What effect that had on the team, who knows?" Neilson said.

Added Colin Campbell: "To be blunt, Mess won."

That seems naively simplistic and almost completely incorrect.

Messier had nothing to do with the soft goals the goalies were letting in. The prior season, the netminders had been brick walls in front of the Ranger net; this season, they just weren't stealing as many games.

Messier had nothing to do with Neilson's loss of confidence in Richter, or Richter's loss of confidence in himself.

Messier had nothing to do with whether Kovalev was allowed to mature naturally, to be himself, to show some personality, or whether he would be bounced back and forth on the Binghamton commuter line.

Messier had nothing to do with the disabling neck/shoulder injury Leetch suffered.

Messier had nothing to do with Jan Erixon, the team's best defensive forward, being injured time and again.

Messier had nothing to do with the extra players Neil Smith added to the team, players for whom Neilson was unable or unwilling to find jobs.

Messier had nothing to do with management's refusal to declare 20 top players, give them responsibilities and have them perform.

Messier had nothing to do with counterproductive lineup selection.

Messier had nothing to do with the team's abysmal underachievement under Neilson in each of the two playoffs before Messier arrived.

Messier had nothing to do with the programmed 70-second timeout that was implemented so stations could show one full 60-second commercial every few minutes. That break provided a free breather to the front-line players, who could play up to the commercial, rest during it, then stay on the ice. The fourth line became obsolete.

Messier had nothing to do with the rest of the league getting better, or Larry Bertuzzi's ruling. Months after Neilson had been fired, months after Bertuzzi had awarded him to Philadelphia, Lindros sat in the Flyers' dressing room and said, "I think Roger Neilson is cool. Something about him is really cool." It might have made a fascinating triangle, worthy of a TV movie: The young phenom, torn between supporting a coach he respects and a captain he idolizes.

But none of that happened, and you cannot properly blame Messier for it. Messier played great in 1991-92, he did not play as great in 1992-93. That has been known to happen.

Campbell's "Mess won" comment made great copy, but not even Campbell believed it fully and he would admit as much a few months later as he sat in his Binghamton office.

"The pressure in New York started from the first day of the (1992) playoffs until Roger was released," he said. "We knew we had to do well in the playoffs because we were favored, and we should have been. We had a great team. We were rolling at the time of the strike and we had two goaltenders at the top of their games. We had a checking line at the top of its game, a defenseman (Leetch) at the top of his game, an offensive line with an MVP (Messier) at the top of his game, a rookie (Tony Amonte) at the top of his game. It was a team that was clicking on all cylinders.

"Then, after the strike, things evened off a bit," Campbell added. "New Jersey got their problems out of the way. We were in a real horse race with New Jersey, and from there on, it seemed like it was a pressure-packed situation.

"When we lost (to Pittsburgh), everyone points to that one goal," Campbell added, referring to the Ron Francis 70-footer that got past Richter in Game 4. "Then they point at Roger and say, 'Roger got outcoached by Scotty Bowman. Roger can't win the big one, can't win the Cup.' So now, the legacy of that becomes, 'You have to win the Cup this year, Roger — or get out of the division, anyway — or you're gone.' When Richter would lose, it was, 'Geez. That big game against Pittsburgh last year, he didn't come through. He can't do it.'

"The GM did what he had to do in the summer. He had a team with a great record over the season and he would have made a major trade (for Lindros). He was trying to acquire the best prospect to come along in years, maybe ever," Campbell said. "When it didn't happen, I don't think it was a bad blow. It was kind of refreshing, because we had a great record and we liked the players we might have lost. When it wasn't done, we dropped the whole thing and never talked about it again.

"So Neil said, 'I'm going to do the next-best thing. I'm going to strengthen our team. I'll get Phil Bourque and we can weaken Pittsburgh a little bit. And I'll entice probably the most talented kid from Russia, Kovalev, to come over right now. We lost one guy, Rob Zamuner, but I'll keep another guy, Tie Domi. And I'll also convince Peter Andersson to come over to North America; we're not sure about him, but he's one of the best players in the Swedish Elite League.'

"Obviously, there were going to be some problems with numbers, but I think with the whole tenuous thing of the Roger watch, the numbers situation just complicated things.

"The first three months were like three years this year. We had a controversy every week, from too many players, to goaltenders . . . We had more controversies than ever," Campbell said. "It just seemed like we were teetering from the start. We won in Ottawa, 3-2 in overtime, and it was like, 'Just squeaking out a win in overtime? In Ottawa? Something's wrong with those guys.' I found myself nervous all the time.

"I think, more than anything, you have to be a confident coach. If you don't have confidence, don't expect your players to have confidence," Campbell said. "Roger'd had two first-place finishes and a second. He was up for Coach of the Year two out of three years. But obviously, the mandate there, with the talent, was success. It comes with the job — the whole package, winning where you are.

"In New York, it's the Cup," he added. "All year long, people didn't care how you were doing. It was, 'Are we going to win the Cup? How about the Cup? Are ya bringin' da Cup to Noo Yawk dis yeer?' That's it, with this job in this city. It's the same in a few cities.

"As a coach, you're allowed to take one step backwards. But when you take the second step backward, no matter what the reasons — injuries, tough breaks, slumps by key players — that comes with the territory and you have to expect that," Campbell said. "If you don't expect it and you don't agree with it, you shouldn't be coaching."

■■■

Neilson wasn't quite as philosophical the day the bullet bit him.

"Last year, Mark came in and gave us all hope for a Stanley Cup. He was really as good a leader as you can ever get on a hockey team," the deposed coach said. "This year, like, he just didn't lead us. And I think that was the difference as far as his contribution.

"Last year, he was right on top of everything — you know, all the little things a leader does — talking to the players, organizing meetings, being right up on everything. He was just excellent. But this year, those things just didn't seem to be getting done."

If Neilson's charge was that Messier didn't lead, the captain's reply was that Neilson didn't coach.

"I certainly don't want to coach the team. I never did want to coach the team when Roger was here, but I thought perhaps we should have been doing some things different than we did," the captain said. "When you play certain teams in your division seven or eight times in a year, you have to change sometimes. Teams eventually start taking things away that they know you're doing.

"And when they start taking things away, you have to adapt and you have to change in order to counteract what they're doing to you, and we weren't doing that," Messier said. "We were becoming predictable. Our record in the division (8-10-0) was becoming clear evidence of that. As good a hockey team as we have, we can't be as bullheaded as to think we can keep running through the wall. Pretty soon, you have to go around it, if that's what's there for you to take."

■■■

Naturally, speculation about Mike Keenan becoming coach began immediately. A Garden bigwig dismissed it out of hand.

■■■

The day he got fired, NHL headquarters announced the result of Gil Stein's strange little witch hunt on the Domi-Probert fight which had occurred more than a month earlier. Neilson was suspended for two days. So was Domi, who, like Neilson, no longer worked in New York.

Two days after losing his job and getting suspended, Neilson lost his beloved dog, Mike, who suffered so long from cancer and finally succumbed as Neilson was taking him home to Ontario.

Neilson has had happier weeks.

■■■

In their first game under Ron Smith, the Rangers still got outshot 40-26, but rallied from a two-goal deficit for a 3-3 tie. The next morning, Watkins, the great facilitator, put together an informal breakfast meeting between Neilson, Campbell, Campbell's wife, and reporters who cover the team.

Neilson had not slept much, which hardly was a surprise. He seemed distracted, disappointed, all the 'dis-' words you can imagine. Still, he mustered some gracious grousing about the headlines in the papers that morning and even provided one of his own: "Coach firings suck."

He also provided, to each guest in attendance, a Roger Neilson Coaches' Clinic T-shirt.

Following is part of the give-and-take between the former coaching staff, Mark Everson of the *New York Post*, Greg Logan of *Newsday*, Walter MacPeek of the *Newark Star-Ledger*, Rick Carpiniello of the Westchester-Rockland Gannett newspapers, Jennifer Frey of the *New York Times*, and your author, representing the *New York Daily News*:

EVERSON: He (Messier) said, 'If he didn't want me to be captain, he should have taken the 'C' away from me.' Should you have?

NEILSON: The thought never entered my mind. I was looking for a way to get the team going. We knew it was very important, that we had to get going that game against Pittsburgh.

MACPEEK: After the game, he (Messier) pretty much said, 'Yeah, I did all the things you suspect I did. I thought it was right.' It just seems to me he set himself up for pretty much a no-win situation unless they win the Cup.

NEILSON: I haven't any comment on that. We didn't have any face-to-face confrontations. We had some discussions. When we met the first day of training camp, he said, 'We may be miles apart in philosophy, but let's not worry about that. I'll play my balls off for you.'

EVERSON: Did he hold true?

NEILSON: Well, who can tell that?

BROWN: You can. You've watched a million hockey players over four decades of coaching. You know when a guy's trying. Did he try? Or did he take you out?

NEILSON: Well, the point was, it was always difficult to tell how injured Mess was.

BROWN: When a player feels less than 100 percent of him is better than anybody else's 100 percent, is he putting himself in front of the team or is he putting the team in front of himself?

NEILSON: No comment.

CARPINIELLO: Do you think any of this would have happened if the Messier stuff never happened?

NEILSON: I think we were fired because the team wasn't playing well enough.

MACPEEK: On breakup day (in 1992), did you think we were misreading him (Messier)? Or did you understand that he was making a big stand?

NEILSON: We knew what was going on.

EVERSON: Your first year as coach, you said something like, you didn't want a superstar on your team. Would you endorse that sentiment today?

NEILSON: Superstars can pose problems for coaches, but that's part of coaching. To be a successful coach, you have to be able to get along with the superstars — whether it be Darryl Sittler or Gil Perreault or Marcel Dionne or Colin Campbell . . .

CAMPBELL: He was always telling me to dump the puck in when I wanted to go end-to-end with it.

NEILSON: I don't think anybody was against Mess, and I don't think anybody was against the coach . . . Everybody wanted the team to play well. Everybody wanted to get going . . . I don't think Mark ever went against the coach. I don't think he ever once went against the coaching staff, whether he agreed with it or not . . . Mark is a player who is one of the more creative players. We never tried to hold him back. When a player like Messier or Leetch tries the things they do, sometimes it's a pretty play and they score and sometimes they try it and it really backfires. When you're not letting them try those plays, where you might not want Kris King or Joey Kocur to try those plays, ever, I don't think we ever said a way not to play . . . I don't think there was ever a problem on the team with him saying, 'Don't do what the coaches say.'

EVERSON: In hindsight, should you have changed captains in camp?

NEILSON: No. Absolutely not. Mark was our leader. No question about it. You don't get a guy very often who commands respect the way he does.

■■■

Before his first practice with the team, Ron Smith called the team leaders into his office and had the good sense to include Messier — unlike Neilson's attempted end-around in Pittsburgh.

"Four of us — myself and Kevin, Leetchie and Garts — met with him this morning, the rest of the team met with him afterward," Messier disclosed. "There's a lot that needs to be done. I think we need to start, basically, from scratch."

- CHAPTER 15 -

WHO'S IN GOAL?

SINCE HE HAD WORKED as assistant at Roger Neilson's postings in Toronto, Buffalo, and Vancouver, Ron Smith was perceived as a Neilson clone in terms of hockey philosophy. Smith was, nonetheless, 10 years younger chronologically than the 58-year-old Neilson, and years older in other aspects.

After practices, for example, Neilson used to hop out of his warmup suit, into a t-shirt and shorts, and lounge barefoot while meeting the media — occasionally casting an eye toward whichever MTV video might be showing silently on the huge screen in the video room. If a camera crew came to interview him at Rye, Neilson would put on a Rangers jacket and baseball cap to provide the facade of big-league formality, but there wasn't a whit of pomp to him. It always was striking how a man approaching 60 could be as spry, fit, and young-looking.

Smith stood on ceremony a bit more. After practice, you could pretty much count on him to be wearing blue nylon pants, a red turtleneck with the Rangers crest at the top. He wore a gold bracelet and wedding ring on one hand, a watch on the other, which is probably three times the jewelry Neilson has owned in his lifetime. The odd time, though, Smith would make his remarks wearing slacks and a sportshirt — as though he might have someplace to go, might actually have a life away from the rink.

Never, not ever, not once, did it appear that way with Neilson. The rink was Neilson's home. Once practice was over, once he was back in those shorts and whatever T-shirt — hockey teams with obscure names were a favorite — he was dressed for the day's remaining hours. There was no mistaking the fact that Neilson, a bachelor, had married hockey. He might take Mike for a walk on the beach outside the back door of his office. He might go to the bank or the post office, might head to Boston Chicken or Dunkin' Donuts. But that was it. Between watching games on the satellite dish, planning practices, running practices, working on the coaches' clinic he runs or checking in with the boss, days always ended up running way short of hours.

Asked how people would notice the difference between him and Neilson, Smith quipped, "I'm 6 feet tall, 200 pounds ... and my dog is a heckuva lot fatter."

Neilson would look down a lot when he spoke, or would look away. Smith was more direct in his expression; he'd make eye contact easily, regularly. When the camera crews came for him, Smith's on-air presence was more viewer-friendly. His answers were more elaborate and illuminating. Good sound bites. And while appearance has virtually nothing to do with coaching, communication skills are tremendously significant, and Smith's, no question, were better.

"I don't have a problem dealing with people one-on-one," he said. "One thing players will always know from me is exactly where they stand. I don't have any problem at all putting my arm around a guy's shoulders—or smacking the opposite end of him. I think that's really important for a player. Obviously, you want to be as positive as you can be most of the time, but when a player needs to hear something, one way or another, he's going to hear it."

Smith wanted to make sure the players knew what he expected of them.

"You're looking for effort, intensity, desperation — whatever you want to call it—consistently, from everybody," he said. "I don't think you can win in this league unless you have that."

There are days and nights you don't win in this league, no matter what you have, and Smith would learn it from the bunch he inherited. After opening his Rangers tenure with the 3-3 tie against New Jersey, Smith supervised his first Rangers victory, a 6-2 decision over Ottawa.

Then, after Richter struggled in Philadelphia, Smith made good on his promise that players would know where they stood.

Defense had become a huge issue with the team, as opponents typically amassed 40 shots or more. This day, the Flyers would manage only 22, a step in the right direction; but Richter

— puzzled, possibly, by so light a workload — would be gone after missing three of the first 10.

Before starting Richter against Ottawa, Smith said, "What we all want to see is him playing like he can." After pulling the Philadelphia-born Richter, in his hometown, Smith said, "Anybody who has ever seen a hockey game would know goaltending was the difference today."

Four days later, the difference in Ranger goaltending would become more pronounced. Richter, 3-7-1 with two no-decisions in his past 13 appearances, would agree to go to Binghamton for two weeks of "conditioning" and Corey Hirsch would be summoned for his NHL debut.

It was January 15. The trade deadline was two months away, but Neil Smith knew he would have to deal Richter or Vanbiesbrouck or face losing either in the expansion draft. Because of his first-year status, Hirsch was exempt from possible claim, but Smith had to see how Hirsch would fare against NHL competition so he could gauge whether Hirsch was up to a backup role if a tempting offer was made for either of the others.

Beyond that, the Rangers were well past the point of being able to wait for a slump to end. They needed results, needed them fast.

"We're clearly looking for a goaltender to emerge and carry us through the playoffs," Ron Smith said. He did not deny Richter could end up being that goaltender.

"Guys with mental strength bounce back," Smith said. "It's how you cope. It's a test, and if he (Richter) passes, he'll be a better player for it."

Richter seemed to do that. He played five games, compiled a 4-0-1 record with a 1.18 goals-against average and a .964 save percentage. And, while at Binghamton, Richter also suggested his play had had little to do with Neilson's loss of confidence in him. In an interview with Jennifer Frey of the *New York Times*, Richter asserted that Neilson questioned his commitment and professionalism because of Richter's decision to live in Manhattan.

"A very big deal was made out of it. I never understood that," he told Frey. "And the thing is, one of the biggest reasons I did it was because I thought it would help me out. I was in this six-bedroom house in Westchester, alone, pulling my hair out (from boredom before moving to the city).

"I'm already the kind of guy who brings my work home with me from the office and I've let it affect me too much," the goaltender said. "If I'm downtown, I can go to a movie or a show, or something like that—just to get out of the house, to have some kind of distraction. But I don't think Roger ever bought the argument.

"Really, it's my fault," Richter said, accepting accountability for the disintegration of his game. "When you're faced with a tough situation, it's up to you to get through that situation. Still, my reaction was to keep working hard, and at the same time, they were questioning whether I was working. That's hard to accept."

Neil Smith said he never ordered Richter not to live in New York.

"We just didn't want to see a landslide of players moving to the city if the practice facility is in Rye," Neil Smith said. "We don't want to segment the team."

How weak an argument is that? Doesn't it segment the team just as much when you start pressuring people to live in a 'tight little Ranger community' up in the suburbs, where you have to get in your car every time you want a sandwich or a newspaper? If you don't trust your players to be of high enough moral character to handle the temptations of a big city, trade them. A tight team is going to be tight no matter where the players live.

It should be noted, also, that Neil Smith lived in Rye when he first took the job. He moved to Manhattan because his wife was miserable and bored in the bucolic Westchester haven of Rye. Sound familiar?

There is a larger issue, too. The players might not live in Manhattan or the other boroughs, but a huge segment of the fan base does. The name of the team isn't Rye Rangers. The name of the team is New York Rangers. The team virtually never practices in the city, and only three of the 25-odd players live in the city. With the team floundering in the public eye — in front of four daily New York newspapers, five New York TV stations and one 24-hour sports radio station — it sends a peculiar message to the sports consumer public in New York if you try to influence players to stay away from their city.

Anyway, someone must have sat on Richter's head after the interview was published, because he would not address it further when approached. And anyway, Richter had other things on his mind.

On January 11, Vanbiesbrouck played a 3-3 Garden tie against Vancouver which was memorable for three things: Mike Gartner's tying goal with 11.5 seconds left in regulation time,

Vanbiesbrouck's overtime stop on a Pavel Bure breakaway, and the puck someone threw out of the stands — and into the Vancouver net — while Messier was taking an actual shot with 22.3 seconds left in extra play. Replays solved the mystery of two pucks being on the ice, and Messier's 'goal' was disallowed; but the Rangers had snatched a point from the contest against a league powerhouse, and that had to be a positive sign.

They followed that with a 5-4 victory over Washington that left them wondering if the glass was half-empty or half-full. The Rangers rallied from a two-goal deficit, scored four straight and won for the first time in seven Patrick Division contests. But after holding their prior three opponents under 30 shots each night, they let the Capitals ring up 51.

"That's wide-open, full-throttle hockey," a weary Vanbiesbrouck said later. "The fans get their money's worth, but it's life-threatening to the goalies."

When the team had its usual out-of-division letdown and dropped a 3-0 decision in Montreal for its sixth straight road loss, it was time to see what Hirsch could do.

He is 20 years old. His hair is a flaming red-orange. His complexion is the definition of fair, his physique (5-10, 160 pounds) the definition of scrawny. Out of uniform, Corey Hirsch looks like anything but what he is, a promising goalie with NHL potential. But for a boy playing goal against men, Hirsch made the difficult look easy in his debut January 19 at Detroit.

A special sendoff from Messier helped break the tension.

Seconds before he would skate to the center circle for the first faceoff, the captain came to the goal crease and tapped Hirsch's padded chest with his glove.

"He said, 'It's time to start your career,'" Hirsch recalled, "and it felt unbelievable for him to come over and say something like that to me."

Then Hirsch started his career. With a precision display of poise, discipline and maturity, the youngster got the Rangers a 2-2 tie with the Red Wings at Joe Louis Arena — where his team had been 1-7-2 its prior 10 visits.

Hirsch stood up confidently. He was well out of his crease, reducing the shooting angles. He used small shuffling steps to move laterally, the motion reminiscent of Flyers great Bernie Parent. After what seemed to be some initial nervousness, Hirsch also did a nice job directing shots into the corners of the rink, and he was smart about the tempo of the game, regularly smothering pucks to prevent scrambles and cause faceoffs that got him and his team a breather.

Regularly there were occasions when Hirsch would freeze the puck, the Rangers would lose the draw, then Hirsch would glove a point shot and hold onto it for another faceoff. So the Red Wings' shot total inflated somewhat, but not as the result of multiple-shot flurries.

Sheldon Kennedy's goal, a wrist shot from between the circles that clanked in off the post, snapped a 1-1 tie at 4:15 of the third period. But the Rangers came back on a shorthanded goal from Darren Turcotte. Jan Erixon chopped the puck off Steve Yzerman's stick at the boards to Hirsch's right, sending Turcotte in against goalie Tim Cheveldae. Turcotte stayed on his forehand, swerved to his left and buried a 10-footer for his third shorthanded goal of the season.

Though the Rangers trailed twice, Hirsch remained eminently composed and came up with a number of critical stops on fine Red Wings scoring chances. In the third period alone, he thwarted a solo rush by Shawn Burr, used fine positioning to make a chest save on a Sergei Fedorov dart from the left-wing circle, and dragged his back leg to get his right foot on a 20-foot shot which Kennedy had slid back against the grain while moving to the goalie's left.

Hirsch made 30 saves, and two of the toughest came after horrific giveaways by his defensemen.

Just 3:39 into the match, Jeff Beukeboom overskated the puck in the circle to Hirsch's right, leaving the puck free for Ray Sheppard to collect for a cut-in. Sheppard was within 10 feet when Hirsch dropped, half on his back, half on his right side, and slammed his blocking glove and stick on the ice to smother Sheppard's attempted stuff shot.

"I think that actually helped me, more than anything," Hirsch said. "After that, I said, 'Hey. I can actually do something. I can play against these guys.'"

The stop was Hirsch's third career NHL save, the first having come 1:24 into the contest, when he used his pads to block Nicklas Lidstrom's 50-footer from the left point.

Hirsch would preserve the tie with 9:26 left in the second period, stopping Steve Yzerman's breakaway after a stunning gaffe by Sergei Zubov turned the puck over barely 20 feet from the net.

When it was over, the youngster said he had dedicated the game to his grandpa, Kasper, who had died over the prior weekend at 75.

"He was an inspiration tonight, because this was the realization of his dream," Corey said of Kasper Hirsch. "I just wish he could have been here."

Having performed nicely in Detroit, Hirsch got a start in the next game, in Los Angeles against the Kings. With Mike Gartner setting an NHL record by reaching the 30-goal plateau for the 14th consecutive season — Leetch, Hardy and Gilhen observed the occasion by giving Gartner a rose after the game — Hirsch beat a Los Angeles team that looked even shakier in goal than the Rangers had before Hirsch's arrival. The guy in the end-arena seat at the Great Western Forum, taking in all the action, looked an awful lot like Roger Neilson.

"I haven't had a chance to be bored yet," said Neilson, who was on his way to Hawaii.

Though Messier had sprained his wrist in Detroit and would miss the next six games, it appeared the Rangers might be getting on a roll. Richter had done his time in Binghamton and had made the most of it. Hirsch had shown the promise the Rangers had hoped he would display. Now, with the trade deadline approaching, it was time to get two goalies in the showcase and see if there were any takers.

"Yes," Ron Smith confirmed, "the other teams out there are wondering what's going on here with our goalies.

"John Vanbiesbrouck just sat and watched this whole experiment happen. He's been very supportive about it," Ron Smith said. "Now, it's back to Mike and him to show us who's our No. 1 starter.

"This is the way we must go," Ron Smith added. "Obviously, our two goalies are the guys who have been here. If we went the other way (with three), somebody isn't going to play.

"Certainly, it's encouraging for everybody what Corey did, what Richter did, and what Vanbiesbrouck was doing," Ron Smith said. "So we're in that 'trilemma' again. It's not a dilemma, it's a 'trilemma.' Is that a word?"

It was as soon as Smith created it.

"We've got to continue with our plan and see where it leads us," Neil Smith said. "Our first priority was to help Mike Richter get his game and his confidence back. So far, so good. He couldn't have played much better for Binghamton and we hope he'll continue that now in the NHL. In the meantime, Corey Hirsch showed us that not only is he an excellent prospect, but that he can do a good job in the NHL right now."

Richter started the next two games and split the decisions. On January 27, in the Garden return of Domi and King, Richter survived a Domi breakaway in the final seconds of the first period and collected a 5-2 victory over Winnipeg. And Neil Smith survived a Domi broadside.

"People don't like to tell the truth around here," Domi said before the game, feeling his oats, since the Jets had gone 11-1-2 — including the 9-0-1 streak they brought to the Garden — since the trade brought him and King to Winnipeg. "People beat around the bush, make excuses and point fingers at the players.

"I got blamed for getting Colin Campbell fired and Mess (Mark Messier) got blamed for getting Roger Neilson fired. The people who actually did the firing, meanwhile, are hiding in the weeds when they should be stepping forward and saying, 'I fired him and that's it.'

"It all started in the summer with the Lindros thing. One minute, he makes a list of untouchable players and the next minute, two of them are going to Quebec in the Lindros deal," said Domi, perhaps ignorant of Page's request for him during the negotiations. "From that point on, everybody began thinking that they were going to be in the next deal. Right from that point, everything was all lopsided and the good feeling from the year before wasn't there anymore. It got worse when he signed too many players and more of our team chemistry went out the window. He put Roger in a difficult position, and look what happened."

■■■

There were two players who did not survive the events of January 27. Jay Wells suffered a badly sprained right knee while defending a rush at the Rangers' blue line. Adam Graves got a bit overeager trying to help out and crosschecked Winnipeg's Evgeny Davydov, who fell hard into the outside of Wells' right knee. The initial forecast was that he would miss six weeks.

Later, James Patrick locked knees with Jets defenseman Phil Housley and suffered a lesser sprain; he'd miss only three.

But with Leetch and Messier out, the Rangers already were without 209 points from the season before (Messier had 107, Leetch 102). They also were without two players who had been named to the Prince of Wales Conference team for the all-star game at Montreal. Kevin Lowe went in Leetch's stead, while Gartner — who was going, anyway, for the lap sprint at the skills competition — replaced Messier.

All Gartner did at the skills competition was win, with a lap timed in 13.510 seconds — way slower than his qualifying time All he did in the all-star game the next day was score four goals and add an assist.

"Mess gets a big handshake and 'Thank you very much,'" said Gartner, who got a chance to show off for wife Colleen and his two children, 8-year-old Josh and 6-year-old Natalie. "I'll buy him dinner."

Leetch is the top defenseman on the left side, Patrick the best skater on the right, and Wells the most consistent hitter. Now the defense was missing half its key components, plus Hurlbut, who had sprained his left knee when he collided with Turcotte during practice two days earlier. The losses put tremendous pressure on Zubov, Beukeboom, and Lowe, who tried gallantly but were overmatched by the challenge of filling such big skates.

Joe Cirella, who had not dressed for 13 games and who went unclaimed when placed on irrevocable waivers the week before, was pressed back into action on the right side. Mark Hardy, an outcast in six of the Rangers' nine games under Ron Smith, went back to the left.

There was something inherently good about that. Cirella had an exemplary attitude during his long stint as a spare wheel, never groused — even when left home from the Detroit-Los Angeles road trip. Hardy bit back his bile, and was returned to action as a result.

"I know it's their job and they're paid well and all that," Ron Smith said, "but still, they've been very upbeat and good in practice."

It didn't help. The Rangers went to Buffalo and threw away two more points; scoring three times in the first 5:15 then watching the Sabres pump five past Richter for a 6-4 victory. It was

January 29; Richter had not recorded consecutive complete-game victories since a Washington/Ottawa perfecta October 21-24.

"They had us dead, and they didn't put us away," Sabres coach John Muckler said. "If New York played three periods like they did the first, I'd be betting on them to win the Stanley Cup."

The next night, Vanbiesbrouck got his first start in exactly two weeks and dropped a 3-1 decision in Toronto. The outcome was historic for the Maple Leafs but routine by now for the Rangers.

It was a memorable night in Toronto, because beer was available at concession stands for the first time since the old cathedral opened in 1931. It was standard for the Rangers as it left them with a 1-8-1 record in their past 10 on the road heading into the usual guaranteed non-win at Nassau Coliseum February 1.

"It's only a half-hour bus ride and we've got to get fired-up," Paul Broten said. "I don't mind the Coliseum at all. There's no better place for us to get things started."

They did not win, of course. They had three leads and lost them all in the 4-4 tie that kept them in third place, two more than the Devils and Islanders.

"A feeling of half-fulfillment," Vanbiesbrouck said. "We're still two points ahead, and that's what the main point is: to stay two points ahead of them — or whoever. (But) We're going to look at the standings, and all that work is going to be just to push a game off the schedule."

Another day, another non-victory. The outcome left them 0-2-1 in three games, all on the road. But the overall slide would reach 0-4-2 — with two of the defeats and both the ties in divisional games — before the injury-depleted bunch would muster a 4-3 victory over the Islanders February 12.

"It's like the Keystone Kops. So many things have happened," Neil Smith said. "We ought to put together a lowlight tape instead of a highlight tape."

There was one point in a game against Philadelphia during that stretch when the five skaters on the power play were Zubov and Peter Andersson, who had been recalled, with Steven King, Alexei Kovalev and Ed Olczyk up front. Not one of them had played for the team on opening night, so many thousand years ago in Washington.

There were two months left, lots and lots of time, but it was time to start looking at the tiebreaking criteria that could determine which Patrick Division teams go to the playoffs and which go home.

The first criterion was victories, and the Rangers' 23 were the fewest of the top four teams.

Next was points earned in the season series. The Rangers trailed Washington, and were even with the Devils and Islanders.

Goal differential for the season was the last tie-breaker. The Rangers had scored seven goals more than they had permitted, which put them behind Washington and the Islanders but left them ahead of New Jersey.

The goal differential was down to plus-four after the Penguins came to the Garden and left with an efficient 3-0 victory. Pittsburgh goalie Tom Barrasso was as sharp as he needed to be to leave the Rangers 1-7-3 in their past 11 games in the division. Worse, they had four victories in their prior 18 games overall (4-9-5), and three of those victories came against Ottawa, Los Angeles and Winnipeg.

They split a home-and-home series with the Islanders — guess where the loss was — but then kicked off a three-game winning streak (their last of the season) with a 4-1 conquest of St. Louis February 15.

The highlight of the game with the Blues was Vanbiesbrouck's Save of the Season. St. Louis center Craig Janney cut in from the right side and started moving across the crease, from Vanbiesbrouck's left to his right, with several of the jelly-jiggly moves that have made Janney famous.

Vanbiesbrouck stayed with him, stayed with him, then went down, ultimately falling on his back. Lying on the ice, he reached his left glove up over his head, so that it was just as much on the ice as the rest of him was as Janney shot.

The puck came to rest on the back of the wrist padding on Vanbiesbrouck's catching glove, forming a frozen sandwich: The ice on the bottom, the puck in the middle, Vanbiesbrouck's glove on top. This all went on behind Vanbiesbrouck's head, which was turned almost completely toward the net as he sprawled. If he had lifted his hand even a fraction of an inch, Janney's shot would have slid under it.

"It was just a desperate action, or reaction," Vanbiesbrouck said.

Desperate times called for desperate measures, and times were growing desperate indeed. They would embark on a five-game road trip needing as many of the 10 available points as possible, and would come back with seven despite another barrage of injuries to defensemen.

After two victories over San Jose, one at the Cow Palace and one in a neutral-site game at ARCO Arena in Sacramento, the Rangers would reach Vancouver for a showdown with the Canucks. The morning of that game, Mark Hardy asked for, and was granted, a meeting with Neil Smith. At that meeting, in Vancouver's Pacific Coliseum, Hardy asked to be traded.

That day, Per Djoos was flown out to Vancouver from Binghamton and dressed, ahead of the healthy Hardy, for the game against the Canucks. Barry Watkins left messages at the hotel, advising the media of the transaction — or at least attempting to. One reporter checked in with the operator and was told, "Yes, a Mr. Pierre DuJones called you from Birmingham."

They would blow a lead late in Vancouver. It was Kovalev's 20th birthday, but he would gift-wrap a giveaway with 3:28 to play and Petr Nedved gave the Canucks a 5-4 triumph. The next day, in Calgary, Djoos was told he was being sent all the way back to Binghamton.

Whereupon he got royally pissed.

"I don't think I messed up that bad on those five shifts. Did I?" he asked, sarcastically. "To bring me out here, play me five shifts and send me back makes absolutely no sense. Is Mark Hardy that bad that he can't play those five shifts?"

They would find out that night, when Hardy dressed and played. But while Djoos was winging back to Binghamton, the Rangers learned they should have kept him. Jeff Beukeboom blocked a shot with his hand, and Sergei Zubov blocked Joel Otto's stick with his neck.

Having lost two more defensemen, the Rangers also would lose a point on a goal off a faceoff in the last five seconds. In the dying seconds of a game on the road, when you're squeezing tightly to a one-goal lead, there are two things you want to do if there's a faceoff in your end: You want to make sure you don't lose that draw and you want to make sure the other team's center doesn't win it. You lift his stick, you fall on the puck, you take a second off the clock, you do anything you have to do, but you don't let that puck get back to the other team's point.

That isn't how it worked out. Adam Graves lost the draw to Theoren Fleury, and you knew that puck was going in even before it got to Al MacInnes at the point. Somebody blocked MacInnes' shot, but Robert Reichel got free for a 10-footer on which Vanbiesbrouck made a fine right-skate save. The rebound went to Gary Suter, who canned a 10-footer and the Rangers had to settle for a 4-4 tie.

They would win 1-0 in Edmonton the next night, however, on an Amonte goal, off a sublime Messier pass from behind the net, and exceptional goaltending by Richter.

This was, however, a season in which few victories came for free. In the closing 10 seconds — again — Oilers' defenseman Igor Kravchuk would catch Messier blindside with a clean and devastating check near the Rangers' blue line. The hit, from the side and to the rear, popped the bones out of the cartilage on the right front of Messier's rib cage and caused what Messier termed the most painful injury he had ever suffered.

That figured. Barely a week earlier, Ron Smith had noticed the captain's improved play.

"He's showed real bursts of that freight-train look he has when he gets going," the coach had said.

In a matter of days, the freight train got derailed.

The team picture, for 1992-93, should have been an X-ray.

CHAPTER 16

MARCH MADNESS

POSTCARDS FROM A MONTH of immeasurably odd Ranger events:

Goodbye handshakes are the worst handshakes. You never want to be the guy getting told, "Hope everything works out. Maybe someone will pick you up," because that means some team has cut you loose. And that, by extension, generally means you weren't quite good enough.

When March began, Mike Hurlbut was the first to get those handshakes and to hear those hopeful expressions of encouragement at Rye. Hurlbut had to pack his gear and spend those awful hours of limbo, waiting to see if some NHL team might want a left defenseman for the stretch, might think Hurlbut worth claiming for the $60,000 waiver price.

No one did. So Hurlbut remained Ranger property and played against Utica in Binghamton as though nothing ever happened.

Cirella got put on waivers in January; nobody claimed him, and Cirella became an important contributor during the spate of Ranger injuries. But Cirella, in his waiver experience, was a victim of numbers — his age, 29, and his salary, $463,000 plus bonuses. Hurlbut, younger at 26 and cheaper at $125,000, ended up leaving because of an injury — the sprained left knee he suffered in a January collision with Turcotte.

"Being here was a great opportunity, but the injury couldn't have happened at a worse time, as it turns out," said Hurlbut, a supplementary draft pick in 1988. "I got a chance to establish myself here, more so than I had. Not that 23 games by any means establishes me as an NHL defenseman, but I played pretty well, and I was just looking forward to getting back in the lineup on a consistent basis. I think that would have happened had I not been hurt."

Hurlbut was injured in a January 25 practice and had not played for the Rangers since. On the just-concluded 3-1-1 road trip, the Rangers went through nine defensemen, and it is difficult to imagine Hurlbut would not have been one of those used had he been healthy. Being in the right place at the right time can change your life; being on the wrong end of what Turcotte called "my first hit of the season" unmistakably changed Hurlbut's life.

"I was kind of surprised (about being placed on waivers)," Hurlbut said. "I expected to get an opportunity to get back in the lineup, but the team is playing pretty well right now and it's pretty tight in the division, so I can see where they don't want to experiment with the lineup," Hurlbut said. "It's probably in my best interest, if I wasn't going to be in the lineup, to get put through waivers. If somebody picks me up, great. If not, I'm back in Binghamton. It's their decision, it's totally up to them, but I can see how it could work out for the best."

It didn't shorten the long drive north to Binghamton, to a smaller paycheck, to a lower caliber of hockey.

Turcotte, meanwhile, had his own problems.

Modern skates generally are built for speed more than protection, which is why Turcotte had a heavy-duty rubberized plastic outer shell molded to the instep of his skates. Turcotte wanted some extra protection, because he kills a lot of penalties and penalty killers take a lot of shots off the feet.

Turcotte took a Garry Galley shot off the left foot in the game against Philadelphia February 3, then absorbed a Larry Murphy blast in the Pittsburgh game a week later.

Didn't the padding work?

"I had changed skates two games earlier," Turcotte replied, "and the shell hadn't been added to the new ones yet."

Turcotte was just testing the new skates to see if he liked them, so he held off on the extra protection.

He shouldn't have waited.

But that's pretty much the way things had gone for him. Just about every Ranger trade rumor involved his name. His collision with Hurlbut ruined the defenseman's season. On top of that, Turcotte waited all year for a salary arbitration hearing, which was supposed to have been conducted and completed before the season began.

Turcotte managed to score 30 goals centering a checking line with Broten and King in 1991-92. He had killed penalties, had worked the point on the power play and had been plus-11. But the arbitration thing hung over him. The Rangers were offering $400,000, and Turcotte, who was at $250,000, was looking for $700,000-plus.

"It's a tough situation for both Neil and myself," Turcotte said. "Salaries are at the in-between stage. Half the guys have re-signed, half haven't, and you can see a $300,000-$400,000 swing. We're making our points on the basis of guys who have re-signed, he's making his on guys who haven't. That's where a lot of the problems are right now, and we figure the best way to go is through arbitration."

Now, here he was, waiting for a hearing, waiting to see if he'd be traded, waiting for his foot to heal, and watching as Ron Smith had come up with three nicely balanced lines — Olczyk with Messier and Amonte, Bourque with Nemchinov and Gartner, Graves with Weight and Kovalev.

So, with the trading deadline scheduled for March 20, the questions Turcotte faced were: Would he be back at all? And where in the lineup could he fit? Hockey had become a three-line game; fourth line is no place for a two-time 30-goal scorer.

"Turc plays 16-18 minutes, no matter where he plays (positionally), because he works the power play, kills penalties, plays a checking role, goes out in offensive situations," Ron Smith said. "The only question is whether you give him a regular line or make him a super utilityman. I was going to sit down and talk about the whole issue with Darren the day he got hurt. I wanted to work it out with him and come to an agreement as to what's best and how he'd be most effective to the team — and for his own career."

Turcotte wasn't the only player awaiting a return, Leetch couldn't keep his eyes off the calendar. March having come in like a lion with a 2-2 tie against Buffalo and a 3-1 victory over Pittsburgh, Leetch was getting spring fever.

"I'm more positive every day, still planning on playing the 13th (in Washington)," Leetch said. "My shoulder's not any stronger than it was before the team went on the (February) trip, but I think just from using weights for the muscles surrounding the shoulder, my rotator cuff's a lot stronger now, so it's easier to do some things."

So you're closer to playing Brian Leetch hockey than any time since the injury?

"Getting there," Leetch said. "Even when I come back, it's not going to be how I would like it to be. It may not come back all the way until the summer.

"I'm going to be able to do the things I'd like to — just maybe not as well," he added. "I won't be able to pass the puck quite as quickly as I'd like in certain situations. I may not shoot as hard, but I never beat guys on strength; it's accuracy and putting it through the traffic, which I can do."

■■■

For a variety of reasons, there was a low turnout at the optional morning skate in Quebec March 6. One was, the team had played the night before, winning an emotional 3-1 game from the Penguins. Another was, the charter aircraft that was to take them from Newark to Quebec was delayed by weather in Toronto. So instead of getting to the airport, getting off the bus and getting onto the plane, the team got off the bus and went in search of methods to kill the hour's wait for transportation.

Most of the players went to the combination Pizza Hut/ Mrs. Fields franchise store, only to learn there was no pizza. It was after 11:30 p.m., and no hot food was available. Mrs. Fields had all but sold out, down to her crumbs. There were some muffins left on a bottom shelf, and the lady behind the counter told equipment manager Joe Murphy, "You have your choice of corn, corn, corn, corn or corn."

"I'll take corn, then," Murphy replied.

There were some salads and fruit cups available in a refrigerated section, along with the standard apple juice, soda or mineral water. The truly adventurous risked the ready-made tuna salad sandwiches. The players gathered at the tables, little groups sprinkled everywhere. And, as usual, they were recognized by clutches of onlookers. The blue canvas Ranger bags, carried by several of them, were one tipoff. Their appearance was another, as generally there aren't many athletically-built men in suits and ties walking through Newark Airport this late.

Some of the players simply went to the gate to await the plane's arrival. They were greeted there by a bunch of college-aged kids who seemingly had plenty of time to kill. Several requested autographs, several wanted their pictures taken with the athletes. Though tired from the game, though interested mostly in just getting to Quebec and getting to bed, the players signed all the papers thrust at them, answered all the questions. And anyway, they were pretty much trapped.

At long last, the plane arrived and the school kids gave a pleasantly energetic sendoff.

As usual, the first few rows of the plane's first-class section were stocked with fruit, cheese, crackers and soft drinks, to be grabbed on the way to seats in the back. After the disappointment at Pizza Hut, the snacks were a smash hit.

For a while, the landing threatened to be one, too. While the bulk of the flight was a smooth sail, swirling winds in Quebec made the landing a wrestling match between the pilot and the plane. There were occasional moments when it seemed the aircraft was going sideways—always fun. The wingtips wobbled almost until the landing wheels touched the runway, at which point somebody — Hardy, most probably — yelled, "Thanks, Garts," a religious man.

Clearing customs and immigration was interesting because it provided a peek at Sergei Zubov's passport. It was a fascinating document with a leathery cover, the color of baked blood, and red-pink pages stamped with visas and laminated permits of several varieties. One of the visas identified him as Serguei. Also in the passport was a photograph of such poor quality it would be difficult to identify the subject as Zubov with any certainty.

Nonetheless, it neither interested nor concerned the inspector, who instantly stamped Zubov's document and sent him off to the bus. By the time the bus reached the hotel, it was 3 a.m.. It was cold. It was snowing, and the wind blew the snow in wispy clouds.

So the only people who ended up at Le Colisee for the skate were Vanbiesbrouck, Joe Kocur, Paul Broten, Steven King and Mark Hardy. The assistant coaches, Al Hill and Dan Maloney, were there early — hoping to gain some intelligence information from the Nordiques' skate. But Quebec was more intelligent than that; the Nordiques' skate was optional as well, affording Hill and Maloney in-depth views only of the players who probably would NOT be playing against the Rangers that night.

There is nothing much good about not playing, but there was one positive for the guys who sat out the Quebec game.

At least no one could blame it on them.

For just when it appeared the team defense had turned a corner, just when the chance was there for a good Ranger weekend to become great, the Nordiques brought the ceiling of Le Colisee down on the visitors' heads. With second-place Washington sitting there, waiting to be tied in points, with a chance to jump five victories over .500 for the first time since December, the Nordiques — Neil Smith's un-favorite team — said, "Excuse us" and plundered their guests, 10-2.

The game brought home, yet again, the flip-flop turn the season had taken. With the fine players Quebec already had, plus the players they got from Philly for Lindros, the Nordiques had hoisted themselves into a tie for second in the NHL overall standings. This night, the Presidents' Trophy champions of the previous season were no match for them. Again, the trip to Quebec wasn't worth making.

It was trouble enough that this was another one of those "letdown" games, the team having given all it had in defeating division rival Pittsburgh the night before. But facing a relatively healthy Quebec team, and doing it without Brian Leetch, Mark Messier (who stayed home, as had been planned) plus Darren Turcotte and Jan Erixon, among others — was a tremendous amount to ask.

Ultimately, it was too much.

The Nordiques got two goals plus an assist from Joe Sakic. They got a goal plus an assist from Mats Sundin. They scored on faceoff execution. They scored on rebounds. They scored on Ranger mistakes — of which there were loads. They scored five times on seven shots during one absurd stretch that began with Sakic's 2-0 goal at 17:36 of the first period and ended when Alexei Gusarov made it 6-2 at 10:06 of the second.

Doug Weight scored twice, and the way the Rangers had defended lately, two goals might have been enough. After all, they had scored just six goals over the three games entering this one and had gone 2-0-1.

But this night, they would face the top offense in the conference; and after two periods the Rangers would need five goals in the remaining 20 minutes to even hope for a lead.

The Rangers had to figure on a wobbly first period. They have a lot of over-30 players and had been at an emotional peak to beat their bitter division rivals from Pittsburgh the night before. A little letdown and a little fatigue were factored in; the Rangers were going to depend on Mike Richter early and he knew it.

At 12:24, Claude Lapointe beat Graves on a draw to Richter's right and Mike Hough snapped in a 20-footer. Barely five minutes later, Sakic broke things open by stepping out of the penalty box, splitting the defense of Lowe and Beukeboom, and rifling a 15-footer in off the post.

Barely a minute later, Sakic got behind Steven King and slam-dunked a crossing pass Mats Sundin had sent from the left-wing sideboards. It was 3-0 and the Rangers could not afford to let the hole get any deeper, but Graves went off for tripping in the last minute of the first period and Sundin made it 4-0.

The deluge never stopped and Richter never got pulled. Smith left him in for all 10.

Not that long ago, Richter might have been flatter than a crushed critter on the highway. It would have been easy for an outsider to think, "He's out of here, for sure. They've got to trade him now or get him back to Binghamton . . . That was his last start."

It would have been easy for Richter to think those things, as well. And such thoughts wouldn't have been hugely far-fetched. Everything with Richter had become life-and-death.

Somewhere along the line, perhaps during the stay in Binghamton, that end-of-the-world outlook simply got up and left. Richter knew there was a game coming up against the Kings in a few days, knew John Vanbiesbrouck probably would be Ron Smith's choice to play it. He knew there would be another contest, in Chicago two days after that, and a goaltender would be required then, too.

But the life-and-death edge, the urgency, was gone. It wasn't a bombshell every time Smith picked a target, the way it was with Neilson. The improved play of both goalies — the Quebec game notwithstanding — may not have been a coincidence.

"I think he looks at it with a real objective, accurate eye," Richter said of the way Smith handled the division of goaltending duties.

"I've tried to be as direct as possible with them about whatever situation," Smith said. "It's near the end of the season, and the focus is on what I can do to get the team in the right state for the playoffs. They (the goalies) are like the other players;

whatever they can do to make it better — whether it's just playing better or staying upbeat and positive, which they've been, they've done."

Vanbiesbrouck, the older of the pair, maintained a more even disposition during the various crises. Richter rode a wildly swerving roller coaster, but the ride seemed to have ended. You could see it in his face, hear it in the words after the blowout.

"I personally felt the first seven were offside," said Richter, who had watched Vanbiesbrouck beat the Penguins.

"I was emotionally a little down after all my yelling last night (Friday)," he added. "The best thing you can say is, they (the Nordiques) ran out of time and couldn't score any more goals."

They were good lines, but Richter wasn't laughing off the loss. Nobody on the Rangers was any darn good. Everybody knew it.

"We're all competitors, we can't stand to lose, and it's hard to stomach being embarrassed," Richter said. "We were absolutely thrashed out there — much of it our own doing, which is worse. But I walked off the ice thinking I'm still a good goalie and we're still a great team — that we'll recover and do fine."

It was starting to look that way.

And there was something else: Brian Leetch was coming back.

■■■

Leetch had been gone so long that Ron Smith, who took over as coach January 4, wrote his name in the lineup for the first time before the March 9 game against the Kings.

Leetch had been gone 82 days. He had been gone so long that the game marked his first as a teammate of Ed Olczyk, who was obtained December 28.

Leetch, who was listed as day to day when this odd ordeal began, finally returned after 12 weeks. He decided the time had come to see what he could do. He put on his No. 2 jersey. He reclaimed the alternate captaincy. He returned to the left of Beukeboom, and he made one very relieved individual of Turcotte.

"Because Brian's coming back," Turcotte said before the game, "nobody will notice how bad I'm going to be."

Due to that fracture in his left foot, Turcotte had missed the Rangers' past 11 games. Compared to the 34 games that the stretched neck/shoulder nerve cost Leetch, that was a relative eyeblink. On the other hand, 34 games without Brian Leetch — even 34 minutes — was an agony the Rangers never wanted to endure again.

"If you look around the league and take the franchise player out of a team's lineup for three months, I think it would affect every team in the league," Messier said. "Guys like that, you just can't replace. His coming back, his popularity in the dressing room and his skill level just add a whole dimension to our hockey club — a guy like that who can play defense and add so much to the attack can really change the complexion of a game."

Leetch had changed the team's complexion by being gone so long. His absence had posed a formidable test of the Rangers' depth, and the team had survived relatively well.

"Guys did a really outstanding job. Efforts like that are how you get around injuries to players of Brian's caliber," Messier said. "Joey Cirella was sitting out, but then he got a chance to play and really, has played his best since I've been here. Mark Hardy, when he's been given his chance to play, has given his heart to it every time. And you've got a guy like Peter Andersson, who might never have had a chance; now, he's seasoned to some degree, and playing with a level of confidence, so that if something happens with an injury in the playoffs, he's right there.

"And now Sergei Zubov got a chance, and he's probably been our best defenseman over the time he's been playing," Messier said. "With him, Leetch, and James Patrick you've got a pretty good defense back there."

The defense hadn't been particularly good before he left, so it could only get better. But certainly, the puck would spend less time in the Rangers' defensive zone with Leetch skating it out every time. And the power play certainly would regain its pulse, as was shown when Leetch set up a power-play score by Gartner with 5:54 left for a 4-3 victory.

"I was just happy they decided to let me play," Leetch said. "I've been talking with coaches a little bit, saying, 'We've got to make a decision and just see how it feels on the ice.' It's different in practice and in the weight room than in a game.

"The shoulder was fine," he added. "I took some hits on it, but I just feel regular soreness from a regular game."

This was anything but a regular game.

The Islanders had won, which made the outcome at the Garden all the more important. If Leetch hadn't come back — along with Messier and Turcotte — if the RANGERS hadn't come back, they'd have fallen to fifth.

Which is not the place you want to be on March 10.

The Kings had leads of 2-0 after 3:31, and 3-2 after two periods. They had been 23-0-3 in games they led after 40 minutes. But Olczyk set up a slam dunk by Nemchinov at 10:02 of the third to tie it, and referee Ron Hoggarth misinterpreted an obvious dive by Alexei Kovalev over Jimmy Carson's stick to give the Rangers a power play and set the stage for the victory.

Leetch, at the left point, fed Patrick on the right. Patrick's diagonal pass to the left-wing circle was slowed by the Kings' Pat Conacher, but Gartner whipped a 15-footer past rookie goalie Rick Knickle and Leetch's comeback was a complete success.

"He looked better than I expected," Smith said. "I thought I'd see some real rough spots and I didn't see any."

Vanbiesbrouck, who had struggled early, made 17 third-period saves to keep the Rangers' heads above water in the turbulent playoff seas.

Vanbiesbrouck had taken a needless penalty just 24 seconds into the game. He had given up a power-play goal, then had whiffed on a 45-footer by Conacher — all in the first few minutes.

"So in the third period," he said, "I felt I had to do my part."

In the game's first minute, Vanbiesbrouck tried to skim the puck off the glass and down the ice, but it went over the boards, leaving Hoggarth no choice but to cite Vanbiesbrouck for delay of game. The Kings' Luc Robitaille got position on Patrick and somehow redirected the pass Wayne Gretzky sent in front from the corner to Vanbiesbrouck's left.

So the Rangers were down 1-0 after 1:26, before the Garden crowd could welcome Leetch back to the season. The fans weren't the only ones happy to see Leetch return. "Believe me," Vanbiesbrouck said, "the welcome mat was long."

But the Rangers were down 2-0 when Conacher, killing a hooking penalty to Tim Watters, scored the first shorthanded goal against the Rangers in 21 games.

Watters was in the box because he hooked Tony Amonte. Amonte had steamed in on a breakaway with a pass from Messier. Messier had gotten the puck thanks to a lovely breakout pass from Leetch. That was one of the many lovely additions Leetch's return provided, on his first shift since December 17. The sequence was: Leetch to Messier to Amonte, opposition penalty, chance to tie the score.

Except Conacher messed up the equation. From the left-wing circle, he took a 45-foot shot through Patrick's legs and the puck went in.

"I lost it for a second," Vanbiesbrouck said, "but those are ones you've got to have."

Other than a Rob Blake shot that squeezed through his pads for a 3-2 Los Angeles lead at 8:43 of the second, Vanbiesbrouck tightened the screws from then on and the Rangers had what they needed: A one-goal victory on the ice and an immeasurable triumph in the dressing room.

Now, they were on a surge of 3-1-2. They were four victories above .500, had a chance to go five up for the first time since Kovalev's hat trick beat Boston for a 19-14-4 record December 27.

Five victories over .500 isn't great, of course, but it's the quickest way of getting to six victories up, and so forth. The team headed to Chicago thinking good things.

■■■

The visitors' dressing room at Chicago Stadium is down-stairs, way downstairs, and it is everything the rest of the place is not.

For so very old a venue, the Stadium is very nicely lit and impeccably well-scrubbed. Way downstairs, the corridor outside the dressing room is dark as a cave. Inside, the visitors' dressing room might have been considered spacious in 1929, when the place opened, but it is about as cramped as any on the tour.

Turcotte reached into his locker stall, grabbed his slate gray suit slacks and shook them vigorously.

"In this place, you've got to check for roaches," he said, nodding at his surroundings. "There's going to be a lot of homeless roaches next year when the Blackhawks move."

Actually, the bugs are safe for a while. Although the framework for the utterly massive United Center is in place across West Madison Avenue, the Blackhawks will spend the 1993-94 NHL season at Chicago Stadium.

Where Turcotte would be calling home was a lot less certain as he verified that his clothing was free of wildlife. The center stared up at the locker room lights and did some quick math in his head after the pre-game workout.

"How many hours to go until the trading deadline? Nine days times 24 hours, that's 216 hours," he said. "What time is it now?"

It was a quarter past one, New York time, which added an hour and 45 minutes to the total, since the deadline was set for 3 p.m., Eastern time, March 20. The center's salary arbitration hearing also was coming up that day, but that was small potatoes compared to the matter of his Ranger survival.

"Here's what I heard," Turcotte said. "I heard me, James Patrick, Joe Kocur, and Mike Richter to Los Angeles for Marty McSorley and Tony Granato."

Granato had been convinced for months he would be returning to the left side of some Rangers line, and there was no mistaking the all-business looks on the faces of Rangers boss Neil Smith, Kings GM Nick Beverley, and Los Angeles owner Bruce McNall a few evenings earlier when the Kings had come to the Garden. It looked like they were talking seriously, but with fewer than 216 hours to the trading deadline, you knew EVERYBODY was talking seriously.

Turcotte had been traded several dozen times, in publications everywhere, over the prior few weeks. Early in the season, Turcotte's agent claimed Neil Smith vowed to trade Turcotte if the arbitrator rules in the player's favor. Coincidentally, a ruling would come well before the deadline.

Sometimes smoke is a sign of fire, sometimes smoke is hot air. Turcotte would know soon. In the interim, the center was on edge.

"Arbitration can wait," Turcotte declared. "Who cares what I'm making, as long as I'm making it in one place."

He wanted the place to be New York.

"Some guys don't want to be here," Turcotte said, refusing to name names, "but some guys don't want to leave. I don't want to leave."

It wasn't his call, wasn't anything he could control. It's a lot easier to shake a bug off your suit than to shake off a trade rumor this close to The Big Day.

There are lots of times when players have superb hearing, lots of times when they get a piece of the deal right — the destination, perhaps, or some of the players involved, but not all of them.

Sometimes, they mess it up all together, which means they have worked themselves into nut cases for nothing.

Neil Smith would have addressed several needs by obtaining McSorley and Granato. While McSorley would be another over-30 former Oiler coming to "Edmonton East" at the Garden, and slow as a slug, he is an exceptional competitor.

Granato, meanwhile, would be the sparkplug the Rangers had not had since the departures of Kris King and Tie Domi. King and Domi were limited players, absolutely, but they could wake up a dozing building, a sleeping bench, by throwing a big hit or creating some type of chaos. The role had gone unfilled since they left and the Rangers had been much the worse for it.

The supposition was, McSorley's toughness would make up for the departure of Kocur, Granato's speed would make up for the loss of Turcotte's. Patrick — about the only Ranger "traded" more times than Turcotte or Richter — presumably would be replaced by a Peter Andersson-level player, although Andersson isn't half the skater Patrick is.

The problem with Turcotte's rumor was, it didn't have a goalie coming back for Richter. You had to think Los Angeles would part with Kelly Hrudey or Rick Knickle, though. Either could finish the season in New York, then be left available in the expansion draft.

It all sounded plausible. That's the great thing about trade rumors. When they actually make sense, they're delicious.

Unless you're in them, unless they come true and you have to leave the people with whom you've played and for so long, have to move the family, try to please a new coach, fit in with a new bunch of guys.

■■■

A night in Chicago Stadium usually is a night of suffering for any visiting team. You figure, going in, that unless you play exceptionally well you will leave the ancient rink with more bruises than the Blackhawks, but fewer goals.

So the fact the Rangers won 4-1, scoring three goals on three shots in a 6:29 span of the third period, suggested several things. And the standings told what the victory didn't: The victory tied the Rangers in points with the Capitals. Each team had 73 heading into a second-place showdown at Capital Centre two nights hence.

The Rangers increased their point total because Nemchinov slid a wraparound past a soft-as-butter Ed Belfour for 2-1 at 7:02 of the third period. And Olczyk, an ex-Blackhawk and a Chicago native, used defenseman Chris Chelios as a screen, then clanked a 25-footer in off the post at Belfour's right for 3-1 at 12:51.

It was an important insurance goal and further evidence that Olczyk, after a long struggle, was coming around. He had started scoring in mid-February, when he was placed in Graves' spot with Messier and Amonte.

"Over the past couple of weeks, Eddie probably has been one of our best players," Messier said. "He drives to the holes, he's strong, he can hang onto the puck deep in the attacking zone, and he plays both ends of the rink. If he can play like that, it frees Adam to contribute on another line."

In the team's 11 games since February 15, Olczyk-Messier-Amonte had been together for 10. Olczyk had points (4-7-11) in eight of those contests and the Rangers had a 7-1-2 record.

"It's an honor to be able to get to play with a guy like Mess," Olczyk said. "I just try to get out of the way and let them do all the pretty stuff and I try to do some of the dirty work, forecheck and play well defensively."

Forty seconds after Olczyk scored, Graves grabbed a Belfour clear at the left-wing sideboards, then drove it into the net before the goalie could get back.

That emptied the rink of a crowd which never really turned into its growling, howling self.

"We took about 35 icings tonight, so that kind of keeps the momentum down for them," said Vanbiesbrouck, on a 6-1-1 roll. "Once we got the lead, we got them frustrated."

Jeremy Roenick, the Blackhawks' firebrand, was held to one first-period shot and was a non-factor the rest of the way. Chelios, another Blackhawk pepperpot, hit the post to Vanbiesbrouck's left at 11:34 of the first period — keeping the Blackhawks' lead at one, thanks to a Jocelyn Lemieux goal.

Maybe if they're up 2-0 after 20 minutes, the Blackhawks pour it on and the Rangers get buried. But it ended up going the other way because the Ranger forwards did a responsible job of slowing down their checks as the puck entered the defensive zone, giving the defense time to stand up.

"As much as possible, you've got to not allow Chicago to pound your face against the glass in your (defensive) end. If you can do that consistently, you've got a chance to play an even game," explained Ron Smith, whose 12-9-7 record was looking gaudier by the game. "If you let them push you up against the glass in your end, you're in trouble."

That rarely occurred. The Rangers were strong in the battles at the wall or the corners. They stayed with the game plan, drove the puck deep into Chicago's ice, and finally pulled even after another obvious dive by Kovalev — has the man NO shame? — created the power play on which Amonte tied it at 11:49 of the second.

Amonte, in the corner at Belfour's left, took a shot that hit the goalie's stick, then his arm, then the post, then rolled across the line. The goal was as bad as the Rangers were good, thanks to overall good play plus the added dimension Leetch gave them.

Referee Don Koharski boxed Roenick for that "hook" of Kovalev at 10:29 of the second period, and Leetch drove the Chicago defense back with a burst of speed and retained possession as he crossed the blue line. Eventually, the puck worked its way to Amonte in the corner to the left of Belfour, and the right wing — his skates almost on the goal line — decided to wing the puck to the net.

The puck struck Belfour's stick. Then it ran up his arm. Then it hit the goalpost at his right. Then it went in to tie the game.

The Rangers never looked back. They won a game in a tough rink. Leetch was back. Olczyk was getting hot. Other than the Quebec game, the team defense had been getting better and better. The Rangers had stretched their hot streak to 4-1-2. Darren Turcotte shook out his pants, put them on and headed to the bus.

After practice the next morning, the team took a flight to Washington, where the weather forecast called for snow.

■■■

Pro athletes put their health and well-being on the line every game night. They think nothing of playing in pain. Most barely notice cuts that require stitches. These are things that come with the territory, the same as travel.

Some of them hate flying, some merely dislike it, but they do it. They pass the time playing cards or reading, or sleeping, or working on the laptop computers many of them have begun taking on the road.

"Great, isn't it?," Hardy said in an airport one day. "I've got a $2,000 computer, and all I know how to do is play the golf game on it."

Nine holes, or even a mini-tournament, might start in the airport's waiting area, continue after the plane had reached its cruising altitude, and last until the runway was in sight — unless the battery ran out.

The travel is very regimented, and very structured, intentionally. First, it is easier for everyone involved to travel in a pack. That way, there is one flight, one bus, one hotel. You're a team, you're a family, you all go together. And that helps keep the chaos to a minimum.

A bus picks the group up at the rink and delivers the team to the airport. A team representative greets the group at the airport and hands each member a boarding pass. At the arrival airport, the team is met by a bus which delivers it to the hotel. At the hotel, the team has been pre-registered and an assistant manager has placed the players' pre-assigned room keys on a table for rapid dispersal.

From bus to lobby to elevator to room rarely takes more than a minute or two. Often, players have been to their rooms, dropped off their bags, come back to the lobby and headed out the door for supper or a snack in five minutes or fewer.

It becomes second nature, a habit. You take the same airlines to the same cities, unless you're chartering someplace. You stay at the same hotels, unless the game-day meal has been found deficient in some manner. Make no mistake, a bad game-day meal can get a hotel "fired."

Still, change is relatively rare. So Matt Loughran took a heap of good-natured ribbing when he changed the Rangers' hotel headquarters in Washington, cancelled the USAir charter flight home that had been scheduled (and paid for), and arranged train transportation to New York.

"It better snow, Matty," players chided Loughran, the Rangers' manager of team operations and the man responsible for moving the skating platoon from city to city. "It better snow."

Eighteen inches of snow had been forecast for the area, along with a dangerous wind-chill factor. Local television stations had broadcast constant warnings from the Maryland State

Highway Administration, cautioning area residents not to venture from their homes because of poor visibility and icy roads. Further testament to the seriousness of the warning was provided when the Capitals moved their office personnel into a hotel near the Cap Centre; they didn't want anybody marooned and unable to come to work in case a storm made things difficult.

And, indeed, it snowed.

It snowed a lot.

The Rangers' hotel in suburban Greenbelt — about a 15-minute bus ride from Capital Centre — was blanketed by snow overnight, then buffeted by sleet that was driven by high winds. The optional morning skate was cancelled, but the players seemed unconcerned when they gathered for the team meal.

Pre-game meals are important on a couple of levels. They are the player's main source of fuel for the day, so the menu must be stocked with enough items to carry the athlete through the afternoon, plus the evening's expenditure of energy. Second, they are yet another time for team togetherness. There is no way every player on a team is going to like every other player, or enjoy the company of every other player — or even seek the company of another player. Still, there are a bunch of tables available, a bunch of open chairs, and there is always a chance to hear a new voice for a change or get a new opinion or renew a debate.

This day, the buffet included a large tureen of soup, an enormous bowl of salad. One chafing dish contained fish, another veal, another the choice of spinach pasta or regular. There were baked and roasted potatoes. There was rice. Cooked carrots. Cottage cheese. There was a huge bowl of bananas, apples and oranges, which players often take to their rooms for dessert or a snack.

The meeting room set aside from dining was not large enough to accommodate both the buffet and all the tables, so the buffet was set up in the hall. Players would serve themselves in the corridor, then adjourn to the room to eat.

As each filled his plate, he would look to the right, through the lobby's massive windows, to survey the storm and evaluate its impact.

"This is NOTHING," said Peter Andersson, used to seeing far worse back home in Sweden.

"It's an every-day occurrence up in Edmonton," said Graves, who played there two seasons.

But this wasn't Edmonton. It wasn't Sweden. This was Greenbelt, Maryland, and there were things at stake other than second place.

Generally, if the teams are in place and the on-ice officials are in place, you play the game — even if nobody comes. The issue that day, however, was that if you play the game, you tempt people to come watch it. Of course, people with common sense wouldn't go, but sports fans don't always have common sense. Then what happened if a fan got into an accident, or even killed?

Of course that could happen on a bright, clear, warm spring day, too. But for once, an ounce of prevention prevailed. As home team, the Capitals had the final decision on postponement, and they announced their decision to do so around 3 p.m. — long before any of the locals would have been tempted to leave their home and hazard the weather.

There was one case where it was too late to turn back. This was a 'Trip with the Rangers' weekend, and somewhere out in the storm was a full busload of folks who had paid for transportation from New York, a reception with team president Neil Smith and others, plus a game ticket.

Except there was no game. And the players who had kidded Loughran all were saying, "Matty was right." And nobody knew where the bus was.

It was the Rangers' fourth postponed game since 1950. On March 3, 1978, the Rangers and Capitals also were snowed out of a game at Capital Centre; the contest was played March 24 and the Rangers powered to an 11-4 victory. A storm postponed the Rangers' visit to Montreal January 10, 1970 and the Rangers lost the rematch the next night, 4-1. The death of King George VI cancelled a Rangers-Maple Leafs game in Toronto February 6, 1952, and the teams tied, 3-3, in the rescheduled game February 19.

■■■

The team had flown in on Friday, but they had done so after practice. The hotel is located in an industrial park in Greenbelt, which means to do anything at all — there are a few restaurants and malls a short ride away — you had to have a car or a cab. There was little chance of a cab being available, given the weather, and there was a good chance of people getting stir-crazy after nearly two days in the hotel.

So Ron Smith scheduled a practice, with the team bus to leave the hotel at 5 p.m. The citizens could stay safe and cozy in their homes, but the team, at least, could get in a workout to keep some sharpness — and get out of the blasted hotel. And anyway, Joe the Bus Driver in Washington is one of the best. He wouldn't let anything happen.

It didn't seem there were 18 inches of snow on the ground when Joe inched the bus away from the hotel, but a bit of trouble arose when he tried to negotiate the slight incline out of the parking lot.

The bus started skidding backwards . . . toward the lobby.

"What've you got? Hush Puppies on this thing?" somebody yelled from the back.

The bus is Joe's pride and joy. You don't insult the bus and you don't insult his driving. His silence shushed any further remarks, as everyone realized it could be a long, cold walk back if Joe got petulant.

After he got up the hill, Joe made the right onto the access road and took the second exit onto I-95 South, which was more or less deserted. People had obeyed the warnings, so the bus had the road to itself. There was a light rain, but the sky actually was getting lighter. Joe made great time, and by the time he eased to a stop at the Cap Centre, not a drop of rain was falling. There wasn't a hint of wind.

It sure looked like they could have played.

But who could have known that in advance?

Who could have lived with himself if ANYONE had gotten hurt?

The Caps made the right call; there can be no question. And though they couldn't have known it at the time, they ended up doing a better job on the Rangers than if they had played the game and won by 15 goals.

Because after that night, the Rangers just weren't the same.

■■■

Practice proved another wrinkle in a strange day for assistant trainers Tim Paris and Larry Nastasi.

"It looked like a short day," Nastasi said. "It ended up being a long one."

Paris and Nastasi had left the team's hotel for Cap Centre at 8 a.m. and arrived by taxi at 8:30 after paying the driver an additional $3 'snow emergency fare.' There was snow on the ground, but the game was still 'on' and the morning skate was just a few hours away.

Paris and Nastasi laid out the practice jerseys, socks, and underwear. They filled bottles with water and athletic drink, made coffee. They set up the bench supplies: Tape, water bottles, sticks, towels. They did the shower supplies — soap, shampoo, towels, razors, shaving cream, hair dryers, etc. Paris sharpened all the skates.

Then they learned the optional practice had been cancelled.

So they got the game stuff ready. They packed the practice jerseys, practice socks, practice sticks, and the warmup outfits the coaches wear.

Then they learned the game had been postponed and started packing everything for the trip home. They had packed the first of the two rooms that make up the visitors' clubhouse at Capital Centre; the goalies and defensemen dress in one half of the double room, the forwards dress in the other. The goalie/defense room was done, packed, when head trainer Joe Murphy called with news of the practice.

So they started the whole drill over. Unpacking. Laying out. Making ready for the scheduled/unscheduled/rescheduled arrival of the team.

They stepped out onto the ice at 10 minutes to seven, which is about the time they would have gone out for the pre-game warmups. They skated at their leisure, waiting for the chirp of Smith's whistle to start their sprints.

As they skated toward you, they were like a herd. And everyone of them had a story to tell.

There was Richter, back from Binghamton, still searching for his confidence.

There was Gilhen, hanging on to his part-time job.

There was Hardy, who had asked to be traded.

There was Weight, who would be.

There was Turcotte, waiting for arbitration.

There was Leetch, back from his injury.

There were Lowe and Gartner, the all-stars.

There was Olczyk, starting to score.

There was Andersson, with his neon yellow laces.

There was Kovalev, the so-promising rookie.

There they all were, skating in circles, spinning their wheels, all dressed up, with no game to play.

"There's not much point in fussing about it," Ron Smith said. "We were coming off a real good road game. We were revved to do something good. The (rescheduled) game could mean a helluva lot less April 15 than it does now.

"A week ago," he added, "we'd have been cheering for this — to get a couple of extra days for people to heal."

At that particular practice, the only person trying to heal was Messier, who shrugged into his Ranger sweatshirt, slipped into a pair of shower sandals and sat in the stands for a while to watch the skate.

Later, Messier would adjourn to his locker and fiddle with his skates, which may be listed in next year's press guide as "favorite off-ice activity."

Messier is always tinkering with his skates, always insisting they are not quite right, that they still need some microscopic adjustment in order to pass muster. This time, he put on a U2 compact disc, sat on the bench connected to his locker and measured the width of the toes on one boot. He called Paris over.

"Timmy," he said, pointing to the blades, "as I suspected: When we put these (blades) back on, it somehow got shifted over."

There was a little black mark on the sole of the skate boot and a little black mark on the top of the plastic blade, which is replaced frequently — constantly in Messier's case. The idea is for the marks to line up, for the maximum sense of balance. That is why they've been drawn on. Paris comes over, for probably the thousandth time since training camp, and checks. He would fix it in New York; Messier wouldn't be needing the skates tonight, anyway.

Messier was wearing his glasses. On his right hip, he wore an electronic muscle stimulator that looked rather like a tape or CD player. On his ribs, he placed a heat pack and strapped it in place with a rubberized blue wrap.

The man was banged up.

"Sunday night, I started getting real light-headed. That's a problem when you take anti-inflammatories for any extended period, and without them, I can't play," Messier said. "It's only masking the injury, anyway. Time is the only thing that can really heal it. I think it's a day-to-day thing right now."

It seemed like more than that.

The pills, he said, "Don't really heal it. All it does is take the swelling down. I'm doing the best I can, but also, it's important that I take the time now, get off (the pills), then get back on."

Still, it didn't demand much exertion to try a hand at the trade rumor festival. The Rangers had gotten him from Edmonton. They had gotten Beukeboom from there as well, along with Lowe and Graves, as Neil Smith and Oiler boss Glen "Slats" Sather had become trading buddies. Now, the Rangers were after defenseman Dave Manson, according to the whispers.

Messier had other theories.

"Let's face it," he said. "We're building our team to beat Pittsburgh.

"Slats is looking five years down the road," he added. "What are we looking at?"

At winning it all, as soon as possible.

Messier mentioned two names. He mentioned McSorley of Los Angeles, as Turcotte had. Then he mentioned Esa Tikkanen from Edmonton.

Messier's hearing was better than Turcotte's.

■■■

When they came out, all showered and shaved and ready for dinner, it was snowing. Snowing hard. And sticking. And the wind was formidable.

"Pretty good evidence for not playing," Ron Smith said.

On the bus trip back, the roads were white and crusted with snow. Joe had four-foot wipers on his giant windows, but ice began to build and visibility was a hardship by the time he reached the hotel. If something that size was going to have trouble, you may imagine properly that a compact car would have been over-matched by these conditions.

The players ate, watched every movie they hadn't seen yet on Spectravision, and went to sleep while Matt Loughran figured out a way home.

The equipment was booked on a train that was to leave the station at suburban New Carollton, Maryland at 7 a.m. Sunday, but it had to be loaded — at Union Station, in downtown Washington, by 10 o'clock Saturday night.

Since Paris and Nastasi had handled the 'day' shift, Murphy took the night, had the gear trucked into the city and placed on a baggage car.

There is a story about the baggage car: It was to have carried the Capitals' equipment to Washington's game against the Islanders Sunday at Nassau Coliseum. When that game was post-poned by the storm, the car became available for the Rangers.

The equipment was loaded pretty much without a hitch, but the trip was not without glitches. Murphy, Paris, and Nastasi got to the station at 6:30 a.m. Sunday, but the train didn't leave until 11:30 and didn't get to Penn Station until 3:30 p.m.

Then there was the matter of getting the equipment from the basement of Penn Station to the fifth floor of the Garden.

You're talking roughly three dozen heavy equipment bags, plus several trunks (the skate sharpening machine, the jerseys, the always-in-use team stereo, the tape-laces-mending kits trunk, etc.) — a few thousand pounds in all.

Baggage handlers used electric carts to get the stuff into an elevator and up to street level, but the Garden van, which was supposed to drive the gear up the curving ramp inside, was snowed in. So the baggage guys guided the carts up the massive incline — the one the circus elephants walk when Ringling Brothers is in town.

Except one of the carts stalled before reaching the top.

It was 6 p.m. before the equipment guys left the building.

Getting the players home had been a different ball of wax.

Flying was out of the question, because high winds had closed the airports. So Loughran set up two options: He had a chartered coach car added to a Penn Station-bound train Sunday, and he ordered two buses to take the team to the train. If the trains weren't moving, the buses were going to cruise up I-95 and take the players back to New York.

The buses waited at the station until Loughran got assurance the train would, in fact, leave. The players got on, the 9:08 train left at 9:17, and the group was on its way.

The train was there only by accident. It had been headed toward Washington, but could get no farther because power lines had been knocked down up ahead. So it turned around and headed back north.

There was plenty of room in the car, but a few players wanted to stretch out. So Brian Leetch, the $2-million player, climbed up into the overhead rack — where people usually keep their belongings — and soon was fast asleep. Olczyk did like-wise. Ditto Graves. Kovalev grabbed a video camera and started taping a travelog, somebody called him, "Alexei Truffaut" as he has all kinds of fun with the camera, getting it as close as possible to the sleeping beauties without waking them up.

With Kovalev occupied, Weight grabbed Kovalev's portable phone and made a call. Later, Loughran would use it to telephone the bus company in New York and order sandwiches for the ride back to Rye.

When the train stopped in Philadelphia, Amonte went to one end of the car, opened the door and grabbed a handful of snow.

Ammunition.

He formed the snow into a ball and just flipped it in the air a couple of times, a weapon waiting to be fired — until he missed a catch and it splattered on the floor.

So it shouldn't be a total loss, he picked up some 'shrapnel' and flipped it in Weight's face.

Ah, the glamor of major league travel.

CHAPTER 17

UNSETTLED AIR

AS THE RANGERS became increasingly familiar with the kind of hockey coach Ron Smith wanted played, they became an increasingly solid defensive team.

They had enough scorers to win an occasional shootout, but the policy was to play as solid a defensive game as possible, wait for a break or two, and make sure to convert when an opportunity arises — which pretty much was what happened in Chicago.

Though they fell behind late in the first period, the Rangers stayed with the game plan. They continually dumped the puck deep into the Chicago zone and forced the Blackhawks to move the puck the length of the ice if they wanted to score again. They played well in the neutral zone, making sure that when the Blackhawks dumped in the puck, they were dragging a Ranger or two along for the ride when they chased after it.

The responsible work by the forwards made it easier for the defense to protect goaltender John Vanbiesbrouck.

"We used to play a lot of games with no holds barred," mused Vanbiesbrouck. "Now, we're barring some holds."

Another explanation was the return of Leetch. With Leetch back as his regular partner, Jeff Beukeboom was able to drift back to the background, where he was more productive. Leetch's mobility compensated for Beukeboom's lack of it, providing the perfect blend on a defense pair: A rover and a stay-at-home, a finesse guy and a banger.

In fact, all three pairs had those ingredients. The fluid Patrick combined with the all-defense Lowe, and Zubov, who roams all over the place, went with the less-gifted, more-gritty Joe Cirella.

With the pairs seemingly set, Mark Hardy and Peter Andersson, who filled in well when injuries required it, returned to depth roles, where they were better-suited. Eventually, management would have to figure out what to do with Wells, who wouldn't be back from his sprained knee for a few weeks but that was a fine problem to have. It could be solved in the week that remained before the trading deadline. There were three home games before then.

In fact, their Garden game against Boston March 15 opened a stretch that had the Rangers playing seven of eight games at home — a stretch that provided the perfect opportunity to pile up points and drive toward a playoff spot.

But the Islanders just had finished wasting a similar run of home games after fighting through a tough road stretch, and the Rangers' poor play in a 3-1 loss to the Bruins suggested they could end up doing the same thing.

True, it was the first game back after that bizarre five-day road trip. But in mid-March, their not-good-enough play represented a blown chance to pass Washington and take second place alone.

Okay, everybody's entitled to miss one chance, the thinking went. Edmonton, struggling mightily, was coming in next. And by then, the Rangers would have their focus back.

Keenan and Neilson, heading Team Canada for the world championships, stopped by the Garden to take in the game. The supposition was that they were there to watch Edmonton, which entered the contest 12 points and seven victories behind fourth-place Winnipeg. Seemingly out of the playoffs, the Oilers could offer lots of players for Team Canada.

The fact was, though, that if the Rangers didn't start doing some winning, lots of New Yorkers could be available for a trip to Munich right after the season-ending April 16 makeup with Washington. There was a priority on the two points available, but the Rangers lost, 4-3 in overtime, blowing a two-goal lead they had carried into the third period.

The only guy who deserved to win was Edmonton goalie Bill Ranford, who faced 59 shots — including a Gartner breakaway with 7.5 seconds left in the third — but stole the game for his team. A day that started with the fulfillment of Messier's prophecy — Tikkanen was obtained from Edmonton for Weight mere hours before the game — ended when Craig MacTavish wristed a right-wing circle shot past Vanbiesbrouck at 32 seconds of extra play.

"Any negative thing you can write about it, that's what happened," said Leetch, who had 11 shots. "A 3-1 game, this late in the season, is no time to be going by our checks and thinking it was going to be easy. It WOULD have been easy if we'd have kept playing the way we were."

Second-period goals 19 seconds apart by Ed Olczyk (25-foot snap shot) and Phil Bourque (cut-in from left wing) had provided a 3-1 lead on the scoreboard and a 45-23 lead on the shot clock. But Shayne Corson scored on a power play 46 seconds into the third and Petr Klima tied it with a redirection from the slot off Todd Elik's pass with 5:47 left in regulation — setting off a Ron Smith tirade.

"We'd be right stupid if we don't wake up and smell the coffee. If this doesn't do it, nothing will," the coach seethed. "We played on the road over a stretch of time when we were hurt, we played with a depleted lineup and played absolutely hard-ass, tight, tough hockey every night and got wins from it. Then we get the talent back, and we decide to even it out by laying off the hard work and the checking game.

"Fourteen games to go in the season, we should be playing every game absolutely desperate," Smith added. "I'll acknowledge we got 59 shots, and a lot of great ones, and Ranford made some great saves. But the fact is, we took 10 minutes off in the second period when we should have been trying to get to six or seven (goals), and not only do we not attack or play aggressively or smart or hard, we let them come into the game and go to us.

"It's different if you say, 'Okay, we're going to shut down for 10 minutes and give them absolutely nothing and frustrate them,' but we didn't do that, either," Smith said. "I won't accept it. I simply won't."

Well, what do you do?

"Get the best players to play their best, and play hard, tight, smart, tough hockey," Smith said. "If they won't do it, we know where we'll be April 16."

■■■

The next day brought tragic news from half a world away. Neil Smith's brother-in-law had been killed in an automobile accident in Sweden. The Rangers' president left the team and accompanied his wife to the funeral. With the trading deadline less than a week away, assistant GM Larry Pleau, who had been at his Connecticut home, travelled to New York to represent Smith in Ranger business matters.

That night, the Rangers played San Jose and did what they had to do. They splattered the Sharks, 8-1, and moved into third place, but not until they had been treated to a little pep talk. The Sharks got 19 shots in the second period, and only some fine work by Richter — in his first game since the rout at Quebec — kept San Jose from stealing points the way Edmonton had.

After a conference during the second intermission, the Rangers outshot San Jose 22-4 and outscored them, 4-0.

Graves had four assists, Kovalev scored twice, Gartner notched his 40th. Afterward, Leetch went out with Amonte, Messier, and some friends.

And some time before he got home, Leetch broke his right ankle.

∎∎∎

The medical term was a spiral fracture of the fibula. Having spent his winter teaching us all about the Brachial Plexus, the network of nerves he had injured with that tumble in St. Louis, Leetch would send us back to the medical glossary: The fibula is a bone that runs from the knee to the ankle along the outside of the lower leg. There are two bones in the lower leg and the fibula is the smaller of the two.

And Leetch's right one was broken, badly enough to require eventual surgery. A fractured left ankle had been repaired surgically with a metal plate, held in place by screws, after he had injured it in Toronto on March 14, 1990. Now, he would have a matched set; there would be a similar rectangular plate on the other side, holding the bones together.

But what would hold the Rangers together now? The trading deadline was days away and the GM was overseas. The power play, without Leetch, took the Rangers out of more games than it won for them. Leetch was so much of their confidence, their hope that a tailspin was behind them.

His return, after so long an absence, had lifted them.

Now, his departure utterly flattened them.

"It just takes the air right out of you," Messier said, standing in a Westchester hotel. It was a Saturday night, the night of the

Ranger Fan Club's dinner dance. Player attendance is mandatory and virtually all came, except for Leetch, who was granted medical leave.

Each Ranger player sat at a different table, the better to mingle with the public. In Leetch's place at his table was the top half of a life-sized rendering of the defenseman, hand-crafted and painted by artist/fan Jackie Cannon.

"I hang it on my door at home. It's two pieces, held together with velcro, but someone made a joke that HE'S held together with it, too," said Cannon, who didn't think it was funny.

"They're just doomed," she said, "to not having everybody for the playoffs."

It was at the dinner dance that Neil Smith reached Barry Watkins. Watkins is the director of communications, but this was one message he wasn't eager to communicate.

Through the phone line from Sweden, where it was 3 a.m., Smith asked, "What the hell happened to Leetchie?"

Smith wasn't the only person who wanted to know. It didn't take long for the rumor mill to start sizzling with assertions that Leetch had gone pub crawling — Avalon, The Tavern, who knows where else? — after the San Jose game and had taken a drunken tumble. Others claimed the fracture was the result of a playful wrestling match between Leetch and Messier. There was hazy stuff about Leetch being injured when chased down a flight of back stairs at a club.

The version Watkins released was that as he stepped out of a cab in front of his apartment building on Manhattan's upper West Side, Leetch slipped on a patch of "black" ice. Ironically, Leetch and Richter live in the same building, which is set in barely 100 feet from Broadway. They are the only two genuine Broadway Blues.

Now, Leetch was Broadway blue.

There was a slight problem with Watkins' recreation of the event:

When you slip on a patch of ice, you might lose your balance and fall. In trying to break your fall, you might injure your hand or your wrist, or you might fall on your backside and hurt your tailbone. But, unless your ankle is planted in some way while you're lurching, it would seem difficult to suffer an ankle injury in the manner Watkins described.

Eventually, Leetch provided a more believable version:

Remnants of snow from the monster storm were piled in

along the sidewalk outside his building. Leetch got out of the cab and stepped onto what he thought was a fairly solid-packed snow, but turned out — to his horror — merely to be a hollow shell, almost an igloo. Leetch stepped through a thin crust of snow, lurched, and came down awkwardly — with all his weight — on the side of his foot.

But Leetch did not provide any comment until virtually forced to by the groundswell of "eyewitnesses" casting aspersions on his behavior.

"It was definitely not because I had too much to drink," he said. "If I ever did something to myself because I had too much to drink, I would have come up with a better story than that.

"I went out with Mess (Mark Messier) and Tony (Amonte) and a couple friends of Tony's, had a couple of beers and that was it: A couple (of beers) at dinner and a couple uptown," Leetch said. "I came back in a cab, got out in front of my building, cut between cars and stepped up on a ridge of snow that was built up.

"I didn't really fall down. I rolled over on it," the 1992 Norris Trophy winner said. "My ankle buckled, and I heard it pop. I thought I sprained it pretty bad. I iced it down. The next morning, I still thought it was sprained, and (team trainer) Dave Smith treated it as a sprain."

Leetch also scoffed at reports he had fallen while being chased down some back stairs at The Tavern.

"It's on street level, so I would have had to have been going under ground for that to happen," Leetch said.

"There's absolutely no way anybody can say that I hurt myself in that bar," he declared. "I just don't know how people can say that (the injury was caused by anything else), unless they see you do it."

Bottom line, the leg was going to be in a cast for four weeks and Leetch was going to be out of the lineup for at least eight.

He was done for the year.

They didn't know it at the time, but so were the Rangers.

"I have to look at it that I'm going to get better sooner than they think, so that I have something to shoot for," Leetch said. "I'm just in shock. I can't believe it. I feel like taking the cast off, getting up and saying, 'Joke's over.'"

It wasn't.

Leetch's injury was a source of agony on several fronts, not the least of which was that it was neither game-related nor opponent-related. If there is one trademark of the entire star-crossed season, it is that so many manpower games were lost to injuries that had little or nothing to do with another team.

There were seven injuries, aside from this one, that qualified under this heading:

February 18 — Kevin Lowe and Alexei Kovalev race for a puck in practice. Kovalev, a step ahead, stops short and throws his shoulder backward into the on-rushing Lowe. Result: Lowe, jolted upright and to the left, suffers back spasms and misses two games.

February 3 — Sergei Nemchinov and Phil Bourque collide at the Philadelphia blue line. Both limp to the bench. Result: Nemchinov returns, Bourque suffers a sprained left knee and misses six games.

January 27 — This one gets an asterisk. At the Rangers' blue line, Adam Graves crosschecks Winnipeg's Evgeny Davydov, who tumbles into Jay Wells' right knee from the side. Result: A severe right-knee sprain for Wells, who misses 31 games.

January 25 — Darren Turcotte and Mike Hurlbut collide in practice. The result: Hurlbut sprains his left knee, misses 14 games, then is assigned to Binghamton, where he remains.

December 17, 1992 — Leetch flies head-first into the St. Louis Arena sideboards after missing a check on Philippe Bozon. Result: Leetch compresses a nerve that starts in the neck and runs down the left shoulder. He misses 34 games.

December 11 — Bourque and Wells collide in warmups at Tampa Bay. Result: Bourque suffers a concussion and misses the game.

November 2 — James Patrick checks Buffalo's Wayne Presley into goalmouth, where Presley collides with John Vanbiesbrouck. Result: Vanbiesbrouck strains groin muscles, misses four games.

That's eight injuries which pretty much were self-inflicted. By its own count, the team would lose 202 man-games due to injury in 1992-93. By our count, 115 of those man-games (56%) had virtually nothing to do with the other team. So there's nobody to blame, no villain, no emotional relief. All injuries are a source of frustration, these were a source of frustration and anger.

"This is just one season," Messier said, "when the fates are going to test our perseverance to the bitter end."

It wouldn't be the first time. Experienced Ranger fans remembered the injury that knocked Jean Ratelle out of the playoffs the year the Rangers got to the finals. They could remember a year Brad Park — another star defenseman, another Ranger who wore No. 2 with such grace — went down. You almost could count on it as part of the Ranger tradition, the Ranger jinx.

"'Jinx' is another excuse for lack of motivation," Messier declared. "If you're good enough, and want it enough, you erase all the jinxes."

But whether the team was good enough now, without Leetch, was very much open to question. Fortunately, the trading deadline had been extended from March 20 to March 22, because March 20 was a Saturday, and why force the office staff of every team — plus league headquarters — to work on a weekend? The 22nd was Monday, and Neil Smith was expected to join the team in Ottawa, in time to make some deals.

"When he gets here," Ron Smith said, "I'm sure Neil will have about 100 messages from people offering to help him out of his dilemma."

During his pre-flight remarks, the captain of the Rangers' chartered plane forecast "some unsettled air" on the way to Ottawa. Then he taxied down the Newark Airport runway and took off — with the injury-dinged Rangers, their interim coach and their stand-in general manager, Larry Pleau.

If that isn't unsettled air, what is?

"Leetchie getting hurt and Neil not being here makes things pretty confusing," James Patrick said. "I don't think anyone can get a real feel for what might happen."

By 3 o'clock, they would know.

"I don't think Neil is sitting there, going, 'Jeez. How am I going to replace Brian Leetch?'" Pleau said. "He's sitting there, saying, 'The direction I was heading, the last little bit, can I continue in that direction? Or do I have to step back, because of what's happened with Brian Leetch?'"

Even before Leetch was injured, Smith was believed to be working on improving the defense.

"But you're not going to replace a Brian Leetch in a trade," Ron Smith said, "unless somebody wants to give you Ray Bourque, Al MacInnis, or Chris Chelios."

There was the chance Neil Smith would go another direction, try to add power up front and keep pressure off what remained of the defense.

"The cause is still there to coldly improve the team, and I think Neil's totally capable," Vanbiesbrouck said. "I think he knows more than any of us put together about the players in this league, by far. I trust everything Neil's done. I trust his foresight. In this game, the toughest thing is foresight."

At practice before the flight to Ottawa, the toughest thing was figuring out which player, if any, would be gone.

"You're aware of the deadline, but you don't deal with it until it happens," Patrick said. "When Dougie Weight got traded (the previous Wednesday), I said, 'I can't believe it. That was the last skate with him, the last pre-game meal with him.' But never before."

The team got to Ottawa Sunday afternoon and practiced at the Civic Centre. Richter and Vanbiesbrouck were the goalies, in black jerseys, as usual. The Olczyk-Messier-Amonte line wore red. Graves, Turcotte and Kovalev formed the green line. Tikkanen and Nemchinov formed two-thirds of the white line, with Broten taking a resting Gartner's place in the drills. The gold line was Bourque, Gilhen, and Kocur. The defense pairs were Hardy and Patrick, Lowe and Beukeboom, Andersson and Cirella. Zubov went without a formal partner.

And if this WAS going to be his last practice with the team, Richter was going to have fun at it. When the formal drills concluded, Kocur, Kovalev, Broten, Turcotte, Graves, Lowe, Andersson, Tikkanen, and Nemchinov formed a semicircle in front of Richter's goalmouth. They worked the puck from player to player until somebody shot. If Richter made the save, the shooter was "out." The last guy left was the winner.

It ended up being Kocur, when a brilliant left kick stop finished Tikkanen in the finals. There was cheering and kibitzing and insults and laughs. They left the ice smiling, but you knew there were people in their last hours with the team.

"It's almost like an unrealistic day," Vanbiesbrouck said. "Everybody jokes about it until somebody's name gets called. Then, all of a sudden, it's not funny any more."

The names were Hardy and Gilhen.

And Turcotte's prediction about a deal with Los Angeles was part right. But he wasn't in the package.

Hardy and a draft pick were sent to the Kings for grinding center John McIntyre. Gilhen was sent to Tampa Bay for left wing Mike Hartman.

With those deals, Smith made the team younger and scrappier, but that was it. No other planned moves ever got beyond the talking stage. Nothing happened, or failed to happen, because of the injury to Leetch, said Smith, who added he "exhausted every effort" to trade a goaltender before the 3 p.m. deadline.

"We had two or three different objectives going into the last couple of weeks," Smith said, "and clearly, we satisfied one of them — which was to get our team grittier and physically stronger."

The deals were aimed at replacing ingredients sent away by previous transactions. Hartman was expected to provide the pugnaciousness Smith swapped in the deal for Olczyk, while providing insurance in case Joe Kocur's battered hands became unavailable.

McIntyre, voted the Kings' top defensive forward by the L.A. media in 1991-92, was expected to add some incendiary grit as the No. 4 center. The pick the Kings got was the fifth-round selection Ottawa handed over in last November's Dave Archibald deal.

"They've got to be gritty, have the mindset to go into the lineup whenever we want them to, and tick off whoever we want them to tick off," Neil Smith said of McIntyre and Hartman.

If Smith got rapped for trading away years when he acquired the 28-year-old Tikkanen for the 22-year-old Weight, it should be noted the 23-year-old McIntyre was secured for a 34-year-old Hardy and the 26-year-old Hartman was gained for the 29-year-old Gilhen. Neither Hardy nor Gilhen was going to play much, and each had asked to be moved.

The Kings had wanted McIntyre to replace Steve Kasper as a checker and Mike Krushelnyski as a grinder, but Los Angeles coach Barry Melrose had grown to question the youngster's commitment.

"John has to decide whether he wants to play in the NHL," Melrose had said. "He doesn't have to compete with Jari Kurri or Wayne Gretzky to play, but with his style of game, he has to do it (compete with intensity) every day and every night."

McIntyre admitted performing that way at times, and did it consistently enough during the 1988-89 OHL season to be named captain of coach Ron Smith's Guelph Platers. McIntyre had 30 goals and 129 penalty minutes as a left wing that season, but hadn't played that position — or come close to that type of production — in the NHL.

The 6-1, 175-pound pivot had eight goals in 69 games over his best pro season, the 1990-91 campaign he split between Toronto and Los Angeles. He broke in with 17 points and 117 penalty minutes with the Maple Leafs in 1989-90, two years after Toronto made him 49th player drafted.

In 49 games before the deal, McIntyre had 2-5-7 with 80 penalty minutes. He seemed the natural choice as center for an all-acid fourth line with Tikkanen and Joe Kocur. In Los Angeles at the start of the season, McIntyre did similar duty when flanked by Warren Rychel and Marty McSorley; but when the Kings made the Paul Coffey deal with Detroit, obtaining center Jimmy Carson plus right wings Marc Potvin and Gary Shuchuk, McIntyre's ice time began fading.

"I feel I can be a lot better player than I am," McIntyre said from Marina del Ray, California.

He would get a chance to show it.

Smith had flown all day Sunday to get back to North America, then spent the rest of his time trying to trade goalies for defensemen.

"I'm not going to stop talking about it, even now," Smith said, referring to a goalie trade. "I know the number of teams that would definitely take one of our goalies. It's just a matter of whether we want to take what they're offering."

The team president promised a deal before the expansion draft, declaring there was no way he would lose one of those assets for nothing.

"I'd rather control where one of these guys went. If I lost one in the expansion draft, he could end up across one of the rivers," Smith said, referring to New Jersey or Long Island. "If you trade a guy, you can trade him with 'an understanding' (that the goalie won't end up back in the division)."

By the time the 3 o'clock deadline passed, Smith looked almost as tired as he had the morning after his first all-night session with Marcel Aubut on the Eric Lindros trade last June.

In the late afternoon, Smith sat shoeless on a sofa in a wood-panelled suite that was nicer than most apartments. Somebody asked if he had just put the finishing touches on a Stanley Cup team.

"No," replied Smith, who made the mistake of saying 'yes' to a similar question a few seasons back, after Joe Kocur had been obtained.

Trade deadline day is a draining experience. You have guys getting traded, though they wanted to stay with the team. You have guys who want out, yet aren't traded. You have guys thinking they're getting traded, but they end up not getting traded. All kinds of things happen.

Gilhen said he got word at 3:10 p.m., after thinking he had survived.

"What I'll remember about being a Ranger was being part of that great year last year, winning the President's Trophy, and how much I enjoyed being part of it," Gilhen said. "I think I'll remember what a classy organization it was and how well I was treated.

"Neil Smith was really good to me; he moved me to a team that wanted me and I have to thank him for that," Gilhen added. "It's still hockey, and hopefully, it's a place where I'll be getting a chance to play. I made a lot of close friends in New York; it was too bad it couldn't have gone on, but nothing is forever."

Not even a Stanley Cup drought?

"The Rangers are a team with a ton of potential," Gilhen said. "There's too much depth there, too many good players not to do well. I can't imagine a team that good not making the playoffs and not, in all honesty, making a run at it."

Turcotte had been "traded" to a different city every day. But when the Rangers dealt Weight for Tikkanen last week, after winning their arbitration argument with Turcotte, it seemed they finally chipped out a definite roster spot for the two-time 30-goal scorer.

Still, the afternoon was a long one.

"I just had to wait, and fortunately, I didn't get The Phone Call," Turcotte said. "I slept, off and on. I woke up at 4 o'clock and the phone hadn't rung."

So he went to work.

Olczyk had been obtained way back in December, so he wasn't likely to be moved. But his two new teammates also were old teammates.

"Johnny McIntyre is good on faceoffs, is a good penalty killer," said Olczyk, who played with McIntyre in Toronto. "And he can fight. He's fought some of the toughest guys in the league. Not many people know that, but he's a tough player. He's a smaller version of Adam Graves and a little more of a kamikaze, who goes out and bangs anything that moves.

"Mike Hartman is one of the most competitive and best team guys I've ever played with," added Olczyk, who played with Hartman in Winnipeg. "He goes up and down his wing, and can shoot a puck pretty well. He's just a top-notch role player and a great team player."

The Rangers needed Hartman to replace Tie Domi.

"When you're behind as often as we are, and you try to get a goal to get back in it, Harts is not the one you play, usually. Brian Bradley is the one who'll get the ice time," said Lightning coach Terry Crisp. "You try to be nice about it, but that's the way it is. When you're behind most games, sometimes your heart-and-soulers and your checkers don't get a lot of ice time. But Mike Hartman is a heart-and-souler."

Being traded to the Rangers officially completed Hartman's NHL "cycle." They say you've hit for the cycle when you've played in each of the league's divisions, and the left wing had played for Buffalo in the Adams Division, Winnipeg in the Smythe, Tampa Bay in the Norris before being sent to the Patrick playoff race.

"I got the call at about 3:05, and I said to myself, 'This team is going to the playoffs,'" Hartman said. "This is a good team.

"I know what they're looking for," the left wing said. "They're looking for someone to create some scoring opportunities and throw some good hits. The most I ever had in a season was 11 goals, so they're not looking to me for scoring."

Hartman had those 11 goals and added 10 assists with Buffalo, the team with which his NHL career began, in 1989-90. Before last season began, he had 38 goals and 1,154 penalty minutes in 300 NHL games.

"When you get the opportunity to play in New York," Hartman said, "you make the most of it."

The Tony Amonte-to-Winnipeg rumors crashed to earth at 3:01 p.m.

"When you get alone, you think, 'Geez. Something might happen,'" Amonte admitted. "But it didn't bother my afternoon nap. I got up to my room at 1:30, fell asleep, woke up at 4 — no calls, no nothing."

Then, of course, there was Mike Richter, who was believed to be offered everywhere, for everyone.

"I felt either I'm going to be here, and at some point be asked to help, or I'll be going somewhere else and be a starting goalie there," Richter said. "I felt either way, when this day came, it would be good. The most positive thing about a trade is, if somebody's trading for me, they want me to play right away; that would have been my consolation for leaving a team and a place that I enjoy so much.

"Who knows how close it was to going down? But I'm glad it didn't take place," Richter said. "I feel I haven't reached my potential yet, and I don't feel I need a change in order to reach it. I still think I can help this team out, I think we have a lot to look forward to, and I didn't want to leave a good situation here."

Of course he meant the general situation of playing for the Rangers, playing in New York. The more-serious facts of life were, after all the deadline-day activity, they were one point out of third — and one point out of fifth — when they skated onto the Civic Centre ice for the game against the Senators.

"Now, it's important that we realize this is our team, this is the team we're going into the playoffs with, and really try to focus in on the task at hand," captain Messier said. "If we do that, I really believe we have as good a chance as anybody in the league to go all the way. But there has to be a total commitment, from everybody here, from here on in."

With the passing of the trade deadline, there are no more rumors, no more trade worries. After months of the marathon, the playoff sprint had begun.

"When you think about it, we've been playing playoff hockey for a month already," Messier said. "That can be good, but sometimes there's going to be a little bit of (an emotional) dry spell."

Almost immediately, it hit. The Rangers collected a graceless 5-4 victory and sneaked out of town.

CHAPTER 18

APRIL FOOLS

THE SCHEDULE DOESN'T JUST FALL out of the sky and onto somebody's desk. There are meetings and phone calls and conferences and arguments, and what you end up with are dates you like, dates you absolutely hate, and dates you live with.

When the Rangers' schedule was released, before all the fun began, April clearly was going to be all those things in microcosm. There were eight games, seven against Patrick Division rivals, in a 13-day span. There was a five-game week which included two sets of games on consecutive dates — a 4/5 Washington-Hartford sequence and a home-and-home set with Pittsburgh on 9/10.

But there was a tradeoff. The first game of the month, on the second, would follow a four-day break in the schedule; that would provide a nice respite if the team had bumps or bruises it needed to heal. And by finishing on the 14th, there would be three full days before the start of the playoffs on Sunday, the 18th. Having been the last team to get their season underway, the Rangers would be the first to get it over with.

Moreover, even if they opened the playoffs on the road, the team still could have a day off April 15, get in two good practices, then leave for whatever city they would have to reach. Of course, travel would be no problem. The Devils or Islanders or Flyers would be a bus trip away, while Washington or Pittsburgh were within an hour by plane. The Rangers would enter the tournament as fresh and rested as possible.

The March 14 snowout erased the convenience factor. Instead of finishing the season with a home game against Washington April 14, they would finish by making up the snowout in

Washington on the 16th. A total nuisance. Now, if they made the playoffs, there probably would be a short-turnaround situation: Game in Washington Friday night, charter flight home, late practice Saturday, then off to whatever city.

As the month began, with the Penguins miles ahead in first place and the Capitals in second by three points over the Devils, the best-case scenario would have been for the Rangers to finish third. That way, they could finish the season at Capital Centre Friday night, then simply stay put until Game 1 of the Patrick Division Semifinal on Sunday. The Rangers were looking ahead, not back. They opened April with a 10-point lead on the last-place Flyers. Why look back? That race was over.

As the month began, Paramount also had made it perfectly clear that the media hounds better clear away from Neil Smith's door. Gutkowski conducted a conference call in which he declared the Garden's support for the job done by the club president/GM — regardless of the fact that as he spoke, the team just had tumbled into fifth place.

The Rangers had been three points out of first place when November began, one point out of second when January began, a point out of third when March began. This was the sixth straight month that opened with the Rangers no higher in the standings.

"Over the last few months, I've had some formal dinners with a couple of different beat writers, and the subject of Neil Smith's position within the organization has come up in all those dinners, and what happens if we get in the playoffs or we don't get into the playoffs," Gutkowski explained. "I've also seen in print from time to time some speculation about what would happen to Neil if the Rangers don't make the playoffs. A lot of guys have come recently and asked for specific quotes, and I thought it's time to address this.

"I wanted to get it out, and get it out to everybody at the same time. I think it's very important to note that I'm speaking for myself, Madison Square Garden, and the total support of everybody at Paramount Communications," Gutkowski added, referring to Stanley Jaffe and Martin Davis when he spoke of Paramount. "We feel Neil Smith has done an excellent job with the Rangers since he arrived four years ago. He's one of the most respected talents in the NHL today. He's assembled an acknowledged group of skilled players, an equally skilled staff. As always, we'll be evaluating the organization after the season's over, but I can assure you Neil will be leading this team when we break camp next September — no matter what the outcome this year. I wanted to say that, get it out in the front, address it now, because I thought it was important to do — and important to do it to everybody at the same time, because I know you've all inquired.

"When you look at anybody's job, you've got to look at the organization they've put together from top to bottom, from a professional level and a league level," the Garden president said. "I think this year, we have collectively said, has been a disappointment. But that there are reasons for it. The injuries have certainly had some play. We have not performed to the level that we would have wanted to, but there's a lot that goes into the decision-making process. We have great faith in Neil, great respect for his ability, great respect for his knowledge. We also know if Neil Smith ever left this organization, he'd be picked up in a New York minute by another organization.

"We're very comfortable with Neil. We think Neil has done a good job overall as far as trades are concerned. He's tried to strengthen the team wherever he could. Whenever you make trades, in any league, there will be some that people will think are good or bad. But overall, we think Neil's done an outstanding job as far as making trades.

"We're not happy about being in fifth place," he added, "but we expect the team to get better, and we're not out of the playoffs yet."

There was one other way of reading Gutkowski's remarks as a direct statement to the players: You may have gotten Neilson fired, but you aren't getting Neil Smith fired. There was only one bullet in your gun and you killed Neilson with it; you've gotten away with all the murder we will allow.

"Neil can't skate for the players, the coach can't skate for the players. Any team becomes the responsibility of the team that's on the field," Gutkowski said. "When you are successful, it's the players who get it done, and when you're unsuccessful, you always have to look to the people who play the game."

There also was a way of reading Gutkowski's remarks as a direct statement to Smith. One juicy little morsel in his expression was, " . . . I can assure you Neil will be leading this team when we break camp next September." That's a lot different from saying, "I can assure you Neil will be leading this team at the end of his contract, four years from now." A devil's advocate would suggest this seemingly unconditional endorsement was, in fact, much more finite.

Except for a very few legacies of the Patrick and Esposito eras, the people who played the game so poorly this season were brought in by Neil Smith. In many respects, they also were the people who had carried the team to 105 points the season before; despite a bad run, there was ample talent on the team, and it had been cultivated from the soil Smith had farmed. If you bring in ANOTHER new GM, you all but start from scratch.

"In any league, it's hard to find a real good executive. And once you've got him, you've got to keep him for a long period of time," Gutkowski declared. "Stability will ultimately lead to winning. That (remaining stable) is one thing we have not done well in the past and one thing we want to do very well in the future. We all believe we have to be a stable organization if we want to win a Stanley Cup."

One issue remained, however. When a corporate executive issues a vote of confidence, the guy who gets it better hire a bodyguard. Because in the warped mathematics of professional sports, an embattled general manager plus a vote of confidence usually equals a kiss of death.

"All I can speak for is the New York Rangers, and why this is being given," Gutkowski said, attempting to end any doubt. "It's because of the absolute support we have for Neil and the respect we have for him as a hockey talent."

If there was any sigh of relief from Smith, he kept it well hidden.

"I'm very flattered and honored that the support I'm shown on a day-to-day basis has been made public by the company — and how supportive they are of the future that's in my hands," Smith said. "It's one thing to be supported in a season like last year, when there were a lot of accolades. It's harder to do it this year, when times have been more difficult.

"Certainly, this company (Paramount) doesn't have a reputation for doing things like this," he added, "so it's very flattering to have that faith expressed."

That faith would be shown again, in a different way, a few days later. But first, there was the matter of the Islanders, April 2.

■■■

The teams were an eyelash apart, but only on the basis of the standings. The Islanders in fourth place with 78 points, the Rangers next at 77 points, but the Islanders held whopping advantages in several other areas. They were ahead in the standings, had more victories in the division, had 17 victories on the road. The Islanders were the team with a 100-point center, Pierre Turgeon, in their lineup. They were the team with unmistakably the better defense, and, with Al Arbour, held a monumental edge in NHL head coaching experience over Ron Smith.

The mathematics were straightforward. A victory would put the Islanders ahead three points and four victories — a critical figure, as victories represent the first tiebreaker criterion should two clubs finish even in points. A victory would leave the Islanders in position to split their eight remaining games, two of which were against Hartford and one of which was against Ottawa. In order to move ahead, the Rangers would have to go 6-2-0, 5-1-2, or 4-0-4 in their remaining eight, with seven of those games against divisional foes . . . against whom the Rangers had won precisely 11 times all season.

"This is even tougher than the playoffs," Adam Graves said. "In the playoffs, you can afford to lose three games and still win a series. We can't do that here. We can't afford to lose three games."

And they certainly couldn't afford to lose this one.

"We've got to play as if our lives are on the line — which they are, basically," Mike Gartner said.

With the usual coverage on MSG Network and SportsChannel, plus additional coverage by ESPN, the scope of the game became notably national — while the emotion was decidedly local: The Rangers and Islanders, the cross-county rivals, doing battle again. Life and death, again, at the Garden. A big-game evening in a big-game arena that knows how to put on a show.

"What better way to spark up an old rivalry than with an old-fashioned barn-burner?" Vanbiesbrouck asked.

There were the Rangers, fighting for their playoff lives, ending a season of unremitting stress. There were the Islanders, fighting to prove that their Sad Sack days were done. The Islanders were nearly 10 years removed from their last Stanley Cup, but that's a lot less than 53 years.

Who had the most pressure on their shoulders?

Take a wild guess.

■■■

The Garden is a striking venue, with its lights, its colors, the enormous scoreboard suspended from the ceiling over center ice. There is constant noise, cheers or boos during the play, loud music during the breaks, all kinds of commercials or video clips on the four-sided Gardenvision screen. And there are two extremely busy visual shows above and around the arena, although it registers on few, if any, of the 18,200 who will fill the building this night.

First, there is the procession of advertisements on the boards that enclose the rink. Budweiser beer. Gulf Oil. Snapple Natural Iced Tea. Sabrett hot dogs. Air Canada. New York lottery. Subaru automobiles. Upper Deck hockey cards. U.S. Health Care. Coca Cola Classic. Paine Webber. Bugle Boy. Met Life insurance. Amtrak. Modell's sporting goods. Sharp electronics. Nobody Beats The Wiz.

Then there are the banners that hang from the ceiling. When the basketball court is in place and Riley's Knicks are competing, the Knicks' bench is at the Eighth Avenue end of the arena and the flags that commemorate the Knicks' accomplishments hover above them in a semicircle from 31st Street to 33rd. There is a blue banner for the 1969-70 world championship team, another for the 1972-73 champs, others still for the Atlantic Division titles of 1970-71 and 1988-89. There are white ones for the players whose numbers have been retired: 15 Monroe. 19 Reed. 22 DeBusschere. 10 Frazier. 24 Bradley. 12 Barnett. 613 Holzman. 15 McGuire.

Since the Eighth Avenue end is the basketball end, the American flag points proudly westward from the Eighth Avenue side of the center scoreboard. Thus the Seventh Avenue side is the hockey end of the building, complete with the Canadian flag that points toward it from the Seventh Avenue side of the scoreboard.

The 11 Ranger banners are arrayed in a semicircle. As you face it from the basketball end, the flag farthest left honors the 1926-27 American Division championship, the one farthest right would celebrate the 1991-92 regular-season championship. The honorees, reading across from your left, would be the 1931-32 American Division winners, the 1941-42 regular-season champions, and then, fourth from the left, the No. 1 flag that commemorates the career of goaltender Ed Giacomin — perhaps the most popular player in team history. Giacomin often credits fan support for gaining him a plaque of honor in the Hockey Hall of Fame, and his departure from the team, when he was claimed on waivers by Detroit on Halloween night, 1975, was one of the bleakest moments in the team's too-often-bleak modern memory.

It was a Friday night, and the Rangers' Fan Club had scheduled one of its bus trips, to follow the team to Montreal.

"As many of us gathered outside MSG to wait for the buses to come, the news reports started hitting our ears," Debbie Rockower recalled. "Our faces were streaked with tears. What was going to be a much-anticipated first trip of the season to Canada almost became a funeral procession.

"How could the Rangers do this to our beloved 'Eddie?' Eddie meant a lot to the members of the Fan Club, when most players could have cared less. We drank ourselves into oblivion, to try to forget about Eddie, but it would not go away," Rockower continued. "We went to Montreal, lost the game, and no one cared."

In an exceptional piece of irony, the Rangers' game after Montreal was the next night — against the Red Wings . . . and Ed Giacomin.

"All we cared about was getting back to New York in time on Sunday to root, not against the Rangers but to root FOR Eddie Giacomin. We got back just in time, too," Rockower said. "I got to the blue seats as the teams skated out for the National Anthem. I never made it to my seat at Eighth Avenue. I stood where I had entered the arena — cheering, crying, yelling, over and over, 'Eddie! Ed-die!'"

The seats in the Garden balcony, where the faithful ones sit, aren't blue any more. They are more a greenish-blue mint color that is described as teal. Still, the tears spilled at the Garden that Sunday night — not only by the fans but by Giacomin, as well — are part of what is memorialized by that banner at the Seventh Avenue end.

The Giacomin banner is significant for what it means, what it makes you remember — the joys of Giacomin's triumphs, the bitterness of his departure, that tearful Sunday night when he got an ovation for every save and recorded a 6-4 victory over the Ranger team that betrayed him. And it is significant because it is the Garden landmark closest to Neil Smith's vantage point near the building's roof.

To reach it, Smith takes an elevator to the luxury box level, walks a bit to his left to an unmarked steel door that looks like it should open into a broom closet. In fact, the door opens onto a ladder of stairs so steep they seem better-suited to a submarine.

At the top of the steps, he heads through another door, out onto an enclosed ledge usually reserved for people who shine the spotlights on whatever performers happen to be playing the Garden on a particular night. There are other spotlight positions, but those are actually inside the ceiling. Still, when he steps out onto the narrow walkway and takes a few strides to his right, Smith is about as high up as one can get.

The circus had arrived a few days earlier, and Smith's normal view of the ice is obscured by the huge rectangular frames from which trapeze artists will swing and sway. For the vista to clear, Smith must move farther to his right, up two small steps, to a countertop before which sits a bar stool.

"I'm just going to sit," Smith said, "and chew my fingernails."

He would have 10 tiny meals, then, as the exceptional event would unfold, five stories below him on a playing floor that is five floors above street level. And he would have the company of Roger Neilson, by now an assistant coach to Mike Keenan with the team that would represent Canada at the approaching World Championships. The team would be made up of players from non-playoff teams, and it was a decent bet one of these clubs might be making sizeable contributions of manpower.

Outside, scalpers knew this could be their last big payday of the season; this was as near an NHL playoff game as the Garden might come.

Inside, the fans watched the pre-game warmups and tried to forget about the three consecutive home losses the Rangers had suffered, the five defeats in the prior six Garden games, with the only victory coming against the just-awful Sharks. This was a one-game season, right here, right now, and they were ready as the players went through their paces.

The music was okay, but there was no menace to it — nothing to add some jolt to the pre-game spirit. It was upbeat, rather "PG" rated when something a little more "R" or "X" rated might have put more fizz in the soda. You wanted a little "Welcome to the Jungle," like at the Spectrum in Philadelphia, but what you ended up with was more like an anthem from a Disney park.

Welcome to the new Garden.

Messier got a hand as he skated off the ice with 1:25 left in the pregame. John McIntyre, Darren Turcotte, and Amonte were the last three Rangers left. Turcotte hit the crossbar with a shot, then hurled his stick into the crowd. Amonte was the last to leave.

It's 7:19 p.m.

Do you know where your courage is?

■■■

In the broadcast booth, Sam Rosen and John Davidson looked at the matchup of Messier and Pierre Turgeon up the middle, the matchup of Richter and Glenn Healy in goal. In Section 54, Stanley Jaffe took his position.

It is always fun to watch Jaffe before a game, although it is a bit easier to do it before a Knicks game, because he sits right on the court. Jaffe sits in the last seat of the celebrity row that virtually always includes another film maker, Spike Lee, and on any given night can feature Maury Povich and Connie Chung, or other athletes or actors — or, before they split, a couple that included one of each: John McEnroe and Tatum O'Neal. John F. Kennedy, Jr. is no stranger to the last seat at the other end.

Jaffe is a man in charge of a huge entertainment business, a man who likely would be an excellent poker player, because you cannot read his face. His moments of rage apparently are reserved for those close to him, as are his moments of great joy. But he gives little signs when he roots, and as singer John Amirante finishes the anthem this night, Jaffe punches both hands forward, a gesture of "We're gonna DO it" as the final notes of music fade away.

Every seat is full, every luxury suite is jammed as the rumble begins. These people don't care about the banners, don't notice the rink ads. Most of them don't know who Jaffe is or where he sits. And they probably don't give much thought to the players Ron Smith has on the ice:

The goalie, Richter, spent time in Binghamton, scraping the bugs off the windshield of his game. Zubov, one of the starting defensemen, was the guy Neil Smith had signed last summer almost as an afterthought. Cirella, the other defender, had been placed on irrevocable waivers but had gone unclaimed. Ed Olczyk had come over from Winnipeg not that many months earlier. Only Messier and Amonte qualified as full-season varsity.

The game was going to boil down, in part, to the Rangers' ability to control Turgeon, the 117-point scorer. Ron Smith wanted Messier matched on him, but knew Arbour would do all kinds of changing on the fly to get Turgeon out against someone else. In fact, when referee Bill McCreary dropped the opening faceoff, he dropped it between Messier and Benoit Hogue — Turgeon having been shifted to Hogue's left-wing position and then, within seconds, off the ice entirely in favor of Ray Ferraro. Forty-one seconds into the game, with no Turgeon for target practice, Messier thumped Hogue in the corner to the right of Islanders goalie Glenn Healy. Just a little attention-getter, a little something to show the captain was prepared to set a tone.

The Rangers wanted to bang this night, wanted to crank up the tempo and put a hard edge on the game. And they wanted to crunch Turgeon whenever possible. The Islanders didn't seem to care very much; they had dressed all the toughness they needed in Mick Vukota, Rich Pilon, plus defenseman Darius Kasparaitis — the man the Rangers love to punch. Islanders captain Patrick Flatley also takes no backward steps; he has been a respected Garden visitor since one of his bodychecks shattered Barry Beck's left shoulder in the 1984 playoffs.

Other matchups started to emerge. It seemed Ron Smith would try to get Lowe and Beukeboom out on defense for an element of physical presence against Turgeon, whose reputation was not one of exceptional hockey courage. Arbour seemed to want Pilon out against Gartner. Kasparaitis and the Rangers' pest-du-jour, Tikkanen, came together about 3:30 into the match — Kasparaitis flinging himself into the air in an attempt to hit Tikkanen, Tikkanen going back at the defenseman and drawing a penalty that gave the Rangers their first power play of the evening.

It would not succeed, of course, and the first period would become a season in microcosm. The Rangers would come up with some good, at times very good, minutes. But they would not play all 20 of a period. And they would not get the clutch goal they needed. So the Islanders just stayed patient. They knew every second they were not behind made it seem as though they were ahead; the longer the Rangers went without the lead, the crankier the fans would get and the more the Rangers would start to press. Eventually, if the first 75 games had been any indication, the Rangers would find a way to self-destruct.

They would do it by getting into penalty trouble late in the session. Gartner would slash Kasparaitis at 16:51 and Joe Cirella would cross-check Turgeon into the corner boards 1:08 later — leaving the Islanders two skaters to the good for 52 seconds.

It would take only half that time for Derek King to score. He accepted a Turgeon pass at the top of the slot, about 35 feet in front of the net, and wound up. King knew he would have to shoot high, that Kevin Lowe would dive out at the shot, because Kevin Lowe dives in front of every shot taken. Richter knew King would be shooting high, because if he shot low he would hit Lowe, which would be a dumb play.

The whole building knew King would have to shoot high. King shot high.

He rifled it under the crossbar for 1-0 Islanders.

Which meant trouble, deep trouble, for the Rangers — trouble that seemed to get deeper with 27.7 seconds remaining and time still ticking on Cirella's penalty. Steve Thomas carried to the top of the right-wing circle and Lowe, true to form, threw himself in front of the puck while Ray Ferraro and Beukeboom went to the net. This time Lowe blocked the shot, but Thomas regained control and threw the disc to Flatley in the high slot.

Flatley fired a 35-foot sizzler past the ever-present Beukeboom screen—and past Richter's right hand. It looked like the Islanders would be taking a 2-0 lead into the intermission.

Except for one thing.

Beukeboom had driven Ferraro into the crossbar while Turgeon was taking that shot. The post to Richter's right had been knocked off its peg. Properly, McCreary disallowed the goal.

It stayed 1-0.

For another 60 seconds.

The first and last five minutes of a period tell you a lot about a team's focus, and the final few minutes of the first period told you how close the Rangers were to losing theirs. They trailed by one — only because a disallowed goal prevented them from trailing by two. They had given the Islanders a two-man power play. They should have been thankful to get to the dressing room with a chance to regroup.

Instead, they came out for the first shift of the second period and watched the Islanders add to their lead.

You want to know about focus this night, you have to look to the Islanders' bench. They could have started feeling sorry for themselves after losing that goal, on the road, just before inter-mission. Instead, they came out harder.

Vladimir Malakhov came late into the play for a wrist shot that sailed wide of Richter from the top of the right-wing circle. The Ranger forwards — Messier, Olczyk, and Amonte — start running around, so the Islanders regain possession of the carom. Messier and Olczyk, at least, are in the same zone as the puck.

Amonte is out in the neutral zone on a mindless sprint to nowhere.

Malakhov, fed again, threads another wrist shot between the legs of the onrushing Olczyk while, at the same second, Zubov skates left-to-right through Richter's line of sight. Zubov provides a perfect field-of-vision screen — just enough to break Richter's focus as Malakhov's shot arrives. Richter moves late on the shot, which bounds off his blocking glove and into the air. As Richter regains focus, the puck floats behind him. His desperate dive knocks it off the goalpost and into the net.

Quickly, you check both goalposts. They both are in place. Anybody in the crease? Nope. This is a goal. It's 2-0 Islanders, 32 seconds into the period. There are nearly 40 minutes of regulation time remaining, but there is Ranger blood in the water.

The Islander sharks start a feeding frenzy.

Richter, left to face a two-on-one Islander break, stops King, then Travis Green at 3:08 of the period.

Twenty-five seconds later, Beukeboom takes a crosschecking penalty and the Islanders get their fourth power play — but not before Richter makes a reflex left kick on Brad Dalgarno off a puck that had bounced out from the endboards. The Islanders are confident, the Rangers tight. If it gets to 3-0 here, the game's over.

Richter gets his left skate on a Steve Thomas 15-foot one-timer from between the circles. Cirella fails to clear a puck, then blocks another Thomas shot into the seats.

The crowd is getting nasty now. Richter seems to be fighting this battle alone. The Islanders are starting to toy with their rivals. They have taken 14 of the game's past 17 shots.

Then, at 4:57, John McIntyre steals a puck and gives Messier a chance in front. But Messier, at a sharp angle to Healy's left, sends his usually-dependable backhand wide. Hope is beginning to wane. The Rangers need a spark.

Who provides it?

The always-surprising Kovalev.

Kovalev has a lot of weapons with which to intimidate a goalie. He has speed. He has slithery moves. He is a skater of exceptional strength and balance, which makes him a tremendous threat one-on-one.

Except this time, Kovalev is pure, straight-ahead powerpunk. Out with Kocur, his body guard, Kovalev drives to the net with the puck. Checked by defenseman Scott Lachance, Kovalev simply cannot stop in time to avoid running over Healy in the Islanders' net.

Healy goes down as though shot. First, he is no dummy; maybe he can steal a charging call from McCreary. Second, his goalie coach is Bill Smith, who perfected over-acting or over-reacting to even the most incidental contact with forwards.

The play boils down to which side you're on. From the Islanders' bench, it's a cheap shot. From the Rangers' bench, you're awake now, up, alert; to this point, Healy hardly has been rattled by any Ranger shots, so you might as well try to rattle him some other way.

The crowd, of course, loves it.

McCreary doesn't. He gives Kovalev two minutes for interference with the goalie and two minutes for roughing Lachance. Lachance is penalized for roughing Kovalev. In a side encounter, Kocur and Pilon get 10 minutes each for misconduct. But some credit should go to Pilon, who wrestled Kocur to the ice and unarguably prevented Kocur from doing what Kovalev ultimately did: knock over Healy.

All this happens with 5:21 left in the period. And while it gives the Islanders a power play and a chance to expand their lead, aggression penalties of that nature often are killed, because they energize a team. According to statistics kept by a Rangers superfan, Tracy Pincus, only 15% of the Rangers' aggression fouls led to power-play goals-against — while 54% of the so-called lazy penalties for restraining opponents (hooking, holding, holding the stick, interference) led to opposition goals.

True enough, the Rangers survived Kovalev's steamroll of Healy. Messier, in fact, hits the post with the rebound of a shot the Rangers get during the penalty.

And just 14 seconds after the penalty expires, Olczyk gets the Rangers on the board. Sergei Zubov drives into the play, draws the attention of three Islanders on the right wing and slides a pass in front to an unchecked Olczyk. Just Olczyk and Healy, outside the goalmouth; Olczyk goes to the backhand and hits the upper corner over Healy's left glove.

So it's a one-goal game with more than 23 minutes to play. The Rangers are reasonably sure Richter will keep giving them miracles; this second period was one of his best in the entire season. They have the crowd back. They have shaken the Islanders, even if they have been generally outpositioned and outplayed. They have gotten one huge break, thanks to the disallowed Flatley goal . . .

Then they get another with 1:37 left in the second when McCreary blows his whistle an instant before Green's third whack of a scramble slides under the left pad of a fallen Richter.

There is more Ranger pressure at the start of the third. The Rangers have been in desperate trouble for several weeks now, but this is one of the few times when they clearly are playing like a desperate team. They are bending the Islanders backward, waiting for them to buckle, when perhaps the biggest break of all pulls them even.

Lachance is canned for interference at 7:27, and at 8:26, Peter Andersson accepts a Messier pass at the center of the Islanders' zone. He winds up for a shot that glances off a body and bounds wildly to Healy's right, where the hulking Uwe Krupp is positioned.

At 6-foot-6, Krupp is the tallest player in the NHL. And while it may be a source of scientific wonder that giraffes can munch the tops of trees while standing on such tiny feet, it is a fact of life that towering humans require greater support.

Krupp's feet are huge.

Andersson's shot hits Krupp's left skate, then the right one.

The puck pinballs past a bewildered Healy at 8:26. The game is tied.

So now it's an 11:34 game, winner-take-fourth at the Garden, and the question is, which team has the jam? Which team WON'T make the game-turning mistake?

The answer isn't provided in regulation time, until both teams have wasted chances to win. Richter makes an exceptional spear of a Tom Kurvers shot from the left-wing circle with 3:48 left in the third period to save the Rangers' bacon. Then the Rangers' own power play saves the Islanders' bacon.

Given a four-on-three advantage with 1:43 left in regulation (Lachance held Tikkanen in front, then Tikkanen and Benoit Hogue went off for jawing at each other), here is the sequence of Ranger opportunities on the advantage:

— Andersson one-timer goes wide of the net.

— Zubov one-timer over the net.

— Gartner shoots wide.

Healy barely was bothered. He could have gone for a drink and watched the Rangers shoot wide all night.

So it goes to overtime. Five minutes or fewer. Winner-take-fourth. You may assume safely that Neil Smith has run out of fingernails.

Then it happens.

Messier has the puck in the Islanders' zone, along the left-wing boards, when he attempts a centering pass that is picked off by Travis Green. Green sends a soft pass to Brian Mullen at the Islanders' blue line and Mullen skates through the neutral zone against the retreat of Lowe and Beukeboom.

Mullen skims a soft dump-in straight at Richter, who sticks the puck to the corner at his right. Beukeboom gets to it there, but he is pursued by Brad Dalgarno, so he reverses the puck toward Lowe, behind the net.

That's trouble, because Lowe is sealed off and smothered by Mullen, pinned against the goal frame. The puck goes free for an instant, is picked up by Dalgarno for an instant at Richter's left, but then Beukeboom eliminates Dalgarno and order apparently is restored.

So Lowe takes the puck again, behind the net again. Despite pressure from Turgeon, he slides a pass to his right-wing boards, to Amonte.

Amonte, on his forehand, his backside against the Paine Webber ad, checks his passing options while under mild pressure from Mullen. Amonte sees Turcotte at the center of the blue line, sees Graves all the way across ice, near the left-wing boards.

Had he seen Malakhov, waiting to poach, like a free safety in football, Amonte obviously wouldn't have made the pass.

But you don't get a do-over.

Malakhov uses his huge stride and his huge reach to make a gamble of his own. If he misses the puck and the pass gets through, Graves and Turcotte are off to the races against Kasparaitis.

Malakhov doesn't miss.

In his positively brilliant book, *The Game*, Hall of Fame goaltender Ken Dryden made a positively brilliant point that was driven home to him during the Challenge Cup series between teams of NHL and Russian stars. It was played in 1979, at the Garden, the very same building where this was unfolding.

"I don't know when it happened. I don't know how. I don't know if I understand it the same way the Soviets understand it. I am convinced the Soviets fundamentally changed their approach to the game, that they understand finally that hockey is not a possession game, nor can it ever be," Dryden wrote. "The puck changes teams more than six times a minute, more than 120 times a period, more than 400 times a game, and little can be done to prevent it. Instead, hockey is a transition game: offense to defense, defense to offense, one team to another. Hundreds of tiny fragments of action, some leading somewhere, most going nowhere."

This one definitely leads somewhere.

Malakhov steals the puck, setting in motion the quick and lethal transition from defense to offense. He makes a backhand pass to Turgeon in the deep slot, and Turgeon shoots while Turcotte and Graves — outside the blue line by now — realize the turnover and begin making their transition from offense to defense.

Beukeboom charges toward Turgeon and drops to his knees, trying to make Turgeon rush the shot. It goes wide, but two things happen.

First, Amonte, trying to cover for his mistake, barges to the front of the net. In his eagerness, he knocks over the kneeling Beukeboom. As Beukeboom rolls onto his belly, he accidentally pins Amonte's stick. For a long moment, Amonte can't get it loose.

Second, Malakhov, a calm eye in this storm, grabs the Turgeon carom and backhands the puck around the boards from Richter's left.

It goes to Dalgarno, in the corner now to Richter's right. Beukeboom is out of the play now, Amonte can't get across to Turgeon, and Lowe, who had gone over to challenge Malakhov's pass, is just coming back to the goalmouth. Dalgarno gets his pass through and Turgeon whips the puck toward the net; he doesn't seem to get all of it, but he gets enough to roll it into the crease.

It hits Lowe's right skate, like a bank shot with a billiard ball in a pool tournament.

The only official shot of overtime goes in at 3:41.

There are shrieks at the Garden, whoops of Islander joy.

Upstairs, behind the Ed Giacomin banner, Neil Smith is paralyzed momentarily. He doesn't want to watch the people file out of the building. He isn't ready to head downstairs, to the fifth floor, to fifth place.

He sits on the two steps that lead up to his catbird seat. Buries his head in his hands.

Smith feels a hand on his shoulder.

It is Neilson, the man who coached the team to 50 victories the prior season, the man he fired January 4.

"Don't worry," Neilson said. "There's a long way to go yet."

CHAPTER 19

EVER DOWNWARD

WHEN TURGEON'S SHOT NESTLED in the netting, three pairs of eyes got very big. Tie Domi, Kris King, and Doug Weight, who started the season as teammates, were sitting in a Don Cherry's pub in Edmonton. Fate had brought them to this city on this night. The following evening, at Northlands Coliseum, they would be opponents — King and Domi playing for the Jets, Weight playing for the Oilers. But for now, they could sit together as friends, have a beverage or two and watch the men who had begun the season as their teammates.

"They went ahead, changed the coach and did everything they had to do, and they're still losing," Weight said after Turgeon's shot went in. "I have a feeling we'll see an awful active summer in New York if they don't make the playoffs."

Domi wasn't going to miss a chance to throw in his two Canadian cents' worth.

"Oh my God! They've got to clean house," he said. "They've got the highest payroll in the league. You win the Presidents' Trophy one year and you're not in the playoffs the next year, you know something's wrong.

"It shows it wasn't Roger Neilson (who was to blame) there," he added.

■■■

There were eight games remaining, but downstairs at the Garden, it was as though the Rangers' world had come to an end.

There stood Ron Smith, coach of a team with four losses in a four-game homestand, every game a must-win. There stood Ron Smith, coach of a fifth-place Rangers team, a man whose destiny may have been cemented by an own-zone giveaway.

Smith wore a gray suit, a white shirt, a tie with red and black brush marks. He said, "I'm trying to be as rational about it as I can possibly be."

There was no point to being rational.

"A cross-ice pass, in your own zone, with 1:25 left to go in overtime isn't my idea of a defensive breakdown. It's a lot worse than that, is what it is," Smith said. "That's just a blatant mistake."

You didn't have to tell Amonte.

"Definitely a low point for me," he admitted.

Three weeks before, the Rangers had been in second place. They were starting a stretch of eight games in which seven would be played at home; they would end up losing six, falling to fifth.

"There's only one state of mind you can have," Smith said, "and if you don't have it, you've got to create it: A determined, optimistic approach to winning eight out of eight."

Bear in mind, in their 105-point season, when they were good — when they won 28 games at home and when they had a healthy Brian Leetch — the best the Rangers could do was win seven out of seven. Now, here they were, scraping their butts near the bottom of the Patrick Division with Leetch recovering from ankle surgery. Who in the world could Smith have thought he was kidding?

"You really have to 'up' your level of play, and we just haven't," Richter said. "The longer we go without winning, the more we have to depend on other teams. We have to find ways to win. Good teams do that, and we haven't been able to."

Now, they had to go to Washington and win one in a row.

■ ■ ■

There was one way of telling how much farther the Rangers could fall in the Patrick Division: By looking at the standings, which showed the last-place Flyers on a hot streak and creeping dangerously near. There was no way of telling how much farther they might fall psychologically, however, and that was true not only of the players but of management.

A short Jaffe story is worth telling here, then:

The Islander game was Friday night, the Capitals game was Sunday afternoon, which left Saturday evening free. Jaffe invited Neil and Katia to spend it in his suburban home. They had dinner, they watched a movie — by Paramount? — in Jaffe's screening room.

This comes on the heels of arguably the worst loss in a season of unrelenting upset. Moreover, here is the Garden, facing the prospective loss of millions in playoff revenue if the Rangers don't qualify for the tournament. If anything, this would seem a time when the Jaffe-Smith relationship might cool. Rather than turn his back on Smith, however, Jaffe extends a supporting hand — seemingly confirming the vote of confidence Gutkowski had issued mere days before.

His spirits boosted, Smith was a touch more spry at the Capital Centre the next day. But before the game, he had to clear up some controversy regarding an earlier comment he had made about Mike Keenan.

Given Ron Smith's designation as interim coach, the Ranger coaching job had become a topic of general discussion earlier in the week and Neil Smith had said, "I don't agree the Rangers need a dictator for a coach."

In fact, that was exactly what they needed, but that's another story.

The 'dictator' comment was relayed to Keenan, who got his nose a little out of joint.

"That's a disrespectful comment by Neil," Keenan said, "in light of the successes we've had."

So Smith had to do some backtracking, and he did it in the Cap Centre media room.

The room in that arena is divided into two parts. Just inside the front door there is a hospitality area which includes a bunch of two- and four-person tables, a cafeteria-style kitchen, a soda dispenser, coffee urn and the like. On the far side of the wall is the work room, and it was in that room that Smith made his clarification.

"I was not directly speaking about Mike Keenan, but in general terms," he said. "I was asked about the type of coach I felt the club might need — whether it would be a disciplinarian or an ass-kicking coach. I replied, I don't think the team necessarily needed a dictator. There was no intention on my part to link that

word, 'dictator,' to any particular person, and I wanted to clear
that up."

But do you consider Keenan a dictator?

"I consider him a hockey coach," Smith replied. "I have no
opinion otherwise.

"Once we get into the process of looking at the coaching, I
think anybody who is not employed and has the credentials that
Mike Keenan has would certainly be considered."

■■■

Entering the contest, there were a few things to consider.

First was, after losing six of their past seven games at home,
the Rangers almost enjoyed a "road-ice advantage." It almost
was good to get away from the pressure at the Garden, the desire
to assuage the disappointment of the fans the Rangers had let
down so many times. The team reached Washington with a 5-2-
1 mark its past eight on foreign ice.

Second was, the utterly unpredictable Capitals were having
a pretty rotten time of their own against Patrick Division teams.
The Rangers arrived at Capital Centre with a repugnant 11-15-3
record in sectional games, but the Capitals' otherwise gaudy
features bore a giant carbuncle of an 11-18-2 Patrick ledger. The
only team in the whole conference with fewer divisional wins
than these two clubs were Ottawa's slapstick Senators, who had
staggered to 4-27-1 in Adams Division contests.

Moreover, Washington entered the match having lost seven
of eight home games against divisional rivals. Here it was, April
4, and the Capitals hadn't beaten a Patrick foe at home since New
Year's Day.

As odd, at 20-12-6, the Capitals were by no means a bad
team at home; but they were no better, victory-wise, than the
Rangers, who had slumped to 20-14-5 at the Garden.

Nonetheless, the Capitals were coming off a 4-0 conquest of
Montreal. The Rangers, meanwhile, were reeling from the devastating overtime defeat and their world was utterly upside down.

Not even a year earlier, the Rangers had been on top of the
hockey world, employers of the league's most valuable player, its
top defensemen and, by acclamation, at least, one of its top coaches.

Now, they were fifth and fading. Since the 1974-75 season,
when the NHL went to its four-division format, no team had

failed to make the playoffs the season after compiling the league's top overall record. Yet here were the Rangers, inching nearer and nearer the wrong kind of history with each additional loss.

There was no way of knowing if the plunge ever would end, if the parachute ever would open. They had gone through so many goalies, so many defensemen, so many combinations, just trying to stop the freefall. And nothing had worked.

So on the way to Washington for the next game, they relaxed. They couldn't have gotten much tighter, anyway.

"We had a couple of laughs on the bus and on the plane," said Messier, who, for emphasis, wore a necktie with smiling faces on it.

"Last night, a few of us went to a little steakhouse," Vanbiesbrouck disclosed, "and we said, 'If we play good hockey, we can still do this thing.'"

"We've got to play with emotion, grittiness and heart," Joe Kocur said. "We've got to play like there's no tomorrow."

No kidding. That had been the case for weeks. Something just happened to get the message through to them for this one angry afternoon.

Graves gave the Rangers the lead when his wheeling shot glanced into the net off Capitals defenseman Shawn Anderson. Since two pivotal goals had gone in off defensemen during the Islander game, it seemed this contest would provide more of the same.

That would prove true. Beukeboom, whose first goal of the season had gone into the New Jersey net off Alexander Semak in February, later would bank his second of the year off Todd Krygier.

But there also was a vital difference between the Islander game and this one.

The Rangers won.

They played hard hockey, in-your-face hockey. They set the terms and the tone and it worked very well.

Just five seconds after giving the Rangers the lead, Graves had a fight with Keith Jones. Once order was restored, Ron Smith pressed the attack; he sent out Beukeboom and the K.O. twins — Kocur and Kovalev.

Kovalev, enjoying his new role as the team's unlikeliest muscle guy, elbowed Alan May and May went after Kovalev, setting off a scrum that led to a misconduct penalty for Beukeboom but left the clubs at four skaters per side. The Rangers may not have done much right all year, but one situation they handled well was four-on-four, and it worked again at 11:21 when Gartner one-timed a Messier pass into the net off the equipment of goalie Don Beaupre. It was the 18th such goal of the Rangers' season; opponents had scored just seven times under those conditions.

It was 2-0 now and the Capitals were getting embarrassed in their own rink — to the degree that coach Terry Murray used his timeout with seven minutes left in the first period. He wanted to know exactly when his team might show some interest in reporting to work.

Now, Ron Smith floored his gas pedal.

At 13:54, Cirella picked a fight with Dale Hunter, and the Rangers again seemed to respond. Olczyk slam-dunked a Messier pass from behind the net at 14:57, his ninth goal in 12 games. It was 3-0, and while this may have been a season of blown Ranger leads, there would be no such event this day.

And good gracious, if Jeff Beukeboom outscores the entire high-powered Washington defense, you better not waste it.

Kevin Lowe picked up the puck at the final buzzer and handed it to Vanbiesbrouck, a souvenir of the 4-0 triumph. As he came off the ice, Messier whooped with joy. Olczyk pumped his fist once. Richter smiled.

"I'm just looking at the standings closely, with some optimism, for the first time in a while," Ron Smith said.

He had good reason. In spite of everything — all the mishaps, all the injuries, all the blown leads and blown points and general blunders, in spite of the schedule still being against them — the Rangers flew back to New York knowing that if they won the next night, at the Garden against Hartford, they would be back in fourth place at least temporarily. And that would set up a mere apocalypse of a game in New Jersey two nights later.

"Strange things happen in the world of sports," Messier said. "That's what we've been trying to say all along — don't get caught up in the standings. Don't get caught up in the big picture of eight games left and wherever you are — we're in fifth place, we're here, we're there, this team is playing that team. We said, 'Let's break it down to games and periods and shifts, and then, little by little, you just whittle away.'"

This was not whittling. This day, the Rangers swung their axes.

"We had everything to lose, and it showed in our play," Kocur said. "We were aggressive, determined and desperate. If you back a rat into a corner, he'll fight his way out."

That's one way of putting it.

"We've played a lot of games trying to score, and it didn't work out," Kocur said. "We changed it up and played a more aggressive, defensive game.

"We need (seven more) games just like that — no backing away, in-your-face hockey."

Suffice it to say, few teams have been as overjoyed to be one point out of fourth place.

"Our task now," Ron Smith said, looking ahead to the Hartford game, "is to absolutely play life-and-death again."

■■■

It turned out to be death.

Painful. Agonizing. Full-out, unabridged suffering. Severed head, fall-off-a-cliff awful, a game you could see and still not believe.

Here's Hartford, eliminated from playoff contention weeks earlier, the last "weak" team on the Rangers' schedule. Here's Hartford, coming to the Garden with 12 road victories all year. Here's Hartford, with 256 goals in 77 games, or 3.32 per contest, to be precise. Here's Hartford, starting its third-string goalie, Mario Gosselin, with a fourth-stringer, Mike Lenarduzzi, on the bench as backup because Sean Burke (back) and Frank Pietrangelo (ribs) were injured.

Here's Hartford, leaving the Garden with a 5-4 victory. After scoring three third-period goals. To take a game the Rangers led 4-2 with 14:38 remaining. To take the two points the Rangers needed so desperately.

It looked like the Rangers were caught in that classic No Man's Land, coming down from a divisional victory the day before, looking ahead to the divisional showdown with New Jersey, and completely ignoring what they may have imagined to be the formality of a victory over Hartford.

It looked like the other Garden giveaways, like all the other times they had failed to finish the job.

It made you wonder: Aside from their mental shape, what kind of PHYSICAL condition were these people in if their tanks went empty after 45 or 50 minutes most nights?

"What you saw tonight has been going on the whole season," Ron Smith said. "This seems to be quite a typical performance and result, the kind that caused the team to get into this jackpot in the first place."

So many times in the season, there were nights when the offense was there but the defense failed. There were times the opposite occurred. This time, while there were any number of mistakes in front of him — another Kevin Lowe dive led to another screen that led to another opposition goal — Vanbiesbrouck's goaltending was suspect. Giveaways by Kovalev turned into the goals by Geoff Sanderson and Michael Nylander that tied the game. Sanderson's was his second of the game and it came while the Whalers were killing a penalty.

Ugh.

Sanderson's was a 40-footer. Nylander's came from 50.

Ugh squared.

"It's hard to believe this is the same team from one night to the next," Gartner said. "It seems this kind of thing has happened several times this year."

Several times in the past few weeks, is more like it. They had the Philadelphia game. They had the Edmonton game, too. They had this one. They didn't finish the job. They got goals from the goal-scorers —Graves, Kovalev, Amonte, and Messier. They got seven shots from Gartner, four of them in the third period as the Rangers tried to extend the 4-2 lead Messier's goal provided.

Instead, they ended up blowing a two-goal lead for the ninth time of the season. Two of those games ended in ties, the other seven in losses, this one coming unglued for good when Pat Verbeek beat Vanbiesbrouck from the right-wing circle with 2:17 left.

The noise you heard at the Garden was the dying gasp of the Rangers' playoff hopes. Unless you were closer to the coaches' office.

Because Neil Smith came down from his perch after the game. He went into the coaches' office. And he wrecked the place.

Vanbiesbrouck, yesterday's hero, was this evening's goat. He had taken a delay-of-game penalty for clearing the puck over the glass just a few minutes into Sunday's game at Washington, but the Rangers had survived the power play and had gone on to win. In this game, Vanbiesbrouck put his team short twice by flipping the puck over the glass, and his play, in general, was just good enough to lose.

To lose his job. To end his Ranger career. Quite a turn-around in 30-some hours.

Then again, this was a season for turnarounds, wasn't it?

Verbeek's shot was a relatively routine one. Sometimes goalies try to make a simple save into a tough play, and Vanbiesbrouck probably would have had the shot in his hip pocket if he simply had stood up. Vanbiesbrouck, instead, got caught halfway — on his way down to his knees, probably his most glaring weakness. When he dropped, Vanbiesbrouck lifted the blade of his stick off the ice. Naturally, the puck slid straight through that hole. It was an awful goal you might live with in November or January. In April, it buys you a bullet. It does so especially when you also lost two-goal home leads to two other non-playoff teams: Edmonton and Philadelphia.

"Do you know what the chances of winning are when you carry a lead into the third period?" Neil Smith asked.

Somebody said about 75 percent.

"And do you know what they are when you carry a two-goal lead into the third?" he asked.

Better, somebody said.

"And do you know what they are when you have a two-goal lead going into the third — and you're at home?"

Really, really good. Right?

"We've lost three games like that in the last two weeks," Smith said.

Vanbiesbrouck was the goalie of decision in each.

Next game, Corey Hirsch was back from Binghamton and back in goal.

■ ■ ■

Ron Smith looked dark and tired, bleak as his team's chances, the next day at Rye.

"Adam Graves got hit (in the leg) with a pass during a drill today," Smith said, smiling thinly. "I went by and said, 'I assume it's broken.' He said, 'No, no.'"

It would not have been shocking. Everything else had gone wrong, just about everyone else had been injured or slumping at one point or other, why not Graves?

"We're getting to be like 'Rocky,'" Smith said. "We're on the canvas, we're up, we're on the canvas, we're up."

The coach elected to remain positive.

"What choice have you?" he asked. "You can expend more energy feeling sorry for yourself than trying to be upbeat."

There is a huge difference, way more than two letters, between being beat and being upbeat. Ron Smith had tried just about everything. Neil Smith had tried just about everything. Nothing had worked outside of the hard-edged, punch-face approach they had applied in Washington, yet, shockingly, they had backed off that tactic and had returned to relatively polite hockey against Hartford.

This is no endorsement of goon hockey, but if you finally stumble on something that works, why abandon it barely a day later when you're desperate to start a hot streak? This game against Hartford was no different from the season's first meeting with Hartford.

Remember the home opener against the Whalers, when the Rangers were coming off a divisional game and looking ahead to another — against New Jersey, ironically? Remember when Burke and Richter had scrapped? When artificial emotion was a mandate? When Kocur stepped up for Kovalev after Kovalev's first goal? Then look at the kinds of penalties the Rangers took against Hartford in this one: interference, delay of game, holding, delay of game.

Joby Messier took a roughing penalty in the first period, Esa Tikkanen took one in the third. That was it.

How sweet.

"There's no coaches' manual for this type of situation," Ron Smith said.

All he needed was a tape of Sunday's game and a copy of the standings. But what materialized was the fuzzy-cheeked Hirsch.

"We don't have any more rabbits in our hat," Neil Smith said.

Aside from his brief tenure with the parent club, Hirsch had been cruising along with the AHL powerhouse in Binghamton. He had built a 35-4-5 record, a 2.79 goals-against average, a .905 save percentage. The previous must-win contest in his career, arguably, had come the prior May, for Kamloops against Sault Ste. Marie in the Memorial Cup tournament that determines the champion of Canadian major junior hockey.

This assignment was just a bit different.

"They have to win. They have to do anything to win,"

Hirsch said. "I'm just going with an open mind. This (a chance to play in the NHL) is what I've been waiting for since I was about six years old."

It was utterly amazing.

Here were the Rangers, paying Vanbiesbrouck $1,135,000 and Richter $900,000 to win hockey games. Yet they were placing their destiny in the hands of a 20-year-old, two-game NHL veteran on a two-way contract that paid him $33,000 at the minor-league level and $170,000 (pro-rated, of course on the basis of a 192-day season) at the NHL level. You could have piled Richter's and Vanbiesbrouck's wallets in front of the net in New Jersey and stood more of a fighting chance.

In defense of the decision, Richter had made some exceptional stops in the Islander game, had kept his team in a match that easily could have been a blowout. But he had not won.

Vanbiesbrouck had pitched a shutout at Washington. How do you NOT start him against Hartford?

Nonetheless, how do you not go back to Richter at New Jersey — even if he had not faced them since the playoffs?

"All I can tell you is what I've surmised: Having a two-goalie system is not as good a situation as having one guy who you give the job to, and maybe you beat him up a little bit, but you come back to him," Ron Smith said. "I would say that both players have had their chance to grab it (the No. 1 job) and carry it on and they clearly have not been able to do it. They just haven't done it."

If these experienced players hadn't 'done it' how could anyone have imagined Hirsch would, under this kind of pressure?

"Sometimes, logic has no place in your mind," Ron Smith said. "It (your thought process) becomes one of desperate measures for desperate times. Any move we make right now would be made without concern for (a young player's) development or (veterans') feelings. We're all big boys. We can take it."

Vanbiesbrouck took it.

"I'm all for it," he said. "I want it to work. That's the bottom line. It's a time to support each other, not be discontent."

Richter took it.

"I have great respect for Corey and his ability," he said. "I have great respect for my own ability, too."

Hirsch got routed the next night.

■■■

It boiled down to two bad stretches in one bad period. The Rangers took their customary two-goal lead on first-period tallies by Tikkanen and Amonte. Tikkanen drove a 15-footer past Chris Terreri's left kick on the Rangers' first shot of the game, at 4:04. And at 15:36, the instant a penalty expired to Bernie Nicholls for interfering with Hirsch, Amonte chopped a Beukeboom rebound in from the doorstep to cap a stretch in which the Rangers outshot the Devils, 13-1.

The goals had come at significant times: In the first five minutes and the last five minutes of a period. Those are the junctures of a session most stressed by Devils coach Herb Brooks, but this was one period in which New Jersey lost some focus.

And there was one juncture in the middle of the period when the Rangers should have enlarged the lead and didn't: Tikkanen had a clean breakaway with a Nemchinov pass 11 minutes into the contest, and Terreri, flat on the ice, got his blocking glove on Tikkanen's shot. Just over a minute later, Terreri made a left-leg stop on a Messier bomb from left wing. It should have been 4-0, which would have been a tougher lead to lose; still, up 2-0 after a period on the road, the Rangers had to feel there was hope. All they had to do was keep up the good work.

Which they did. For 23 seconds of the second period.

The trouble started when Cirella was beaten to a Scott Stevens dump-in by the Devils' Valeri Zelepukin. Cirella had a step on the puck, but for some reason let Zelepukin get there first. The Russian zipped a pass to Alexander Semak in the right-wing circle and Semak's quick shot dropped just a bit and banked into the net off Hirsch's right arm.

It was a bad goal against Hirsch, but the youngster was guilty with an explanation. This was his first time in the building, and his first time at that end of the ice. The pre-game warmup and the first period had been spent at the other end, and sometimes the shooting angles change from one end to the other. Sometimes the lights are a touch brighter at one end than the other.

That doesn't absolve Hirsch of blame on the play. He was a little deep and a little slow, let the shot play him instead of playing it aggressively. Again, though, this was not a pace to which he was accustomed. The American League is good hockey, but it's nowhere near NHL speed. The skaters are faster, they release their shots quicker, and they are much more accurate with those shots. That's why they're in the NHL. The same play could have happened in an AHL game, Hirsch could have played it the same way and made the save, but NHL shooters can make the net as big as a soccer goal.

And they don't ask, "Are you ready yet?"

You better BE ready, at all times. For a puck from anyplace. Hirsch wasn't.

"Usually, I like to go off by myself into another room between periods, think about the last period, what I did wrong and what I did right," Hirsch said, "but after the first period, I felt a little too good about myself," the goalie said. "It was like, 'Wow! I'm winning this game 2-0, things are going well,' and I didn't maintain the focus I wanted to keep."

Anyway, Cirella should have won the race to the puck.

The period, and the game, were full of should-haves for the Rangers. Zubov got trapped on a two-on-one Devils break at 3:13, and Semak skated around the prone Cirella to feed Zelepukin for the tying slamdunk.

Ten seconds later, Tikkanen interfered with John MacLean, and it took just over a minute for the Devils to take the lead. Beukeboom overplayed himself into the corner, leaving room for Stevens and Stephane Richer in front of Hirsch. Cirella covered as much ground as he could, but did not block the Stevens pass that Richer slammed in off Hirsch's toe at 4:34 for the third goal on four Devils shots.

Zelepukin's one-timer from 25 feet — a little on the soft side but again, a quick release — finished things at 16:59. As before, the first and last five minutes told the tale, and this time it was a sad one for the Rangers. The bottom line was the saves Terreri made and the ones Hirsch didn't.

"I couldn't blame him on any of the goals," Ron Smith said. "We'd have loved to have had him be miraculous and stop all four."

It didn't happen.

"I learned a lot," Hirsch said, "and the biggest thing is, to be ready at all times — even when the play is in the other end, because they bring the puck up so fast.

"I have to be a little smarter reading plays and thinking what guys are going to do," he added, "and I have to play a lot more aggressive.

"And after a goal goes in, I have to let it go (mentally)," Hirsch said. "All the goals I've given up in the NHL have been scored in bunches. I've got to learn to let it go, and as soon as the puck drops, get ready for the next shot.

"Live and learn," he said. "That's my theory. If I'm going to play in the NHL, I'm going to have to get used to situations like this," the goalie said. "We had a good first period, but I didn't play for five minutes in the second and it cost me. I can get away with it, maybe, in the minors . . . but not up here. As soon as they know you've let your guard down for a second, they jump all over it. That's professional sports."

■■■

Words were losing their meaning now.

"We've tried everything, and we're going to continue to try everything," Gartner said. "You can say it's hard to believe. You can say it's a nightmare. It's whatever. We are where we are."

Gartner was in the dressing room, ready for the long walk to the bus. Neil Smith was in the hallway.

"I've seen this so much in the last few weeks," the team president said. "It's like a never-ending tape that goes on and on, and I keep watching it. It's a recurring nightmare.

"It's tough to take, but we'll try to get through somehow," he added. "There's still some life in the old body."

Not much, somebody said.

"No," Smith replied.

And now, the last-place Flyers were only six points behind.

CHAPTER 20

ROCK BOTTOM

YOU KEPT ASSUMING it couldn't get any worse, that it had to get better, but it kept getting worse. This collapse had crossed the border from mere calamity to utter disaster.

There were just five games to go, now, and all those tiebreakers not already lost were slipping away. If teams finish even in points, the first tiebreaker is victories and the next is record in the season series — discarding the first home game of the team with the greater number of home games. The next tiebreaker was goals differential, the number of goals surrendered subtracted from the number of goals scored.

"Maybe," Terreri mused, "we've pushed them far enough that they can't come back."

They were three points behind the Islanders, who needed seven points over their concluding six games to clinch a spot. By winning, the Devils reduced their playoff Magic Number to five points. The best the Rangers could do was 89 points and 39 victories, but this victory was the 39th for the Devils, and the Islanders already had 38.

And now, the Rangers could conclude their five-game week with a home-and-home series against the Pittsburgh Penguins, who would come to the Garden two nights later with nothing better to do than go after an NHL-record 16th consecutive victory.

■■■

It was sad. Sad enough to be almost funny. Because the Rangers were a joke. Pittsburgh won, 10-4. Ranger checking limited Mario Lemieux to five goals against two goalies, Hirsch for two periods, then Richter. Tikkanen was minus-five.

It was 3-3 after 28 minutes, believe it or not. But then the Rangers got a five-minute power play, and it killed them.

You couldn't help but think back to that five-minute power play they had in Pittsburgh in the playoffs. Could it only have been a year ago?

There was one shot during the entire advantage this night. Lemieux took it. And scored, naturally.

It was 5-3 after two periods, which is when the Rangers left. They quit on their fans, their interim coach, their goalies, and, of course, themselves.

"I was trying to think of another time in my athletic experience when I've been more embarrassed about a team's performance," Ron Smith said. "I couldn't.

"I'm sure there was SOME effort, but from the neck down, only," he added. "From the neck up, we were bad, bad, bad. I would never accuse a team of quitting, but mentally, every bad habit anyone ever had surfaced in a short span."

So the Rangers lost their sixth straight at home, seventh in their past eight.

The mathematics were getting easier and easier to compute, the chances were spinning away from slim and heading directly toward none. Yet you could walk into Ron Smith's office the next morning and the first thing to catch your eye would be the paperback on the top of a waist-high book case.

The title?

Being Positive: How to Start Making Life Say Yes to You.

■■■

They lost again in Pittsburgh the next night, but not before Neil Smith sat in the lobby of the Hilton and made clear his feelings.

"I've already been angry this season," the Rangers' president said. "I was very angry, very angry — FURIOUS — when I had to let Roger Neilson go. I'm past anger now. The minute this season ends, the scaffold's going up."

You see scaffolds around construction sites and around hangings. It seemed there might be some of each.

"It's no secret what this organization expects, and obviously, we didn't perform up to our expectations," he said. "Therefore, there will be the appropriate adjustments and changes so we can live up to those expectations."

Another day, Smith would say, "Excuses are unacceptable. I hate excuses. It burns me up to have this quality of a team and not be in it."

It puzzled some people, pleased some others.

"I'm surprised they're not in the playoffs," the Penguins' Kevin Stevens said. "I think everyone in hockey is surprised they're not in the playoffs."

Not everybody.

The Islanders were preparing for a salary arbitration hearing with right wing Mick Vukota, and wanted to compare him to Vancouver wing Gino Odjick in terms of minutes played. Canucks assistant coach Ron Wilson compiled Odjick's figures, and added a brief hand-written message to Darcy Regier, the Islanders' assistant director of hockey operations.

In part, the message read, "Good luck driving the nail in the Rangers' coffin."

Which didn't make much of a positive impression when it showed up, by accident, on the RANGERS' fax machine.

■■■

Another ignominy awaited. You could see it coming a mile off and know what it would be. Around the corner was a Battle for Fifth Place. With the Flyers. And Eric Lindros.

Of course they lost it. What did you expect? They were a disaster. They didn't even score. They lost, 1-0, and mathematically were eliminated from the playoffs by a Flyers team that would win its sixth straight — a team that would use the victory to pull into a tie for fifth with their victims.

In the Flyers' quarters, Lindros critiqued the Rangers' showing.

"At the start of this year, everybody looked at them and Pittsburgh to be the (Stanley Cup) contenders," he said. "It seemed like there was no significance out there from their side. I've seen that team play a whole lot better.

"That's a troubled group, down there."

With his chin, Lindros motioned down the hall, toward the Rangers' dressing room. Outside it, Ron Smith was confirming Lindros' suspicions.

"It boiled down, to me, to two problems basically resurfacing," Ron Smith said after his record dropped to 15-20-7. "(One was) the inability to really play a good defensive game — which was the problem in the first half, clearly, and which we thought we got under control, but which really resurfaced at crunch time, at every position.

"The second problem, quite frankly, I don't think the turmoil in the dressing room ever totally disappeared," Smith added. "There were a lot of feelings left over from what happened (the coaching change), and it's difficult to erase that. From a coach's point of view, it's very difficult to erase, and from the inside, it's tough as well.

"There's a lot of currents flowing in the dressing room. You have to say that," the coach disclosed. "I have no complaints about our players dealing with me (but) I have to assume there were a lot of currents floating around there that made it difficult for the team to really get its act together as a team. That's always magnified, certainly, by injuries. Winning cures a lot of ills, but there's no question it (injuries) was a factor.

"I think it affects everybody. I don't care if you've played in the league for 15 years, or you're a first-year player. When things are going on, it's going to affect you. Some people become more determined, some people are confused, some people are bitter, some people are angry. There's a lot of emotions that come up."

And they got in the way of the emotions needed for productive play.

"I never in my life, in any sport, went through a game feeling more sick," Smith said. "Whatever sport it is, at any level, it's a sick feeling (to face being out of the playoffs).

"At times we had some spunk and at times we didn't," he said. "A lot of things happened — breakdowns, and reflected how the team has performed all season.

"If you're a good team, you should never, ever, put the game up for grabs," Smith said. "And our team, too often, had the same problems night after night."

Nobody knew that better than Neilson, who watched the game from the press box. He knew the Flyers would be missing the playoffs, and had chosen this night to notify the five players he and Keenan had chosen for the team. After the game, Neilson spent a VERY long time in the Rangers' coaching office, speaking with Neil Smith — the Rangers' bus long since having left for New York.

"People come up to me and say, 'I guess you're really smiling, eh?' and that isn't the case at all," Neilson had said before the game, addressing the Rangers' plight. "I must admit I wasn't hoping they'd win every game after I got fired, but seeing the way it's been going lately is really depressing. I feel really bad. When you're with a team for 3 1/2 years and see the bottom fall out, it's really depressing. Nobody likes to see that.

"It looks like it's been one of those years for the Rangers, where whatever could go wrong, did," Neilson said.

That was one way of putting it, and probably, in its simplicity, it came closest to telling the story. The players and staff worked hard to come up with something better, something more profound. It was as though a simple answer wasn't satisfactory — that because of the money involved and the profile of the team involved and the agony of the fans involved, there had to be some type of paralysis by analysis so this collapse could be understood, at last, and never, ever repeated.

The next morning at Rye, the season was referred to in past tense, which was appropriate. Just as Neil Smith was past anger, the players were past being tense after so many months under the stress of simply trying to survive. Several sat at their lockers and tried to make sense of it all.

A tour of the room was a journey through the world headquarters of misery, starting just inside the blue doorway near which Tie Domi used to sit. Looking down that row, from Domi's old spot — vacant now — there were seven compartments, each of which had a story to tell.

James Patrick's stall was idle, as well. Back surgery had finished him for the year. Gartner's spot was next, then Graves'. Then came Leetch and Kocur and Wells and Amonte, then an unoccupied spot. Across a shorter row on the far wall were Nemchinov, Olczyk, Richter and Vanbiesbrouck, the goalies getting broader compartments in deference to the bulkier gear they wear.

To their right, as the goalies sat in their nooks, was a nine-player row: Andersson, Hartman, Cirella, McIntyre, Lowe, Erixon, Mark Messier, Turcotte, Zubov. Then, completing the rectangle that leads back to the doorway, Kovalev, Broten, Joby Messier, Bourque, Tikkanen, Beukeboom.

They were men of different sizes and shapes, backgrounds and religions, skills and weaknesses, positions and ages, brought to this room under this roof at Rye for the purpose of winning games and championships for the New York Rangers hockey team. The common sweater and the common environment are supposed to create a common spirit and a focus, but that did not happen in a way that fostered commonality of heart and soul and commitment and channeled it toward productivity.

"I don't dispute the fact that we did have a lack of chemistry," Gartner said. "We had it at times, we fought hard for it at times, but were unable to maintain it.

"I never felt there was any division on our hockey team at all," he added. "I know that's what people are trying to portray, but it's simply not true. I can't say it any clearer or simpler than that, from my perspective.

"But yes, there was turmoil. I think those are different things," he said. "Division is different groups of players, going their own ways and not getting along, and that just wasn't the case with our hockey team. Turmoil is the problems that were created by the way we were playing, that precipitated Roger getting fired, the problems we had after that, the high expectations that everyone had for us and that we had for ourselves. We were fighting against that the entire year.

"We always said we felt we were a great hockey team, but the fact of the matter for this year is, we were not. Although we didn't think we were overestimating ourselves, we obviously did, because we're in the position we're in right now," Gartner said.

"One of the reasons why we got into trouble in the middle part of the season was, we were not playing, as a team, the way we were supposed to be playing. I really blame us as a team. I don't think we can really blame anybody. We can't point the finger at anybody but ourselves. I don't think Roger was the majority of the problem, I don't think Ron Smith was. The players accept the majority, if not all, the responsibility for what happened this year.

"Certainly, without a Brian Leetch, it's going to affect your team. But I don't want that to appear as an excuse, because I don't think it is. And I don't really believe in excuses at all. It's just a fact, rather than an excuse."

Gartner dismissed any notion that the mid-year transition from Neilson's methods to Ron Smith's had anything to do with anything.

"There's no question Ron wanted to play a more aggressive game, but those are minor changes that have to be made. You talk about that (style of play) being a major adjustment, it really isn't. Everybody's played different systems, and all a system is organized hard work. No matter what system you put in, it's not difficult to do; it's strictly execution. It should be a very short time period of adjustment," Gartner said. "I would certainly hope the players were trying to play the same system the coach put in. It doesn't matter what coach you have; if all the players are not playing the same system, it's not working.

"We didn't execute for Roger OR Ron, as a team. It's a very sad statement to have to make, but it's true," he said. "As a professional player, you have to realize there is someone in control and we, as a team, have to go out and perform for that individual. And when we don't, we have no one to blame but ourselves. There are no excuses, no fingers to be pointed, other than to point them directly at ourselves. We're the players who go out on the ice to play and we're responsible for what happened. You can look yourself in the mirror and say you tried; there are some guys, I think, who can say they legitimately tried. But we, as a hockey team — I'm talking of a collective body — obviously, we can't say that we did our best."

Obviously you can't, when you finish sixth for the first time since that glorious 18-41-11 season in 1965-66. But that season was different from its three predecessors to only a slight extent: The Rangers had finished fifth those preceding seasons, the fall to last in the league was far gentler than this one, which left broken glass and twisted metal everywhere.

"This is the first time, in junior hockey, in minor hockey, EVER, that I've missed the playoffs," Lowe said. "It gives you an empty feeling, the feeling of having failed.

"You make the playoffs, go out and battle and whatever happens, happens. There's some sort of accomplishment," he said. "But with this, there's very little sense of accomplishment. It's very strange.

"Now that I've actually experienced the feeling firsthand, I probably know, subconsciously, why I never experienced it before. It's pretty shitty. You feel sick," the defenseman added.

"When you win it all, you don't need to say it to anyone, but you kind of have this feeling in your mind, 'Hey — No one can say anything bad about you or the hockey team. No one. Because you're the best.' And that's a very satisfying feeling. It's a huge accomplishment," Lowe said. "This is the exact opposite. You know in your own mind that how things are perceived by others isn't necessarily true. But you've got to suck it up. They, basically, have a right to say anything they want.

"I think the effort was here all year. That's what's sort of mind-boggling. Sometimes you look at baseball players and go, 'They're lazy lugs. They're not doing anything.' But I'm a pretty good reader of character, you know? And I feel everyone was doing their best to right the ship. We unfortunately got in a downward spiral 13-14 games ago, and never were able to right the ship — whether we were understaffed or we panicked or whatever, I don't know."

Teams with character don't panic. They right themselves before downward spirals reach 13 or 14 games. They find a way to dig deeper and get the job done. This team supposedly was stacked with 'character' players, brought to New York for their experience, their tenure in winning environments. All you hear about the Rangers is character, character, character.

Where the hell was it while the ship was sinking?

"Maybe one way of looking at it," Lowe replied, "is if we didn't have the character players we have, it might have gotten worse, sooner. Who's to say?"

It was bad enough that it got worse, irretrievably worse, when it did. The rest of the division simply sat around and waited for the Rangers to beat them, to catch them, to take a playoff spot from somebody. All it might have taken was a two-game winning streak.

To save you from having to look it up, the Rangers' final two-game winning streak of the season came in the games of March 19 and 22. They defeated San Jose and Ottawa, who combined to win 21 times in 1992-93.

"When I look at the whole situation, it just seems like we let a few games go, then we let it snowball, and we were in a division where you can't take a night off," Graves said. "We lost a lot of games late. We lost a lot of games to teams, no offense, that we shouldn't have lost games to. It was a different set of circumstances every night, but it was a team thing. You can have all the talent in the world, but if you don't do what you have to do, it doesn't really matter. Ron was very positive, very upbeat, and we didn't respond.

"There's no excuses. I'm not a coach and I don't profess to be," Graves said. "There are so many intangibles when it comes to team sports. Whatever they may be, we didn't seem to generate them and it cost us.

"I've never gone through this before and I don't want to go through it ever again. It's not something that is very enjoyable," the star forward said. "We only have to look at one thing, and that's ourselves.

"The only thing that turns anything around is hard work," Graves continued. "So if that means working out eight hours a day in the summer to get ready for next year, or it means going to see a shrink five hours a day to get your head in shape, you have to work harder on whatever you feel you have to improve on to contribute, because it's not going to be one guy that wins it or loses it, it's going to be 24 guys. The New York Rangers lost as a team."

They did it 39 times, and only five teams did it more. Edmonton lost 50, Hartford lost 52, Tampa Bay lost 54, followed by Ottawa (70) and San Jose (71). It should be blood-chilling to remember that the Rangers went 1-1 with Edmonton, the victory coming in that exceptional 1-0 game that cost Messier his health March 17. They went 1-1-1 against Hartford and 2-1-0 against Tampa Bay — losing the game that set off Messier's tirade November 9, then squeaking out 6-5 and 5-4 victories on late Steven King goals in December. Neilson himself said Tampa would have won those games if its goaltending had been any good.

The Rangers managed three-game sweeps of mighty San Jose and Ottawa. But, again, two of the Ottawa victories were one-goal decisions (the first in overtime). And Ron Smith ripped the team after the first conquest of the Sharks.

All told, that's a 10-3-1 record against teams with a total of 297 defeats last year, and the question is, where are the Rangers without THOSE victories, THOSE 21 points? An alleged contender for anything wouldn't have pissed away those three losses and the tie. That's seven points which certainly would have helped the cause — points which were on the table, only to be snatched by the so-called lesser lights.

"I wish I COULD explain this, because I sure as hell don't want it ever to happen again," Joe Cirella said. "Everyone expected it to be the year when you win the Stanley Cup. There's only a few teams that really, honestly believe that, and when we started this season, we were one of those teams, obviously, who believed that. I don't think there was ever a doubt. It might sound stupid or whatever; obviously things didn't happen, but I still don't doubt that we're good enough as a team to be Stanley Cup champs.

"Last year, everybody played within their limitations. Every part of the puzzle fit together uniquely in the sense that everyone knew the job everyone did the job and did the job well," Cirella said. "This year, there were higher expectations, maybe a little more peer pressure — in that other teams played a little more hard against us, [they] weren't just in awe.

"Last year, we had very few injuries; this year, we had key injuries where players got hurt, players played hurt," Cirella added. "When that happens, maybe other players tried to do too much, and that takes away from the puzzle."

It takes away from the puzzle, but leaves the puzzlement. The pieces didn't fit together, never formed the winning picture.

"I've heard of (good) teams that are totally non-existent in unity, and I've played on (bad) teams that did everything together," Cirella said. "There have been different mixes of success. But as far as I know, there was no dissension."

One player didn't just shrug, sigh, and throw up his hands. He didn't want his name used, but wanted his version of the record straight:

"When you lose a two-goal lead, it has nothing to do with Leetchie being hurt or James Patrick. It's how hard you work. And the work ethic here was for shit," the player said. "There's no excuse for that. You have to do everything to win. Nobody was in shape all year — not in winning shape.

"When you're in top physical condition, you never get mentally tired. When you start getting mentally tired and making those lazy mistakes, it's because your body's tired. Not enough oxygen's coming to your brain. You're breathing so heavy that you're not sharp, you're not making those quick, instinctive decisions," the player continued. "Nobody worked. Guys would come to practice, get here five minutes before they're supposed to be here, throw their gear on. And when the coach says, 'That's it,' they're off the ice and home.

"But where does that come from, if a guy doesn't have it here (the player points to his heart)?" the player asked. "Is a coach supposed to say to a guy, 'Get yourself in the weight room?' I don't think so."

The weight room at Rye is spacious, modern and sparkling bright — full of every possible contraption that could help make you fit or maintain your fitness. There are exercise bikes and free weights and resistance machines to challenge every muscle in your being. There are mirrors and music and a large Ranger crest in neon light at the back wall. It is the first room on your right when you walk in off the ice. You walk past it, then, at least twice a day; the idea, is to walk into it, occasionally, on a voluntary basis for the sake of your craft.

Past the weight room is the stick rack, and past the stick rack (the second door on the right), is another entrance to the locker room. If you walk past that threshold, you reach a different dressing room, where each player places his street clothes in a wooden locker which bears, at the top, a brass circle with the players' uniform number on it.

On a day of retrospection and remorse, Mark Messier stood at his locker in that dressing area, the top of his head near the brass "11," and answered every question sent his way. He wore khaki chino pants, a white T-shirt, tied a navy sweatshirt around his waist.

"Right now, I don't feel like ever playing another game in my entire life. My mind's ready to about explode," he said. "This is probably the toughest week I've ever had in my career.

"Right now, I don't feel too good about myself, I don't feel too good about the way the year happened, the way things unfolded," he said. "It's been a very long year, it hasn't been a very fun year, but time will heal everything. It doesn't feel good now, but I know it'll pass.

"I'm not giving up. I still feel I have a lot of gas left in the tank. I can play at an extremely high level for a long time," Messier continued. "I still have an incredible desire to win and I think that, more than anything, is vital. I don't think I've lost my leadership qualities.

"All my years in hockey, this is the least amount of fun ever," he said. "I don't play hockey because I have to, I don't play hockey because I'm getting paid. To me, it's always been fun, I've enjoyed practicing, I've enjoyed playing the games. This year was just a real bad year for injuries. I haven't had a chance to practice . . . I like to practice. I like working out in the weight room."

Somebody asked Messier his greatest regret, everyone around him imagining it would be something to do with the way the Neilson thing was handled. Messier paused for a moment, considering the question and the answer, as he would regularly during the session.

"Probably, beating the shit out of Brian and breaking his ankle," he said.

Everybody laughed. The whole year had been so completely strange, enough bizarre stuff for five seasons having been crammed into one, just about all you could do is laugh.

"At that point, I couldn't come within two feet of anybody, my ribs were so sore," Messier said when the giggles subsided. "I would never have been wrestling around with him."

Then he answered the question.

"Regrets? Not being able to carry the team. To me, that's the most disappointing thing," he said. "I'm learning that the most important thing is what you actually do on the ice. If you're the guy your teammates are looking for to score the big goal or lead the game in any facet, it's really frustrating if you can't do it.

"I needed to take some time (off) at some point, and I just couldn't get it," he said. "We couldn't seem to buy a break or buy a win, and we were fighting for our lives and a playoff spot. No use being rested if you're not going to be in the playoffs.

"We got ourselves into some tight spots down the stretch, got ourselves into a position where we just couldn't get it done. I couldn't get involved physically, and that obviously hurt my game," he said. "I built my game around that (physical play); it's what made me effective for most of my career. And when I pulled those muscles off my ribs, it's a six-week minimum injury. I lost a lot of strength. I never was able to do a situp or do anything for the last six weeks or ride a bike. That hurt. To lift a guy's stick or pull or push, that's the whole game right now (and Messier couldn't do it)."

Still, there was one genuine regret regarding the Rangers' premier defenseman.

"I just can't tell you how much it would have meant to our team to have Leetch," Messier said. "Our team just takes on a whole different dimension."

Now, the whole story was two more games and see you later.

"I don't want to end my career in New York on this note," Messier said, confronting that possibility. "Hopefully, I'm going to be back, and I'll try to make it happen again. I don't want to go out this way.

"I really like it here. It's been a great experience," he continued. "Obviously, this is a down side of playing in New York; but last year was the upside. It was great. I was taken in by my teammates from the first day, and the fans, and we went on to have a great year.

"It's easy to be a great team guy, a great leader and a great player when you're 50-25-5. This is the other side of the coin," Messier said. "So what do you do next, when you are under a little adversity. Do you fold your tent and say, 'I want to leave?' Or stick to your guns, fight back and try to make it better? That's what I intend to do.

"It may sound crazy," he said, "but I don't think there's a lot wrong."

That, Messier knew, would be for the next coach — the Rangers' third in 12 months — to determine.

"I am willing to perform for whoever they decide to have coach," he said, "but I'm not going to sit here and say I thought the direction we were taking (under Neilson) was beneficial to our hockey club. I'd be a liar."

Ron Smith's office was at the other end of the complex, through the hockey locker room, past the large video room with its giant-screened TV and blue carpet, through a short hallway. He, too, answered all the questions, and he had a lot to say.

"I couldn't say I did a great job, because the results aren't there," he said, "but I think evaluation should be based more on how I handled the situation and your estimation of my teaching abilities, ability to deal with people, relationship with management. You measure all the qualities that are there, all the aspects that it takes to coach NHL hockey, and do it in New York. If someone comes along who measures up on all those qualities AND has winning credentials at the NHL level, that person should be hired."

Smith knew his only chance of getting the job on a more permanent basis had rested on somehow getting to the playoffs and somehow doing well in them. He knew "that person" would not be him, that he would be heading back to Binghamton and the AHL next season.

"Players are always skating around with your paycheck in their pocket. That's a given," Smith said. "I didn't covet the job.

I could never do that. In fact, I wasn't real thrilled to get the job, given the circumstances — with the relationship to Roger and also with the knowledge that coming aboard in mid-season is not ideal. If you had your choice of a coaching job you wanted to take, it certainly wouldn't be in mid-season for anybody. I can't say I'm angry, because I didn't covet the job and I wasn't thrilled to get it, in the sense of how it came about."

He inherited a team in turmoil, a condition that subsided briefly but never really vanished. Smith resumed an explanation of the "currents" he had mentioned in Philadelphia the previous night.

"There are always currents in the dressing room, and at times, they become waves," he explained. "A situation like that happened here, where the coach got fired, and the obvious split that we know was there (between Messier and Neilson), there were a lot of waves flowing around. And it settled for a while, but then clearly, under the heat, they started to turn up again. The currents keep swirling.

"There's some guys with guilt about it," Smith said, "there are some guys with worry about their own future. There are some guys doubting other players on their team. There are some guys doubting the new coach. There are some guys wondering about the management. There's this, that and the other thing, and all those things get magnified under the circumstances, and the injury things compound everything and they blow up bigger. They're all sort of settled when things are going okay and you're winning in spite of it. But once things go bad, it all snowballs.

"It's a hard thing to overcome. Winning helps. We looked like we were ready to go (on a tear) after that Chicago game. And it would have been real interesting to see, had those circumstances not happened, where we would be sitting right now," Smith said, speaking of the snowout, the Leetch injury, and the home games the team virtually threw away. "If we had folded regardless, boy, I would be angry and bitter and wondering about bad apples and so on. But I came in with a fresh look, and I have no complaints."

And he made no apologies.

"Some of the things were technical screwups. Let's face it," he said. "A giveaway in overtime, twice, to cost us games we shouldn't be losing. There were two or three soft goals here. A complete letdown for 10 minutes there. This is all after we'd spent 10 or 12 games playing really smart, tight hockey.

"Now, my assumption — right or wrong — is that the weight of playing a long time, under less-than-ideal circumstances, and the psychological whacking we took with Leetch's second injury had something to do with it," he said. "And if you're really, really, really strong, maybe it wouldn't affect you. But maybe, with the group we were playing with, we weren't quite good enough on the ice to parlay the array of character we had into better performance."

Without Leetch or Patrick or even Wells, demands were made of players to play unaccustomed roles. Lowe may have been well-rested from his long holdout, but he played entirely too much. He and Beukeboom often were matched against the opposition's top lines, because there simply wasn't anybody else deemed capable of handling the assignment. Beukeboom, who banked both his goals into opposing nets off opposing players, got time on the power play in one game — yet in another, Per Djoos was brought from Binghamton all the way to Vancouver, then barely used. The Rangers went through more than a dozen defensemen over the course of the season and still didn't seem to have enough.

"I think we have to add one or two physical defensemen; Joby Messier could be one of them," Smith said, "and you probably need one or two forwards of that type. Contact is an indication of eagerness to play, generally speaking. It's an indication of how 'up' you are, but it's also an indication of the kind of player you are, and some players aren't contact players.

"I don't know if there were a tremendous amount of games we got outhit. We're not even a middle-of-the-road team in terms of the physical. Jay Wells missing 35 games was a helluva lot bigger loss than anybody knew, including me," he said. "My information was that he was one of the best defensemen on the team over the first half of the season, and along with all the talk about missing Brian Leetch, forgotten was a guy who gave you six or eight or 10 crunches a game and who played the game the way it was meant to be played by a good, solid defenseman. That contributed to the lack of a real physical presence.

"We had a three-hit quota for every guy, which adds up to 54 minimum if you all get your quota, and 75 is a nice number to get," Smith said. "I'm sad to say, a lot of nights, the quota wasn't met. Again; with some of our players, it's not their game. But you're asking for the minimum; you're asking for a level that's not reaching for the moon."

The Rangers never reached it. Some nights, they never even approached it.

"Coaches are good coaches if they pick the style that best suits their team," Smith said. "They recognize that within that team, there are going to be individuals who need some freedom to do their own thing and to play a certain way, and I tried hard to pick a style that was best for the team and leave some room for individual talent to come out.

"Our attempt to play up-tempo was reflected far more in the defensive game than it was in anything else — a more aggressive, chasing, pressing defensive game, because, let's face it, the other style (go-for-broke offense) was already there, like it or lump it, to an extreme. We had to go to a much more conservative game when we lost Leetch and Patrick. Then, we went to 'Plan B' quite successfully. We had 31 goals-against in 11 games and 10 (goals-against) were in the Quebec game (March 6).

"Any player should be able to adjust, or play within the system that's best for the team — as long as he isn't being asked to totally go away from his game. No player on our team was ever asked to go away from his game totally — except in certain situations that made sense," Smith said. "If you decide you're going to play a trapping, four-back conservative checking game for a period or five minutes or a game or two or three, you better be able to do it. I don't care who you are. But you're wrong if you try to do that consistently with a player or group of players not suited to that style. You have to play to the strength of your team.

"I don't think we were asking someone to completely change what was best for them. We asked for two or three simple things to be done right from the start, and one was clearly a more forcing type of defensive game — a more chasing, harassing, aggressive type of checking game. We asked them to put speed in their game coming both ways of the rink, and commitment in the game both ways.

"And frankly, I don't think there was that commitment," Smith said, his most condemnatory assertion. "We got a fair bit of it (commitment) for some period of time. The statistics somewhat back it up, but that could have been some guilt, too.

"On offense, we worked hard to make it a more direct, simplified, less stylistic game, which doesn't go away at all from the kinds of players we have; it should enhance what they could do," he said. "If you've got a speed guy who can shoot the puck, why would you want to waste time swirling and drop-passing when you've got a direct, fast attack? It makes sense for less-skilled people, but it makes even more sense for skilled people to take that approach, knowing once you've got that established, all those other things will be available to you. I would have a hard time accepting there was a major, major style change being asked to the degree that people couldn't fit into it.

"Any coach will tell you: The more talented people you have, the more difficult it is to simplify your game, because they have the ability to do wonderful things, and the inclination is to do that; they've spent their whole life doing that and they're optimistic about it and positive about it, no matter what," the coach said. "They're much harder to convince than someone who has no options in his game — a guy like Mike Hartman or Paul Broten, heart-and-soul, plug-away guys. You're always battling with talented players to make the most of their talents, and because you expect so much of them, because you see so many great things, it's more hurtful when it doesn't happen. When you lose with a good team, it's a lot more hurtful than with an ordinary team."

This was not an ordinary team. This was about the best-paid team in pro hockey. This was the defending Presidents' Trophy winner. And it crumbled to powder. And it wasn't only the rookies who made the mistakes.

If a chat with Richter is like word golf, his overview of the season was a full 18 holes.

"I certainly haven't taken it all in," Richter said, "but I feel there's quite a few factors — some of them out of our control, like some injuries, and the fact that the coaching change happened and the turmoil. Still, we're responsible for how we play, and for whatever reason, we just haven't been playing as furiously as we can.

"A lot of people made a lot about division in the locker room, for and against Roger. I don't think it was as black-and-white as that. I think individuals had mixed feelings. The team wasn't going. You're in there, going, 'Geez. I don't want Roger to get fired, but I don't want to keep losing.' It's an odd feeling, and it was a disruptive feeling, no doubt about that.

"Some people say, 'Are we an over-rated team?' Maybe we were, maybe we weren't, but (after being) number one in our division, we were certainly capable of making the playoffs. And if not, we were certainly capable of doing a better run than we made of it," Richter added. "I suppose everyone's going to say, 'Well, obviously they WERE over-rated, because if we had rated them accurately, we wouldn't have expected them to do very well.' I think we under-achieved.

"I think at the end of the year, a lot of the problems that have been there all along came to a head," Richter said. "We were not the intense team that we were last year, right off the bat. We were getting away with it for a while, but then it caught up to us. Given all the injuries and everything else, we still didn't play as well as we could. That's as far as I've gotten so far. I'm sure there's more.

"I know it was disappointing to watch us and I know we didn't look as intense as we should have been, and I think that's accurate: We weren't," Richter said. "But I know nobody said, 'I don't care what goes on out here, I don't care whether we win or lose.' We're all professionals, with jobs. Everybody, even if they play at a selfish level, wants to perform well. It was not happening, and I suppose when it's not happening, you have to dig down and make it happen. And, for whatever reason, we didn't do that. Whether the chemistry wasn't right or whatever, I don't believe we ran into some bad luck. That happened and that hurt, no question, but it doesn't (explain) a whole season.

"If we were playing better, we would have at least won at home; it's supposed to be easier there.

"I just know this: There were so many times during the year where we started off okay — not great, not as intense as we should play, but okay. But then, the first instance I can remember was losing here to Tampa Bay and the Capitals — badly. And I remember scraping up the pieces after that and coming back and trying to play again, and we'd get it going a little bit and then we'd have another little setback. Leetchie got hurt in November, then we had that terrible game in Buffalo and Roger was fired. Then we picked it up in Ron's first game.

"We did respond to some of the adversity we had this year, and I don't know, by the end, after Brian got hurt again, what happened somewhere in the back of players' minds. For me to speculate right now is just going to make it sound like I'm making excuses, and I just think we're all ultimately responsible. So I can't say. It's just a terrible disappointment, like I've never experienced.

"I just want to play, whether it's here or somewhere else," Richter said. "I just want to get my game improved and play like I'm capable of playing. I had the most disappointing year I've ever had in my life and I never want to repeat it. I called Team USA (to ask about playing in the World Championships) before they called me. I wanted to get on that team badly. I just didn't want to finish with this taste in my mouth."

Richter wasn't the only one who wanted to gargle.

"When Ron took over, I think everyone was mentally down because of how we were playing, the long skid we went on at the end with Roger, and Roger getting fired," Jay Wells said. "I think there were some people who liked Roger and there were some people who didn't like him. When Ron came in, we had a positive attitude that we were going to go and pull it out. Then we found we were doing the same mistakes and making the same mental errors and losing close games and still not winning.

"Then, I think it was just a sheer case of guys trying to do too much, playing outside their capabilities and never coming back to the basic skills they used to get to the league," Wells added. "The odd game, we'd do that, but then we'd get full of ourselves and then we'd be trying to do too much. I'm trying to carry the puck like crazy, and that's just not my job. It's just not me, my game. The more I try to carry the puck, the more trouble I get into, the more frustrated I get and the worse I play. That, I think, was the majority of my problem.

"You just force so much, you get yourself in trouble — not only myself, but everybody," the defenseman said. "We just never, ever regrouped and figured it out. Whether that's the main problem, I don't know; but it's one of the things. Injuries hurt us a little bit, but we had great players to fill in; other teams (overcome injuries), we should, too.

"It's unfortunate that guys like Zuby (Zubov) or Alex (Alexei Kovalev), first-year guys, had to be in a position to carry this team," Wells continued. "Mess can't do it all himself; I know he tried. But here's a couple of young guys, and not putting them down or anything, but they don't really know the NHL. They don't really know the dedication some people put in to play in this league. They've got so much talent — they're bubbling over with talent. They did for a while, but they need more experience before they can do it for a whole season. They're going to be great players, but they need some schooling. They need to learn what it means to win a Stanley Cup. Everybody has to learn that. Some guys on this team won't get another shot at it, and some guys might be done. They might be finished. Whenever you're on a last-place team, or close to it, who wants you?

"There's gonna be a few players who, you're not sure whether they're going to go anywhere, or do anything or come back next year," Wells said. "For me, personally, it's another screwed-up summer where you don't know what's going to happen."

For Brian Leetch, it already had been a screwed-up winter and spring. Almost literally, he was beset from head to toe, with the nerve injury in December and the leg fracture in March.

"Chemistry has a lot to do with it, execution has a lot to do with it, coaching has a lot to do with it," Leetch said, resting his ankle on a crutch but not using any for the way the season had gone. "We had plenty of injuries and plenty of excuses — none of them worthy of us being where we are."

- CHAPTER 21 -

CONCLUSIONS

BY NOW YOU KNOW the events of a remarkably strange hockey season. By now you know what the key participants thought. Now, here's what I think, making no excuses for the 20-20 hindsight.

I think it is utterly misguided to paint Mark Messier as the villain in the mess with Neilson. I don't think getting rid of Neilson was a bad thing at all. I think it was long overdue. If Neil Smith had fired Neilson after the 1992 playoffs, when it was an obvious option, there is reason to doubt the catastrophe of 1992-93 would have occurred.

I don't think the Rangers had a prayer of winning the Stanley Cup with Neilson as their coach. He wasn't the right coach for this team in this city. He'll probably do very well in Florida with the Panthers, and people will say "What a mistake the Rangers made getting rid of him." I disagree, in advance. I also disagree, in advance, with people who will see the Rangers improve under Mike Keenan and be convinced they could have been just as good for Neilson last season. It isn't that simple.

When you obtain a Messier, you are playing the game for very, very high stakes. You are moving up from a jalopy to a Lamborghini. If you aren't willing to risk hairpin turns on two wheels at 120 miles per hour, if you aren't willing to risk crashing, don't enter the race. Neilson has a good driving record because he almost never exceeds the speed limit.

Of course Messier has an enormous ego. And it's doubtful he is as smart as he thinks he is. His heavy-handed handling of the Neilson affair was like a bullfight by a bad matador; the bull doesn't die right away, so the guy has to keep hacking away until the grim job is done.

But I think teams which accomplish things do so because they have Messiers in their clubhouse. Players such as Messier have tremendous energy; the issue is whether the energy will be challenged and channelled negatively or positively by his superiors. Last year, it wasn't channelled at all and the Rangers paid a maximal price.

I think now, in Keenan, the Rangers have absolutely the right coach. And who knows if that would be the case had Messier not pressed the issue? I think Keenan will steer Messier properly, will harness his power, will bite back when Messier barks. And the Rangers will flourish with those two heading the pack because the team will, at long last, gain the element of personality they have utterly come to lack.

Last year, any semblance of personality was suppressed. Kovalev's originality, his Kovalev-ness, got him a regular commute to Binghamton. Domi, a squeaky wheel but a unique one, was sent away. Richter was branded a heretic for having the nerve to move into the city where he plays. Messier, who at least had the jam to speak up and do something he thought was right — thus displaying the hard-edged, aggressive demeanor for which he was obtained originally — was labelled an assassin.

And people wonder why last year became a mush of dead hockey by dud players. How do you avoid that fate when management's philosophy is, "Be yourself, but not too much."

Hey! Wake UP! This is New York!

With all due respect to Peterborough, this ain't Peterborough. Don't try to make it Peterborough.

I almost hope Keenan and Messier DON'T get along, because then you'll see sparks fly. You'll see two strong personalities butt heads instead of having two disparate personalities act like buttheads. Regardless, there will be a dynamic. The team will have a pulse.

That doesn't mean the team will win, that the decades of waiting will end. The Rangers spent the spring of 1992 erasing their playoff credibility, spent all of 1992-93 erasing their regular-season credibility. Which means they will spend 1993-94 working from Square One.

They won't get the benefit of a single doubt. They don't deserve it.

They won't be over-rated for any reason. They don't deserve it. They finished last. They cheated the fans. They stole their salaries. They were Broadway Blew.

And if they are to change their fortunes, each and every one of them — from Neil Smith to Keenan to Messier, right down to the stickboys — dare not even speak the words "Stanley Cup" until April. You can think about it all you want, work toward it all you want, but don't DARE place that big a cart in front of so fragile a horse. To win the Stanley Cup tournament, you first must respect yourself enough to earn entry into it.

Get that Stanley Cup poster off the shower room door at the Garden. Get that Stanley Cup poster off the equipment room door at Rye. If you want something for motivation, put up a four-foot copy of the 1992-93 Patrick Division standings. And pay close attention to the bottom line.

The team has bright spots. Messier, Graves, Kovalev, Leetch, and Zubov, to name five. Other spots will brighten if the players are used properly and if all pull a fair share of the load instead of reaching for the nearest excuse when their performance comes up short — again.

The team has holes. It needs a No. 2 center, a No. 4 defenseman, a No. 1 goalie. These are the same holes it had last year at this time, and Neil Smith is accountable for not having filled them.

He finally got rid of a goalie, finally rid himself of a counter-productive situation, then recreated it in a matter of days by obtaining Glenn Healy. Now, you tell me: How can Mike Richter be considered the team's No. 1 goalie when it was Healy who played in the playoff semifinals last year? Now, instead of Richter/Vanbiesbrouck, it's Richter/Healy. Virtually nothing is new. The fact is, Richter looks more like trade bait now than when Vanbiesbrouck was here. How is that supposed to create a relaxed mindset for a kid who thinks too much?

Drawing conclusions after a season is like blaming a referee for a bad call after you watch the replay in slow motion. The ref didn't have the luxury of that camera angle, and he had to make a judgment as the event occurred at normal speed, in the span of an eyeblink. His view of the play might have been obscured by a player or another official, and I have no doubt my view in certain instances may be similarly obscured.

I don't know all the deals Neil Smith tried to make, the ones that fell through at the last minute or other circumstances beyond his control which prevented him from easing the congestion in his dressing room. I just know there were too many players around, it became a core issue, the problem didn't get fixed, and Smith is accountable.

He had improved the quality of his roster with his off-season transactions — several of which were pivotal in keeping the team alive as long as it was. But if he gets praise for that, Smith takes the hit for not doing other things that had to be done.

I also have no concrete evidence Brian Leetch DIDN'T slip on a snowbank and break his ankle. I don't know how many nights Roger Neilson picked absolutely the right lineup and gave it an absolutely flawless gameplan — only to have the boulderheads in the dressing room blow it for him. I think, in a lot of ways, Neilson ended up hitting the nail on the head: Anything that could go wrong, did go wrong.

And then some.

There is no way in the world it can happen again the way it did in 1992-93. There will be much closer scrutiny of every deal Neil Smith makes this season, close attention paid the power triangle of relationships: Keenan and Smith, Keenan and Messier, Messier and Smith. Close attention will be paid the health of Brian Leetch, as well, and the ultimate shape taken by the rest of the defense behind him.

But it will take the whole first half for the players to learn Keenan and Keenan to learn the players. The second half and the playoffs, if the Rangers make them, will paint the brushstrokes in the team portrait for 1993-94.

THE SEASON IN QUOTES

■■■
1992
JUNE

"I find that Philadelphia made an enforceable deal with Quebec with regard to (Eric) Lindros' rights and other considerations." — *NHL arbitrator Larry Bertuzzi, June 30, 1992.*

■■■
SEPTEMBER

"If communication breaks down between the players and the coach, (the team) will die a slow death." — *Captain Mark Messier, September 14.*

"Although Kevin Lowe is a great player, he's 33 and we already have two defensemen who are around that age." — *GM Neil Smith, September 23.*

"If I had $10,000, I'd put it down on the Rangers to win the Cup." — *Eddie Galeski of Brooklyn, a Ranger fan for 26 years, at a Garden open house September 27.*

"We'll win the Stanley Cup before they (the Rangers) do." —*New Jersey Devils owner John McMullen, September 29.*

"A lot of players are going to have to suffer through not dressing every game." — *Coach Roger Neilson, September 30.*

"I don't want to be the fifth guy in a deal. If I get traded, I want to be the main guy in a deal." — *Center Doug Weight, who was in the nullified Lindros trade package over the summer and ended up getting traded to Edmonton in March for Esa Tikkanen.*

■■■
OCTOBER

"He's going to take quite a while to adjust to our team and our hockey." — *Neil Smith, speaking of Alexei Kovalev, upon signing the right wing October 5.*

"What I've seen, in the time I've been here, is a team that's pretty hungry. You can sense from everybody that they haven't forgotten that last game. That's good, because it means they're bitter about it." — *Left wing Phil Bourque, who was with Pittsburgh when the Penguins eliminated the Rangers in that 'last' game of the 1992 playoffs.*

"I get a sense that having a good year isn't going to be enough for this team. We need to win it this year." — *Messier, October 7.*

"Rangers Begin Inexorable March to the Stanley Cup!" — New York Times *headline of October 10, 1992 after season-opening 4-2 victory at Washington.*

"Not too many teams are going to come in and get points from New York." — *Montreal coach Jacques Demers, October 23, after his Canadiens became one of several teams to rally for ties or victories at the Garden.*

"Players get upset when they don't play, but the fact is, they get paid whether they do or they don't." — *Neil Smith, October 25.*

"For four or five games in a row, we've gotten worse instead of better." — *Brian Leetch, October 29.*

■■■
NOVEMBER

"If there was a fairly clear-cut (consensus) on which 20 should play, we could go with the same lineup. You wouldn't want to do this all season. We might have to go half a season until something breaks." — *Neilson, November 2.*

"We've been getting by playing lousy hockey. We've had a couple of meetings about it, and we realize we haven't played to our potential." — *Darren Turcotte, November 2, after overtime 7-6 victory over Buffalo.*

"It has been pretty obvious for a while that some kind of a deal is coming. We just don't know when." — *Turcotte, November 8.*

"I'm ready to talk (trade) to people, because we have a surplus. There's no sense sitting with your shelves overstocked and not trying to get customers to buy." — *Smith, November 8.*

"Instead of having four players unhappy, we have 24 unhappy. It's been becoming a problem for a long time now; it's starting to catch up with us." — *Messier, November 9, referring to the effect of the player surplus on the team.*

"I've got to do the right thing. And if that means it takes two more weeks or three more weeks or even two more months, then we'll all have to live with that. The move to make is to improve the hockey club, not to dump players. That would be foolish — to simply get rid of your depth because it is causing some disgruntlement." — *Smith, November 10.*

"I know one thing: There'll be no instigator in this fight." — *Tie Domi, November 19, anticipating December 2 visit of NHL heavyweight champ Bob Probert.*

"It's the feeling of the coaches and myself that he, a lot of the time, is playing a different game than the rest of the team is." — *Neil Smith, November 23, upon sending Alexei Kovalev to Binghamton.*

■■■
DECEMBER

"I think it's great . . . For people going home, that's one of the things they'll be talking about." — *Neilson, December 2, after Probert hammered Domi.*

"I did all my talking on the ice. We didn't win the game, and that's what counts." — *Probert, December 2.*

"I said I'd show up and I guess I showed up." — *Domi, December 2.*

"As a team, we're backpedaling. It's too easy offensively for the other teams." — *Jeff Beukeboom, December 4, after 8-4 loss to Washington.*

"We don't want to believe things can get that bad. But sometimes, the truth hurts." — *Goalie John Vanbiesbrouck, after same game.*

"Most of the time, we're playing without direction." — *Brian Leetch, December 5.*

"There had been some pretty poor play on the part of a lot of our players. We weren't happy with the way things have been going. It called for drastic action." — *Neil Smith, December 6, explaining lineup shakeup.*

"By adding Kevin Lowe, I think we've improved the area where we're the weakest." — *Smith, December 11, after obtaining Lowe from Edmonton.*

"I haven't been in anything less than the Stanley Cup semifinals the last number of years, and I don't expect that to change." — *Lowe, upon signing.*

"It's just a tough situation, with all these players here. What they've done is (they've) made people start doubting themselves. It's a mental thing. You start doubting yourself; you start second-guessing yourself as a player." — *Phil Bourque, December 11.*

"Messier sucks." — *Opinion inserted into the scoring summary of the Rangers-Lightning game in certain editions of the December 12* Newsday.

"I expect the Rangers to advance further in the playoffs than last year. Anything less would be unsuccessful." — *Kevin Lowe.*

"After reviewing the tape (of the Domi-Probert fight), I believe the referee was right in saying there was no instigator." — *NHL President Gil Stein, December 15.*

"I don't want to sit here and rot . . . I thought I was going to get a fair shot at playing." — *Domi, December 16.*

"We're hoping it's not that bad." — *Neilson, December 17, referring to the injury Brian Leetch suffered in St. Louis.*

"If there was ever a game we didn't deserve to win, this was it." — *Neilson, December 22, after 3-1 lead became 5-4 overtime loss to Devils.*

"Colin Campbell really had a lot to do with getting me traded. I can guarantee it." — *Domi, December 28, after being dealt to Winnipeg.*

"I wasn't down on Tie at all." — *Campbell, December 28.*

"It would have been nice to stay in bed this morning if we had won. But we're here, in this old arena, skating hard while everyone else is sitting in front of the TV, watching football and eating dip." — *Rangers assistant coach Colin Campbell at practice that followed 11-6 embarrassment in Buffalo on New Year's Eve.*

■■■
1993
JANUARY

"I don't think Mark (Messier) liked the way I coached, and this year, I didn't always like the way he played." — *Neilson, January 4, after being fired.*

"I respected Roger. I just don't think, the way things were going, he was getting the best out of the team." — *Messier, January 4, referring to his relationship with Neilson.*

"We've got to make the playoffs, and the way things were sliding, that was questionable. I really felt this whole season was going to slip away if I didn't do something. I didn't want to wait until Game 78 and then say, 'Oh, something has to be done.'" — *Neil Smith, January 4, explaining why he fired Neilson.*

"I'm 6 feet tall, 200 pounds, and my dog is a heckuva lot fatter." — *Interim coach Ron Smith, January 4, on differences between him and Neilson.*

"When things are bad, any time there's a change, you hope it's for the better." — *Goalie Mike Richter, January 5, the morning after Roger Neilson is fired.*

"We're very capable of losing to anybody — and losing BIG." — *Richter, January 6.*

"I still think we will be able to receive some kind of reasonable value if we decide to trade one of our goalies." — *Neil Smith, January 16.*

"I'm trying, really, not to be in awe of these guys. It's hard." — *Goalie Corey Hirsch, January 19, after tying Detroit 2-2 in his NHL debut.*

"I've seen it happen before. Instead of us saving his butt, he saves ours." — *Veteran defenseman Kevin Lowe, after Hirsch's debut.*

"I'll be having the garden salad and a glass of water." — *Hirsch, January 20, before the annual team dinner for which rookies pick up the check.*

"We're in that (goaltending) 'trilemma' again. It's not a dilemma, it's a 'trilemma.' Is that a word?" — *Ron Smith, January 25, on three-headed goalie depth chart of Hirsch, Richter and John Vanbiesbrouck.*

"Should we get names and numbers for the backs of our sweaters?" — *Joe Kocur, January 25, after a practice at which there were three coaches, three goalies, 10 defensemen and 12 forwards.*

"A milestone is something other people have done before. A record is something nobody has ever done before." — *Right wing Mike Gartner, after setting an NHL record by scoring 30 or more goals in a 14th consecutive season.*

"Maybe I got too popular for my own good." — *Tie Domi, January 27, upon returning to the Garden with Winnipeg.*

"It's just a matter of time before we start dominating games again." — *Adam Graves, January 30.*

■■■
FEBRUARY

"The problem is, do you just move a goalie for the best offer you can get, which may not seem to you like it's enough, just for the sake of getting the issue over with? I've never operated that way, so it's something I guess I'm resisting. However, if you hesitate too long, then you run into other problems." — *Neil Smith, February 4.*

"We ought to put together a lowlight tape instead of a highlight tape." — *Neil Smith, on the star-crossed season.*

"It's still our goal to win the Stanley Cup this year." — *Messier, February 7, with Rangers one point out of second and three points out of fifth.*

"This was a lousy game by our team, pure and simple." — *Ron Smith, February 20, after a 6-4 victory over San Jose became closer than it should have been.*

"Ever since I've been here, I've given everything I had, always tried to be positive, and now I'm just getting buried." — *Mark Hardy, February 25, after asking to be traded.*

■■■
MARCH

"There's going to be a lot of homeless roaches next year when the Blackhawks move." — *Center Darren Turcotte, March 11.*

"I can assure you that Neil (Smith) will be leading this team when we break camp next September." — *Garden president Bob Gutkowski, March 31.*

■■■
APRIL

"I think Roger Neilson is cool. Something about him is really cool." — *Eric Lindros, April 1.*

"If we lose, but win our last eight, we probably assure ourselves a playoff spot." — *Kevin Lowe, April 1, before critical contest against the Islanders.*

"All I can tell you is what I've surmised: Having a two-goalie system is not as good a situation as having one guy." — *Ron Smith, April 6.*

"I think this team is clearly good enough to be in the playoffs. But just saying that doesn't mean you should be in the playoffs. We have to go out and win our games, and we're not." — *Neil Smith, April 7.*

"I was trying to think of another time in my athletic experience when I've been more embarrassed — and I couldn't — about a team's performance." — *Ron Smith, April 9, after 10-4 loss to Pittsburgh at the Garden.*

"People come up to me all the time and say, 'I guess you're really smiling now,' but that's not the case at all." — *Neilson, April 12.*

"We had chemistry last year. This year, we didn't have it." — *Gartner, April 12, after the Rangers were eliminated from the playoff race.*

"I don't think the turmoil in the dressing room ever totally disappeared." — *Ron Smith, April 12.*

"I don't want to end my career in New York on this note . . . I really like it here. It's been a great experience. Obviously, this is a down side of playing in New York; but last year was the upside. It was great. I was taken in by my teammates from the first day, and the fans, and we went on to have a great year. It's easy to be a great team guy, a great leader and a great player when you're 50-25-5. This is the other side of the coin. So what do you do next, when you are under a little adversity? Do you fold your tent and say, 'I want to leave?' Or stick to your guns, fight back and try to make it better? That's what I intend to do." — *Messier, April 13, after Rangers' playoff hopes end.*

"Players are always skating around with your paycheck in their pocket. That's a given." — *Ron Smith, April 13.*

"We didn't execute for Roger OR Ron, as a team. It's a very sad statement to have to make, but it's true. As a professional player, you have to realize there is someone in control and we, as a team, have to go out and perform for that individual. And when we don't, we have no one to blame but ourselves. There are no excuses, no fingers to be pointed, other than to point them directly at ourselves. We're the players who go out on the ice to play and we're responsible for what happened. You can look yourself in the mirror and say you tried; there are some guys, I think, who can say they legitimately tried. But we, as a hockey team — I'm talking of a collective body — obviously, we can't say that we did our best." — *Gartner, April 13.*

"When you win it all, you don't need to say it to anyone, but you kind of have this feeling in your mind, 'Hey — No one can say anything bad about you or the hockey team. No one. Because you're the best.' And that's a very satisfying feeling. It's a huge accomplishment. This is the exact opposite." — *Defenseman Kevin Lowe, April 13.*

"Whenever you're on a last-place team, or close to it, who wants you?" — *Defenseman Jay Wells, April 14.*

KEY DATES IN THE RANGERS' SEASON

■■■
1992
JUNE

30 — After 10 days of hearings and deliberations, NHL arbitrator Larry Bertuzzi rules the Philadelphia Flyers made an enforceable deal with the Quebec Nordiques for the rights to Eric Lindros.

■■■
AUGUST

31 — Sign free-agent LW Phil Bourque.

■■■
SEPTEMBER

1 — Sign C-LW Dave Archibald.
2 — Sign G John Vanbiesbrouck.
8 — Sign G Mike Richter, D Jay Wells, RW Tie Domi.
11 — Coach Roger Neilson and captain Mark Messier meet before the team leaves for training camp at Glens Falls, N.Y. "There never was a problem (with Neilson) in my mind," Messier says. "I learned a long time ago you respect your coach. I think we have a mutual respect for each other."

13 — Defenseman Brian Leetch, coming off a Norris Trophy season, signs a seven-year, $19-million contract.

15 — After showing up at camp with neon-green skate laces, Red Army defenseman Sergei Zubov signs a multi-year contract. "I will try my hardest to play well here and I will try my hardest to play the way they (the coaches) want."

29 — D Mark Hardy and RW Paul Broten sign contracts.

■■■
OCTOBER

4 — The NHL uses two referees (Kerry Fraser and Paul Stewart) in an exhibition-game experiment as the Rangers host Toronto. Defenseman Peter Andersson receives the Lars-Erik Sjoberg Award for being the first-year player voted by the media to have performed best in training camp.

5 — Though prepared to return to Russia as negotiations appear near collapse, rookie RW Alexei Kovalev signs a five-year contract.

9 — Rangers are the last of 24 teams to get their season underway, one of several built-in scheduling benefits provided by GM Neil Smith.

12 — Banners honoring the regular season Patrick Division championship, plus the overall NHL season title, are raised to the Garden roof before the home opener against Hartford. Kovalev gets the first goal of his NHL career. D Joe Cirella and RW Joe Kocur sign new contracts.

■■■
NOVEMBER

3 — After Vanbiesbrouck is injured during a game against Buffalo, Corey Hirsch is summoned from Binghamton.

4 — LW Jan Erixon misses the first of 18 consecutive games due to back/hip strain.

6 — Trade Dave Archibald to Ottawa Senators for fifth-round pick.

9 — After the team's awful performance in a 5-1 Garden loss to expansion Tampa Bay, team captain Mark Messier declares there are too many unhappy players on the team.

13 — Hirsch returns to Binghamton.

23 — Kovalev is assigned to Binghamton.

25 — Rangers return to Pittsburgh for first game since the 1992 playoffs and win, 11-3. Adam Graves, a villain in Pittsburgh, scores three goals and a career-high five points; Messier gets two goals, four assists. Roger Neilson bars Pittsburgh media from Rangers' dressing room.

■■■
DECEMBER

2 — Rangers host Red Wings and Tie Domi battles Bob Probert in one of hockey history's least spontaneous fights. Shortly thereafter, NHL president Gil Stein announces a just-as-spontaneous inquest.

6 — In response to the team's failure to play even rudimentary defense, management summons wings Steven King and Kovalev, defenseman Sergei Zubov, and goalie Corey Hirsch from Binghamton. Richter is scratched from lineup.

11 — To bolster their defense corps, the Rangers obtain veteran Kevin Lowe from Edmonton for a third-round pick in 1993 draft and Russian prospect Roman Oksyuta.

13 — Hirsch and Zubov return to Binghamton.

17 — Brian Leetch crashes into boards in St. Louis and injures a nerve that runs from the neck into the left shoulder. He will miss 34 games.

27 — Zubov is recalled.

28 — LW Ed Olczyk is obtained from Winnipeg for LW Kris King and RW Tie Domi. Steven King returns to Binghamton. Rangers spend their last day of the season in second place.

31 — Rangers are crushed 11-6 in Buffalo.

■■■
1993
JANUARY

2 — Rangers drop 5-2 decision in Pittsburgh and suffer fifth loss in six games. It is Roger Neilson's last as coach.

4 — Neilson is replaced, on an interim basis, by Binghamton coach Ron Smith. Colin Campbell, who had assisted Neilson, is assigned to replace Ron Smith as Binghamton

coach. President Stein announces he is suspending Neilson and Domi, though neither actually works for the club any longer.

15 — Richter is assigned to Binghamton for conditioning. Corey Hirsch is recalled.

18 — D Per Djoos recalled from Binghamton.

19 — D Mike Hurlbut is returned to Binghamton. Mark Messier sprains his wrist in Detroit and misses six games. Corey Hirsch makes NHL debut, ties Red Wings 2-2 and dedicates performance to his late grandfather.

20 — Kovalev is returned to Binghamton.

21 — Steven King is recalled.

23 — At Los Angeles, Gartner becomes first player in NHL history to score 30 or more goals in 14 consecutive seasons. Hirsch backstops an 8-3 victory.

25 — Richter and Hurlbut are recalled, Hirsch is returned to Binghamton. Hurlbut suffers sprained knee in collision with Turcotte at practice and will miss 14 games.

27 — During game against Winnipeg, Wells suffered sprained knee and will miss 27 games.

31 — Kovalev and D Joby Messier are recalled.

■■■
FEBRUARY

3 — Djoos is returned to Binghamton, Peter Andersson is recalled.

4 — Andersson and Kovalev are sent to Binghamton.

5 — With a lap timed at 13.510 seconds, Gartner wins fastest skater competition as all-star weekend at Montreal begins.

6 — Gartner scores four goals and is named all-star MVP.

8 — Andersson and Kovalev are recalled.

12 — C Darren Turcotte suffers a broken foot and misses 11 games.

13 — C-LW Craig Duncanson is recalled.

16 — Duncanson is returned.

25 — D Dave Marcinyshyn is recalled and Hurlbut is returned.

27 — Rangers complete 3-1-1 western road trip with 1-0 victory in Edmonton. Messier suffers ribcage injury when crunched by defenseman Igor Kravchuk in final 10 seconds.

28 — Marcinyshyn is returned.

■■■
MARCH

10 — Steven King is returned.

11 — With Lowe playing in his 1,000th NHL game, Rangers win 4-1 in Chicago and pull into second-place tie with Washington Capitals at 73 points.

13 — Snowstorms in northeast cause postponement of second-place showdown in Washington.

17 — Obtain LW Esa Tikkanen from Edmonton for C Doug Weight. Rangers get season-high 59 shots against Oilers, 11 by Leetch, lose, 4-3. Arbitrator awards Darren Turcotte a salary of $500,000 per season on a two-year contract; total is $100,000 above what the team offered, about $300,000 below what Turcotte sought.

19 — Gartner scores 40th goal of season, becoming first Ranger ever to collect 40 or more goals in three consecutive campaigns. Leetch breaks his ankle, reportedly after slipping on some ice outside his Manhattan apartment building after the contest, and is lost for the season.

22 — Obtain C John McIntyre from Los Angeles for D Mark Hardy, obtain LW Mike Hartman from Tampa Bay for C Randy Gilhen. Though they win 5-4 at Ottawa, this is the Rangers' last day as high as third place. Rumors run rampant that Leetch either was drunk or was horsing around with Messier the night his ankle was broken.

23 — Disgusted by performance against Ottawa, Neil Smith breaks tradition and calls meeting with team.

24 — Joby Messier is recalled.

26 — D James Patrick leaves lineup due to a herniated disc that ultimately requires surgery. He is out for the season.

30 — Idle Rangers fall out of fourth place permanently.

31 — Garden president Bob Gutkowski gives Neil Smith a vote of confidence. Leetch undergoes surgery on his right fibula. A metal plate and screws are attached to the healing fracture.

■■■
APRIL

5 — John Vanbiesbrouck blows 4-1 third-period lead and loses 5-4 Garden decision to Hartford. It is his final game appearance in a Ranger uniform.

6 — Corey Hirsch is recalled from Binghamton.

7 — Messier plays 1,000th NHL game in 5-2 loss at New Jersey.

9 — Mario Lemieux scores five goals in 10-4 Penguins runaway at Garden which drops Rangers below .500 permanently.

12 — Rangers lose 1-0 in Philadelphia, fall to last place permanently.

14 — Kovalev and Joby Messier are returned to Binghamton. James Patrick undergoes surgery to remove a herniated disc from his back.

16 — Rangers complete season with their seventh consecutive loss and 11th in the concluding 12 games, a 4-2 defeat at Washington. Zubov is assigned to Binghamton.

17 — Rangers introduce their new coach, Mike Keenan.

Check out these other exciting sports titles from Sagamore Publishing.

To order with check or money order:

Send order (book cost plus $3.50 shipping for 1st book; $.50 for each additional book) to:

Sagamore Publishing
P.O. Box 647
Champaign IL 61824-0647